2276C: Implementing a Microsoft® Windows Server™ 2003 Network Infrastructure: Network Hosts

Information in this document, including URL and other Internet Web site references, is subject to change without notice. Unless otherwise noted, the example companies, organizations, products, domain names, e-mail addresses, logos, people, places, and events depicted herein are fictitious, and no association with any real company, organization, product, domain name, e-mail address, logo, person, place or event is intended or should be inferred. Complying with all applicable copyright laws is the responsibility of the user. Without limiting the rights under copyright, no part of this document may be reproduced, stored in or introduced into a retrieval system, or transmitted in any form or by any means (electronic, mechanical, photocopying, recording, or otherwise), or for any purpose, without the express written permission of Microsoft Corporation.

The names of manufacturers, products, or URLs are provided for informational purposes only and Microsoft makes no representations and warranties, either expressed, implied, or statutory, regarding these manufacturers or the use of the products with any Microsoft technologies. The inclusion of a manufacturer or product does not imply endorsement of Microsoft of the manufacturer or product. Links are provided to third party sites. Such sites are not under the control of Microsoft and Microsoft is not responsible for the contents of any linked site or any link contained in a linked site, or any changes or updates to such sites. Microsoft is not responsible for webcasting or any other form of transmission received from any linked site. Microsoft is providing these links to you only as a convenience, and the inclusion of any link does not imply endorsement of Microsoft of the site or the products contained therein.

Microsoft may have patents, patent applications, trademarks, copyrights, or other intellectual property rights covering subject matter in this document. Except as expressly provided in any written license agreement from Microsoft, the furnishing of this document does not give you any license to these patents, trademarks, copyrights, or other intellectual property.

© 2005 Microsoft Corporation. All rights reserved.

Microsoft, Active Directory, Excel, MS-DOS, PowerPoint, Windows, Windows Media, Windows NT, and Windows Server are either registered trademarks or trademarks of Microsoft Corporation in the United States and/or other countries.

The names of actual companies and products mentioned herein may be the trademarks of their respective owners.

1 2 3 4 5 6 7 8 9   QWE   9 8 7 6 5

Course Number: 2276C
Part Number: X11-48917
Released: 09/2005

END-USER LICENSE AGREEMENT FOR OFFICIAL MICROSOFT LEARNING PRODUCTS – STUDENT EDITION

PLEASE READ THIS END-USER LICENSE AGREEMENT ("EULA") CAREFULLY. BY USING THE MATERIALS AND/OR USING OR INSTALLING THE SOFTWARE THAT ACCOMPANIES THIS EULA (COLLECTIVELY, THE "LICENSED CONTENT"), YOU AGREE TO THE TERMS OF THIS EULA. IF YOU DO NOT AGREE, DO NOT USE THE LICENSED CONTENT.

1. **GENERAL.** This EULA is a legal agreement between you (either an individual or a single entity) and Microsoft Corporation ("Microsoft"). This EULA governs the Licensed Content, which includes computer software (including online and electronic documentation), training materials, and any other associated media and printed materials. This EULA applies to updates, supplements, add-on components, and Internet-based services components of the Licensed Content that Microsoft may provide or make available to you unless Microsoft provides other terms with the update, supplement, add-on component, or Internet-based services component. Microsoft reserves the right to discontinue any Internet-based services provided to you or made available to you through the use of the Licensed Content. This EULA also governs any product support services relating to the Licensed Content except as may be included in another agreement between you and Microsoft. An amendment or addendum to this EULA may accompany the Licensed Content.

2. **GENERAL GRANT OF LICENSE.** Microsoft grants you the following rights, conditioned on your compliance with all the terms and conditions of this EULA. Microsoft grants you a limited, non-exclusive, royalty-free license to install and use the Licensed Content solely in conjunction with your participation as a student in an Authorized Training Session (as defined below). You may install and use one copy of the software on a single computer, device, workstation, terminal, or other digital electronic or analog device ("Device"). You may make a second copy of the software and install it on a portable Device for the exclusive use of the person who is the primary user of the first copy of the software. A license for the software may not be shared for use by multiple end users. An "Authorized Training Session" means a training session conducted at a Microsoft Certified Technical Education Center, an IT Academy, via a Microsoft Certified Partner, or such other entity as Microsoft may designate from time to time in writing, by a Microsoft Certified Trainer (for more information on these entities, please visit www.microsoft.com). WITHOUT LIMITING THE FOREGOING, COPYING OR REPRODUCTION OF THE LICENSED CONTENT TO ANY SERVER OR LOCATION FOR FURTHER REPRODUCTION OR REDISTRIBUTION IS EXPRESSLY PROHIBITED.

3. **DESCRIPTION OF OTHER RIGHTS AND LICENSE LIMITATIONS**

    3.1 *Use of Documentation and Printed Training Materials.*

    3.1.1 The documents and related graphics included in the Licensed Content may include technical inaccuracies or typographical errors. Changes are periodically made to the content. Microsoft may make improvements and/or changes in any of the components of the Licensed Content at any time without notice. The names of companies, products, people, characters and/or data mentioned in the Licensed Content may be fictitious and are in no way intended to represent any real individual, company, product or event, unless otherwise noted.

    3.1.2 Microsoft grants you the right to reproduce portions of documents (such as student workbooks, white papers, press releases, datasheets and FAQs) (the "Documents") provided with the Licensed Content. You may not print any book (either electronic or print version) in its entirety. If you choose to reproduce Documents, you agree that: (a) use of such printed Documents will be solely in conjunction with your personal training use; (b) the Documents will not republished or posted on any network computer or broadcast in any media; (c) any reproduction will include either the Document's original copyright notice or a copyright notice to Microsoft's benefit substantially in the format provided below; and (d) to comply with all terms and conditions of this EULA. In addition, no modifications may made to any Document.

    Form of Notice:

    Copyright undefined.

    © 2005. Reprinted with permission by Microsoft Corporation. All rights reserved.

    Microsoft and Windows are either registered trademarks or trademarks of Microsoft Corporation in the US and/or other countries. Other product and company names mentioned herein may be the trademarks of their respective owners.

    3.2 *Use of Media Elements.* The Licensed Content may include certain photographs, clip art, animations, sounds, music, and video clips (together "Media Elements"). You may not modify these Media Elements.

    3.3 *Use of Sample Code.* In the event that the Licensed Content include sample source code ("Sample Code"), Microsoft grants you a limited, non-exclusive, royalty-free license to use, copy and modify the Sample Code; if you elect to exercise the foregoing rights, you agree to comply with all other terms and conditions of this EULA, including without limitation Sections 3.4, 3.5, and 6.

    3.4 *Permitted Modifications.* In the event that you exercise any rights provided under this EULA to create modifications of the Licensed Content, you agree that any such modifications: (a) will not be used for providing training where a fee is charged in public or private classes; (b) indemnify, hold harmless, and defend Microsoft from and against any claims or lawsuits, including attorneys' fees, which arise from or result from your use of any modified version of the Licensed Content; and (c) not to transfer or assign any rights to any modified version of the Licensed Content to any third party without the express written permission of Microsoft.

3.5   *Reproduction/Redistribution Licensed Content.* Except as expressly provided in this EULA, you may not reproduce or distribute the Licensed Content or any portion thereof (including any permitted modifications) to any third parties without the express written permission of Microsoft.

4.   **RESERVATION OF RIGHTS AND OWNERSHIP.** Microsoft reserves all rights not expressly granted to you in this EULA. The Licensed Content is protected by copyright and other intellectual property laws and treaties. Microsoft or its suppliers own the title, copyright, and other intellectual property rights in the Licensed Content. You may not remove or obscure any copyright, trademark or patent notices that appear on the Licensed Content, or any components thereof, as delivered to you. **The Licensed Content is licensed, not sold.**

5.   **LIMITATIONS ON REVERSE ENGINEERING, DECOMPILATION, AND DISASSEMBLY.** You may not reverse engineer, decompile, or disassemble the Software or Media Elements, except and only to the extent that such activity is expressly permitted by applicable law notwithstanding this limitation.

6.   **LIMITATIONS ON SALE, RENTAL, ETC. AND CERTAIN ASSIGNMENTS.** You may not provide commercial hosting services with, sell, rent, lease, lend, sublicense, or assign copies of the Licensed Content, or any portion thereof (including any permitted modifications thereof) on a stand-alone basis or as part of any collection, product or service.

7.   **CONSENT TO USE OF DATA.** You agree that Microsoft and its affiliates may collect and use technical information gathered as part of the product support services provided to you, if any, related to the Licensed Content. Microsoft may use this information solely to improve our products or to provide customized services or technologies to you and will not disclose this information in a form that personally identifies you.

8.   **LINKS TO THIRD PARTY SITES.** You may link to third party sites through the use of the Licensed Content. The third party sites are not under the control of Microsoft, and Microsoft is not responsible for the contents of any third party sites, any links contained in third party sites, or any changes or updates to third party sites. Microsoft is not responsible for webcasting or any other form of transmission received from any third party sites. Microsoft is providing these links to third party sites to you only as a convenience, and the inclusion of any link does not imply an endorsement by Microsoft of the third party site.

9.   **ADDITIONAL LICENSED CONTENT/SERVICES.** This EULA applies to updates, supplements, add-on components, or Internet-based services components, of the Licensed Content that Microsoft may provide to you or make available to you after the date you obtain your initial copy of the Licensed Content, unless we provide other terms along with the update, supplement, add-on component, or Internet-based services component. Microsoft reserves the right to discontinue any Internet-based services provided to you or made available to you through the use of the Licensed Content.

10.   **U.S. GOVERNMENT LICENSE RIGHTS.** All software provided to the U.S. Government pursuant to solicitations issued on or after December 1, 1995 is provided with the commercial license rights and restrictions described elsewhere herein. All software provided to the U.S. Government pursuant to solicitations issued prior to December 1, 1995 is provided with "Restricted Rights" as provided for in FAR, 48 CFR 52.227-14 (JUNE 1987) or DFAR, 48 CFR 252.227-7013 (OCT 1988), as applicable.

11.   **EXPORT RESTRICTIONS.** You acknowledge that the Licensed Content is subject to U.S. export jurisdiction. You agree to comply with all applicable international and national laws that apply to the Licensed Content, including the U.S. Export Administration Regulations, as well as end-user, end-use, and destination restrictions issued by U.S. and other governments. For additional information see <http://www.microsoft.com/exporting/>.

12.   **TRANSFER.** The initial user of the Licensed Content may make a one-time permanent transfer of this EULA and Licensed Content to another end user, provided the initial user retains no copies of the Licensed Content. The transfer may not be an indirect transfer, such as a consignment. Prior to the transfer, the end user receiving the Licensed Content must agree to all the EULA terms.

13.   **"NOT FOR RESALE" LICENSED CONTENT.** Licensed Content identified as "Not For Resale" or "NFR," may not be sold or otherwise transferred for value, or used for any purpose other than demonstration, test or evaluation.

14.   **TERMINATION.** Without prejudice to any other rights, Microsoft may terminate this EULA if you fail to comply with the terms and conditions of this EULA. In such event, you must destroy all copies of the Licensed Content and all of its component parts.

15.   <u>**DISCLAIMER OF WARRANTIES.**</u> **TO THE MAXIMUM EXTENT PERMITTED BY APPLICABLE LAW, MICROSOFT AND ITS SUPPLIERS PROVIDE THE LICENSED CONTENT AND SUPPORT SERVICES (IF ANY)** *AS IS AND WITH ALL FAULTS,* **AND MICROSOFT AND ITS SUPPLIERS HEREBY DISCLAIM ALL OTHER WARRANTIES AND CONDITIONS, WHETHER EXPRESS, IMPLIED OR STATUTORY, INCLUDING, BUT NOT LIMITED TO, ANY (IF ANY) IMPLIED WARRANTIES, DUTIES OR CONDITIONS OF MERCHANTABILITY, OF FITNESS FOR A PARTICULAR PURPOSE, OF RELIABILITY OR AVAILABILITY, OF ACCURACY OR COMPLETENESS OF RESPONSES, OF RESULTS, OF WORKMANLIKE EFFORT, OF LACK OF VIRUSES, AND OF LACK OF NEGLIGENCE, ALL WITH REGARD TO THE LICENSED CONTENT, AND THE PROVISION OF OR FAILURE TO PROVIDE SUPPORT OR OTHER SERVICES, INFORMATION, SOFTWARE, AND RELATED CONTENT THROUGH THE LICENSED CONTENT, OR OTHERWISE ARISING OUT OF THE USE OF THE LICENSED CONTENT. ALSO, THERE IS NO WARRANTY OR CONDITION OF TITLE, QUIET ENJOYMENT, QUIET POSSESSION, CORRESPONDENCE TO DESCRIPTION OR NON-INFRINGEMENT WITH REGARD TO THE LICENSED CONTENT. THE ENTIRE RISK AS TO THE QUALITY, OR ARISING OUT OF THE USE OR PERFORMANCE OF THE LICENSED CONTENT, AND ANY SUPPORT SERVICES, REMAINS WITH YOU.**

16.   <u>**EXCLUSION OF INCIDENTAL, CONSEQUENTIAL AND CERTAIN OTHER DAMAGES.**</u> **TO THE MAXIMUM EXTENT PERMITTED BY APPLICABLE LAW, IN NO EVENT SHALL MICROSOFT OR ITS SUPPLIERS BE LIABLE FOR ANY SPECIAL, INCIDENTAL, PUNITIVE, INDIRECT, OR CONSEQUENTIAL DAMAGES WHATSOEVER (INCLUDING, BUT NOT**

LIMITED TO, DAMAGES FOR LOSS OF PROFITS OR CONFIDENTIAL OR OTHER INFORMATION, FOR BUSINESS INTERRUPTION, FOR PERSONAL INJURY, FOR LOSS OF PRIVACY, FOR FAILURE TO MEET ANY DUTY INCLUDING OF GOOD FAITH OR OF REASONABLE CARE, FOR NEGLIGENCE, AND FOR ANY OTHER PECUNIARY OR OTHER LOSS WHATSOEVER) ARISING OUT OF OR IN ANY WAY RELATED TO THE USE OF OR INABILITY TO USE THE LICENSED CONTENT, THE PROVISION OF OR FAILURE TO PROVIDE SUPPORT OR OTHER SERVICES, INFORMATION, SOFTWARE, AND RELATED CONTENT THROUGH THE LICENSED CONTENT, OR OTHERWISE ARISING OUT OF THE USE OF THE LICENSED CONTENT, OR OTHERWISE UNDER OR IN CONNECTION WITH ANY PROVISION OF THIS EULA, EVEN IN THE EVENT OF THE FAULT, TORT (INCLUDING NEGLIGENCE), MISREPRESENTATION, STRICT LIABILITY, BREACH OF CONTRACT OR BREACH OF WARRANTY OF MICROSOFT OR ANY SUPPLIER, AND EVEN IF MICROSOFT OR ANY SUPPLIER HAS BEEN ADVISED OF THE POSSIBILITY OF SUCH DAMAGES. BECAUSE SOME STATES/JURISDICTIONS DO NOT ALLOW THE EXCLUSION OR LIMITATION OF LIABILITY FOR CONSEQUENTIAL OR INCIDENTAL DAMAGES, THE ABOVE LIMITATION MAY NOT APPLY TO YOU.

17. **LIMITATION OF LIABILITY AND REMEDIES.** NOTWITHSTANDING ANY DAMAGES THAT YOU MIGHT INCUR FOR ANY REASON WHATSOEVER (INCLUDING, WITHOUT LIMITATION, ALL DAMAGES REFERENCED HEREIN AND ALL DIRECT OR GENERAL DAMAGES IN CONTRACT OR ANYTHING ELSE), THE ENTIRE LIABILITY OF MICROSOFT AND ANY OF ITS SUPPLIERS UNDER ANY PROVISION OF THIS EULA AND YOUR EXCLUSIVE REMEDY HEREUNDER SHALL BE LIMITED TO THE GREATER OF THE ACTUAL DAMAGES YOU INCUR IN REASONABLE RELIANCE ON THE LICENSED CONTENT UP TO THE AMOUNT ACTUALLY PAID BY YOU FOR THE LICENSED CONTENT OR US$5.00. THE FOREGOING LIMITATIONS, EXCLUSIONS AND DISCLAIMERS SHALL APPLY TO THE MAXIMUM EXTENT PERMITTED BY APPLICABLE LAW, EVEN IF ANY REMEDY FAILS ITS ESSENTIAL PURPOSE.

18. **APPLICABLE LAW.** If you acquired this Licensed Content in the United States, this EULA is governed by the laws of the State of Washington. If you acquired this Licensed Content in Canada, unless expressly prohibited by local law, this EULA is governed by the laws in force in the Province of Ontario, Canada; and, in respect of any dispute which may arise hereunder, you consent to the jurisdiction of the federal and provincial courts sitting in Toronto, Ontario. If you acquired this Licensed Content in the European Union, Iceland, Norway, or Switzerland, then local law applies. If you acquired this Licensed Content in any other country, then local law may apply.

19. **ENTIRE AGREEMENT; SEVERABILITY.** This EULA (including any addendum or amendment to this EULA which is included with the Licensed Content) are the entire agreement between you and Microsoft relating to the Licensed Content and the support services (if any) and they supersede all prior or contemporaneous oral or written communications, proposals and representations with respect to the Licensed Content or any other subject matter covered by this EULA. To the extent the terms of any Microsoft policies or programs for support services conflict with the terms of this EULA, the terms of this EULA shall control. If any provision of this EULA is held to be void, invalid, unenforceable or illegal, the other provisions shall continue in full force and effect.

Should you have any questions concerning this EULA, or if you desire to contact Microsoft for any reason, please use the address information enclosed in this Licensed Content to contact the Microsoft subsidiary serving your country or visit Microsoft on the World Wide Web at http://www.microsoft.com.

Si vous avez acquis votre Contenu Sous Licence Microsoft au CANADA :

DÉNI DE GARANTIES. Dans la mesure maximale permise par les lois applicables, le Contenu Sous Licence et les services de soutien technique (le cas échéant) sont fournis *TELS QUELS ET AVEC TOUS LES DÉFAUTS* par Microsoft et ses fournisseurs, lesquels par les présentes dénient toutes autres garanties et conditions expresses, implicites ou en vertu de la loi, notamment, mais sans limitation, (le cas échéant) les garanties, devoirs ou conditions implicites de qualité marchande, d'adaptation à une fin usage particulière, de fiabilité ou de disponibilité, d'exactitude ou d'exhaustivité des réponses, des résultats, des efforts déployés selon les règles de l'art, d'absence de virus et d'absence de négligence, le tout à l'égard du Contenu Sous Licence et de la prestation des services de soutien technique ou de l'omission de la 'une telle prestation des services de soutien technique ou à l'égard de la fourniture ou de l'omission de la fourniture de tous autres services, renseignements, Contenus Sous Licence, et contenu qui s'y rapporte grâce au Contenu Sous Licence ou provenant autrement de l'utilisation du Contenu Sous Licence. PAR AILLEURS, IL N'Y A AUCUNE GARANTIE OU CONDITION QUANT AU TITRE DE PROPRIÉTÉ, À LA JOUISSANCE OU LA POSSESSION PAISIBLE, À LA CONCORDANCE À UNE DESCRIPTION NI QUANT À UNE ABSENCE DE CONTREFAÇON CONCERNANT LE CONTENU SOUS LICENCE.

EXCLUSION DES DOMMAGES ACCESSOIRES, INDIRECTS ET DE CERTAINS AUTRES DOMMAGES. DANS LA MESURE MAXIMALE PERMISE PAR LES LOIS APPLICABLES, EN AUCUN CAS MICROSOFT OU SES FOURNISSEURS NE SERONT RESPONSABLES DES DOMMAGES SPÉCIAUX, CONSÉCUTIFS, ACCESSOIRES OU INDIRECTS DE QUELQUE NATURE QUE CE SOIT (NOTAMMENT, LES DOMMAGES À L'ÉGARD DU MANQUE À GAGNER OU DE LA DIVULGATION DE RENSEIGNEMENTS CONFIDENTIELS OU AUTRES, DE LA PERTE D'EXPLOITATION, DE BLESSURES CORPORELLES, DE LA VIOLATION DE LA VIE PRIVÉE, DE L'OMISSION DE REMPLIR TOUT DEVOIR, Y COMPRIS D'AGIR DE BONNE FOI OU D'EXERCER UN SOIN RAISONNABLE, DE LA NÉGLIGENCE ET DE TOUTE AUTRE PERTE PÉCUNIAIRE OU AUTRE PERTE

DE QUELQUE NATURE QUE CE SOIT) SE RAPPORTANT DE QUELQUE MANIÈRE QUE CE SOIT À L'UTILISATION DU CONTENU SOUS LICENCE OU À L'INCAPACITÉ DE S'EN SERVIR, À LA PRESTATION OU À L'OMISSION DE LA 'UNE TELLE PRESTATION DE SERVICES DE SOUTIEN TECHNIQUE OU À LA FOURNITURE OU À L'OMISSION DE LA FOURNITURE DE TOUS AUTRES SERVICES, RENSEIGNEMENTS, CONTENUS SOUS LICENCE, ET CONTENU QUI S'Y RAPPORTE GRÂCE AU CONTENU SOUS LICENCE OU PROVENANT AUTREMENT DE L'UTILISATION DU CONTENU SOUS LICENCE OU AUTREMENT AUX TERMES DE TOUTE DISPOSITION DE LA U PRÉSENTE CONVENTION EULA OU RELATIVEMENT À UNE TELLE DISPOSITION, MÊME EN CAS DE FAUTE, DE DÉLIT CIVIL (Y COMPRIS LA NÉGLIGENCE), DE RESPONSABILITÉ STRICTE, DE VIOLATION DE CONTRAT OU DE VIOLATION DE GARANTIE DE MICROSOFT OU DE TOUT FOURNISSEUR ET MÊME SI MICROSOFT OU TOUT FOURNISSEUR A ÉTÉ AVISÉ DE LA POSSIBILITÉ DE TELS DOMMAGES.

LIMITATION DE RESPONSABILITÉ ET RECOURS. MALGRÉ LES DOMMAGES QUE VOUS PUISSIEZ SUBIR POUR QUELQUE MOTIF QUE CE SOIT (NOTAMMENT, MAIS SANS LIMITATION, TOUS LES DOMMAGES SUSMENTIONNÉS ET TOUS LES DOMMAGES DIRECTS OU GÉNÉRAUX OU AUTRES), LA SEULE RESPONSABILITÉ 'OBLIGATION INTÉGRALE DE MICROSOFT ET DE L'UN OU L'AUTRE DE SES FOURNISSEURS AUX TERMES DE TOUTE DISPOSITION DEU LA PRÉSENTE CONVENTION EULA ET VOTRE RECOURS EXCLUSIF À L'ÉGARD DE TOUT CE QUI PRÉCÈDE SE LIMITE AU PLUS ÉLEVÉ ENTRE LES MONTANTS SUIVANTS : LE MONTANT QUE VOUS AVEZ RÉELLEMENT PAYÉ POUR LE CONTENU SOUS LICENCE OU 5,00 $US. LES LIMITES, EXCLUSIONS ET DÉNIS QUI PRÉCÈDENT (Y COMPRIS LES CLAUSES CI-DESSUS), S'APPLIQUENT DANS LA MESURE MAXIMALE PERMISE PAR LES LOIS APPLICABLES, MÊME SI TOUT RECOURS N'ATTEINT PAS SON BUT ESSENTIEL.

À moins que cela ne soit prohibé par le droit local applicable, la présente Convention est régie par les lois de la province d'Ontario, Canada. Vous consentez Chacune des parties à la présente reconnaît irrévocablement à la compétence des tribunaux fédéraux et provinciaux siégeant à Toronto, dans de la province d'Ontario et consent à instituer tout litige qui pourrait découler de la présente auprès des tribunaux situés dans le district judiciaire de York, province d'Ontario.

Au cas où vous auriez des questions concernant cette licence ou que vous désiriez vous mettre en rapport avec Microsoft pour quelque raison que ce soit, veuillez utiliser l'information contenue dans le Contenu Sous Licence pour contacter la filiale de succursale Microsoft desservant votre pays, dont l'adresse est fournie dans ce produit, ou visitez écrivez à : Microsoft sur le World Wide Web à http://www.microsoft.com

Contents

Introduction
Course Materials 2
Prerequisites 3
Course Outline 4
Setup 5
Demonstration: Using Microsoft Virtual PC 6
Microsoft Learning 7
Microsoft Certified Professional Program 10
Multimedia: Job Roles in Today's Information Systems Environment 13
Facilities 14

Module 1: Reviewing the Suite of TCP/IP Protocols
Overview 1
Lesson: Overview of the OSI Model 2
Lesson: Overview of the TCP/IP Protocol Suite 10
Lesson: Viewing Frames by Using Network Monitor 21

Module 2: Assigning IP Addresses in a Multiple-Subnet Network
Overview 1
Lesson: Configuring IP Addressing for Simple Networks 2
Lesson: Configuring IP Addressing for Complex Networks 13
Lesson: Using IP Routing Tables 25
Lesson: Overcoming the Limitations of the IP Addressing Scheme 35
Lab: Assigning IP Addresses in a Multiple-Subnet Network 47

Module 3: Configuring a Client IP Address
Overview 1
Lesson: Configuring a Client to Use a Static IP Address 2
Lesson: Configuring a Client to Obtain an IP Address Automatically 10
Lesson: Using Alternate Configuration 20
Lab: Configuring Hosts to Connect to a Network Running the TCP/IP
Protocol Suite 26
Course Evaluation 35

Module 4: Configuring a Client for Name Resolution
Overview 1
Lesson: Overview of Name Resolution 2
Lesson: Resolving Host Names 7
Lesson: Resolving NetBIOS Names 18
Lab: Configuring a Client for Name Resolution 31

Module 5: Isolating Common Connectivity Issues
Overview 1
Lesson: Analyzing Client Startup Communication 2
Lesson: Determining the Causes of Connectivity Issues 10
Lesson: Using Network Utilities and Tools to Isolate Connectivity Issues 20
Lab: Isolating Common Connectivity Issues 39
Course Evaluation 45

About This Course

This section provides you with a brief description of the course, audience, suggested prerequisites, and course objectives.

Description

The goal of this two-day course is to provide students with the skills and knowledge necessary to configure a Microsoft® Windows®–based computer to operate in a Microsoft Windows Server™ 2003 networking infrastructure.

Audience

The target audience for this course includes individuals who are either employed or seeking employment as systems administrators in medium to large organizations. The entry critera for this course include that the attending individuals are:

- Entry-level IT professionals, new to hands-on Windows server and network administration.
- Preparing for Exam 70-291: *Implementing, Managing, and Maintaining a Microsoft Windows Server 2003 Network Infrastructure*, a core requirement for the MCSA and MCSE certification credentials.

Student prerequisites

This course requires that students meet the following prerequisites:

- A+ certification or equivalent knowledge and skills
- Completion of Course 2274: *Managing a Microsoft Windows Server 2003 Environment* or equivalent knowledge and skills

Course objectives

After completing this course, students will be able to:

- Describe the Transmission Control Protocol/Internet Protocol (TCP/IP) protocol architecture.
- Convert Internet Protocol (IP) addresses between decimal and binary.
- Calculate a subnet mask.
- Create subnets using Variable-Length Subnet Mask (VLSM) and Classless Inter-Domain Routing (CIDR).
- Configure a host to use a static IP address.
- Assign IP addresses in a multiple subnet network.
- Describe the IP routing process.
- Configure a host to obtain an IP address automatically.
- Configure a host so that automatic private IP address configuration is disabled.
- Configure a host to use name servers.
- Isolate common connectivity issues.

Student Materials Compact Disc Contents

The Student Materials compact disc contains the following files and folders:

- *Autorun.inf*. When the compact disc is inserted into the compact disc drive, this file opens StartCD.exe.
- *Default.htm*. This file opens the Student Materials Web page. It provides you with resources pertaining to this course, including additional reading, review and lab answers, lab files, multimedia presentations, and course-related Web sites.
- *Readme.txt*. This file explains how to install the software for viewing the Student Materials compact disc and its contents and how to open the Student Materials Web page.
- *StartCD.exe*. When the compact disc is inserted into the compact disc drive, or when you double-click the **StartCD.exe** file, this file opens the compact disc and allows you to browse the Student Materials compact disc.
- *StartCD.ini*. This file contains instructions to launch StartCD.exe.
- *Addread*. This folder contains additional reading pertaining to this course.
- *Appendix*. This folder contains appendix files for this course.
- *Flash*. This folder contains the installer for the Macromedia Flash browser plug-in.
- *Fonts*. This folder contains fonts that might be required to view the Microsoft Word documents that are included with this course.
- *Media*. This folder contains files that are used in multimedia presentations for this course.
- *Mplayer*. This folder contains the setup file to install Microsoft Windows Media® Player.
- *Webfiles*. This folder contains the files that are required to view the course Web page. To open the Web page, open Windows Explorer, and in the root directory of the compact disc, double-click **StartCD.exe**.
- *Wordview*. This folder contains the Word Viewer that is used to view any Word document (.doc) files that are included on the compact disc.

Document Conventions

The following conventions are used in course materials to distinguish elements of the text.

Convention	Use
Bold	Represents commands, command options, and syntax that must be typed exactly as shown. It also indicates commands on menus and buttons, dialog box titles and options, and icon and menu names.
Italic	In syntax statements or descriptive text, indicates argument names or placeholders for variable information. Italic is also used for introducing new terms, for book titles, and for emphasis in the text.
Title Capitals	Indicate domain names, user names, computer names, directory names, and folder and file names, except when specifically referring to case-sensitive names. Unless otherwise indicated, you can use lowercase letters when you type a directory name or file name in a dialog box or at a command prompt.
ALL CAPITALS	Indicate the names of keys, key sequences, and key combinations—for example, ALT+SPACEBAR.
`monospace`	Represents code samples or examples of screen text.
[ ]	In syntax statements, enclose optional items. For example, [*filename*] in command syntax indicates that you can choose to type a file name with the command. Type only the information within the brackets, not the brackets themselves.
{ }	In syntax statements, enclose required items. Type only the information within the braces, not the braces themselves.
|	In syntax statements, separates an either/or choice.
▶	Indicates a procedure with sequential steps.
...	In syntax statements, specifies that the preceding item may be repeated.
. . .	Represents an omitted portion of a code sample.

Introduction

Contents

Introduction	1
Course Materials	2
Prerequisites	3
Course Outline	4
Setup	5
Demonstration: Using Microsoft Virtual PC	6
Microsoft Learning	7
Microsoft Certified Professional Program	10
Multimedia: Job Roles in Today's Information Systems Environment	13
Facilities	14

Information in this document, including URL and other Internet Web site references, is subject to change without notice. Unless otherwise noted, the example companies, organizations, products, domain names, e-mail addresses, logos, people, places, and events depicted herein are fictitious, and no association with any real company, organization, product, domain name, e-mail address, logo, person, place or event is intended or should be inferred. Complying with all applicable copyright laws is the responsibility of the user. Without limiting the rights under copyright, no part of this document may be reproduced, stored in or introduced into a retrieval system, or transmitted in any form or by any means (electronic, mechanical, photocopying, recording, or otherwise), or for any purpose, without the express written permission of Microsoft Corporation.

The names of manufacturers, products, or URLs are provided for informational purposes only and Microsoft makes no representations and warranties, either expressed, implied, or statutory, regarding these manufacturers or the use of the products with any Microsoft technologies. The inclusion of a manufacturer or product does not imply endorsement of Microsoft of the manufacturer or product. Links are provided to third party sites. Such sites are not under the control of Microsoft and Microsoft is not responsible for the contents of any linked site or any link contained in a linked site, or any changes or updates to such sites. Microsoft is not responsible for webcasting or any other form of transmission received from any linked site. Microsoft is providing these links to you only as a convenience, and the inclusion of any link does not imply endorsement of Microsoft of the site or the products contained therein.

Microsoft may have patents, patent applications, trademarks, copyrights, or other intellectual property rights covering subject matter in this document. Except as expressly provided in any written license agreement from Microsoft, the furnishing of this document does not give you any license to these patents, trademarks, copyrights, or other intellectual property.

© 2005 Microsoft Corporation. All rights reserved.

Microsoft, Active Directory, Excel, MS-DOS, PowerPoint, Windows, Windows Media, Windows NT, and Windows Server are either registered trademarks or trademarks of Microsoft Corporation in the United States and/or other countries.

All other trademarks are property of their respective owners.

Introduction

- Name
- Company affiliation
- Title/function
- Job responsibility
- Networking experience
- Windows experience
- Expectations for the course

Course Materials

> - Name card
> - Student workbook
> - Student Materials compact disc
> - Course evaluation
> - Assessments

The following materials are included with your kit:

- *Name card*. Write your name on both sides of the name card.
- *Student workbook*. The student workbook contains the material covered in class, in addition to the hands-on lab exercises.
- *Student Materials compact disc*. The Student Materials compact disc contains Web page that provides you with links to resources pertaining to this course, including additional readings, review and lab answers, lab files, multimedia presentations, and course-related Web sites.

   Note To open the Web page, insert the Student Materials compact disc into the CD-ROM drive, and then in the root directory of the compact disc, double-click **StartCD.exe**.

- *Course evaluation*. Near the end of the course, you will have the opportunity to complete an online evaluation to provide feedback on the course, training facility, and instructor.
- *Assessments*. There are assessments for each lesson, located on the Student Materials compact disc. You can use them as pre-assessments to identify areas of difficulty, or you can use them as post-assessments to validate learning.

  To provide additional comments or feedback on the course, send e-mail to support@mscourseware.com. To inquire about the Microsoft® Certified Professional program, send e-mail to mcphelp@microsoft.com.

Prerequisites

- A+ certification or equivalent knowledge and skills
- Completion of Course 2274, *Managing a Microsoft Windows Server 2003 Environment*, or equivalent knowledge and skills

This course requires that you meet the following prerequisites:

- A+ certification or equivalent knowledge and skills.
- Completion of Course 2274: *Managing a Microsoft® Windows Server™ 2003 Environment*, or equivalent knowledge and skills.

Course Outline

- Module 1: Reviewing the Suite of TCP/IP Protocols
- Module 2: Assigning IP Addresses in a Multiple-Subnet Network
- Module 3: Configuring a Client IP Address
- Module 4: Configuring a Client for Name Resolution
- Module 5: Isolating Common Connectivity Issues

Module 1, "Reviewing the Suite of TCP/IP Protocols," reviews the suite of Transmission Control Protocol/Internet Protocols (TCP/IP) protocols. By understanding the function of each protocol and how the protocols relate to each other, you have the context for understanding network administration tasks and network troubleshooting.

Module 2, "Assigning IP Addresses in a Multiple-Subnet Network," explains how to construct and assign IP addresses and how to isolate addressing issues associated with the IP routing process.

Module 3, "Configuring a Client IP Address," discusses how to configure an Internet Protocol (IP) address for a client computer running Windows Server 2003 on a network running the TCP/IP protocol suite. System administrators must be able to configure a client to use a static IP address and configure a client to obtain an IP address automatically.

Module 4, "Configuring a Client for Name Resolution," discusses how Network Basic Input/Output System (NetBIOS) names are resolved into IP addresses. To ensure that clients can communicate on a TCP/IP network, system administrators must know how to configure clients to use the various types of name resolution mechanisms provided by the Microsoft Windows® operating systems.

Module 5, "Isolating Common Connectivity Issues," describes the most common types of connectivity issues and how to isolate them by using a variety of network utilities.

Setup

> - The virtual environment is configured as one Windows Server 2003 domain: Contoso.msft
> - DEN-DC1 is the domain controller
> - DEN-SRV1 is a member server
> - DEN-CL1 is a workstation running Windows XP Professional, Service Pack 2
> - Server computers are running Windows Server 2003, Enterprise Edition, Service Pack 1

Classroom setup

Each student machine has Windows XP Professional installed and is running Microsoft Virtual PC 2004.

The name of the domain is contoso.msft. The domain is named after Contoso, Ltd., a fictitious company that has offices worldwide.

The domain controller is named DEN-DC1, and there is a member server named DEN-SRV1. Both computers are running Windows Server 2003 Enterprise Edition with Service Pack 1 (SP1). The workstation computer is named DEN-CL1 and is running Windows XP Professional with Service Pack 2 (SP2).

The domain has been populated with users, groups, and computer accounts for each administrator to manage.

Demonstration: Using Microsoft Virtual PC

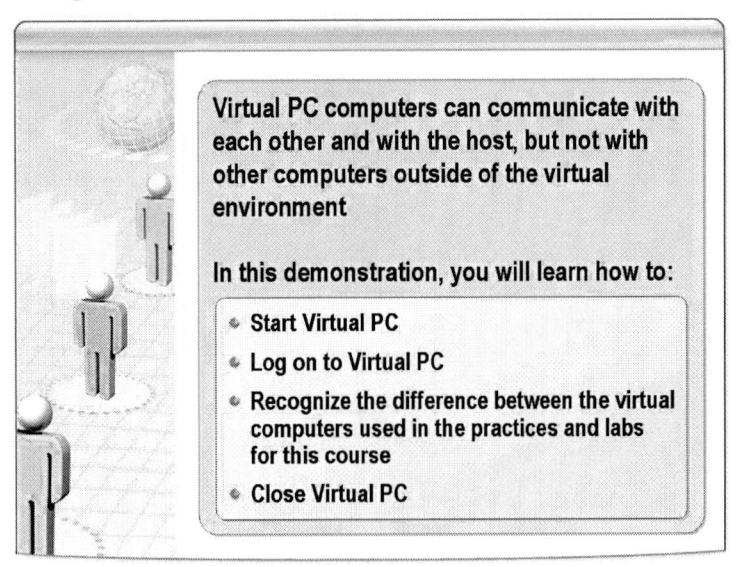

> Virtual PC computers can communicate with each other and with the host, but not with other computers outside of the virtual environment
>
> In this demonstration, you will learn how to:
> - Start Virtual PC
> - Log on to Virtual PC
> - Recognize the difference between the virtual computers used in the practices and labs for this course
> - Close Virtual PC

In this demonstration, your instructor will help familiarize you with the Virtual PC environment in which you will work to complete the practices and labs in this course. You will learn:

- How to open Virtual PC.
- How to start Virtual PC.
- How to log on to Virtual PC.
- How to switch between full screen and window modes.
- How to tell the difference between the virtual machines that are used in the practices for this course.
- That the virtual machines can communicate with each other and with the host, but they cannot communicate with other computers that are outside of the virtual environment. (For example, no Internet access is available from the virtual environment.)
- How to close Virtual PC.

Keyboard shortcuts

While working in the Virtual PC environment, you may find it helpful to use keyboard shortcuts. All Virtual PC shortcuts include a key that is referred to as the HOST key or the RIGHT-ALT key. By default, the HOST key is the ALT key on the right side of your keyboard. Some useful shortcuts include:

- ALT+DELETE to log on to the Virtual PC
- ALT+ENTER to switch between full screen mode and window modes
- ALT+RIGHT ARROW to display the next Virtual PC

For more information about Virtual PC, see Virtual PC Help.

Microsoft Learning

> 2274: Managing a Microsoft Windows Server 2003 Environment
>
> 2275: Maintaining a Microsoft Windows Server 2003 Environment
>
> 2276: Implementing a Microsoft Windows Server 2003 Network Infrastructure: Network Hosts
>
> 2277: Implementing, Managing, and Maintaining a Microsoft Windows Server 2003 Network Infrastructure: Network Services
>
> http://www.microsoft.com/learning/   Microsoft | Learning

Microsoft Learning develops Official Microsoft Learning Products for computer professionals who design, develop, support, implement, or manage solutions by using Microsoft products and technologies. These learning products provide comprehensive, skills-based training in instructor-led and online formats.

Additional recommended learning products

Each learning product relates in some way to other learning products. A related product may be a prerequisite; a follow-up course, clinic, or workshop in a recommended series, or a learning product that offers additional training.

It is recommended that you take the following courses in this order:

2274: *Managing a Microsoft Windows Server 2003 Environment*

2275: *Maintaining a Microsoft Windows Server 2003 Environment*

2276: *Implementing a Microsoft Windows Server 2003 Network Infrastructure: Network Hosts*

2277: *Implementing, Managing, and Maintaining a Microsoft Windows Server 2003 Network Infrastructure: Network Services*

Other related learning products may become available in the future, so for up-to-date information about recommended learning products, visit the Microsoft Learning Web site.

Microsoft Learning information

For more information, visit the Microsoft Learning Web site at http://www.microsoft.com/learning/.

Microsoft Learning Product Types

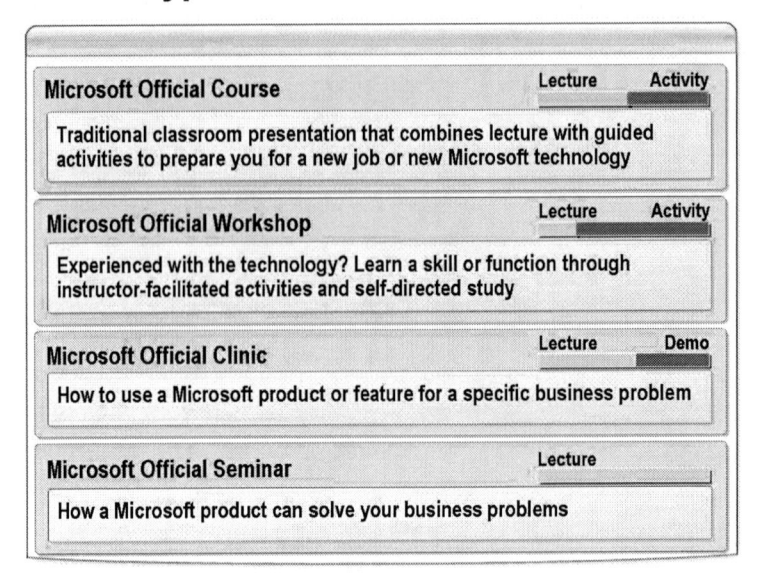

Microsoft Official Course	Lecture / Activity
Traditional classroom presentation that combines lecture with guided activities to prepare you for a new job or new Microsoft technology	
Microsoft Official Workshop	**Lecture / Activity**
Experienced with the technology? Learn a skill or function through instructor-facilitated activities and self-directed study	
Microsoft Official Clinic	**Lecture / Demo**
How to use a Microsoft product or feature for a specific business problem	
Microsoft Official Seminar	**Lecture**
How a Microsoft product can solve your business problems	

Microsoft Learning offers four types of instructor-led products type. Each is specific to a particular audience type and level of experience. The different product types also tend to suit different learning styles. These types are as follows:

- Microsoft Official Courses are for information technology (IT) professionals and developers who are new to a particular product or technology and for experienced individuals who prefer to learn in a traditional classroom format. Courses provide a relevant and guided learning experience that combines lecture and practice to deliver thorough coverage of a Microsoft product or technology. Courses are designed to address the needs of learners engaged in planning, design, implementation, management, and support phases of the technology adoption lifecycle. They provide detailed information by focusing on concepts and principles, reference content, and in-depth, hands-on lab activities to ensure knowledge transfer. Typically, the content of a course is broad, addressing a wide range of tasks necessary for the job role.

- Microsoft Official Workshops are for knowledgeable IT professionals and developers who learn best by doing and exploring. Workshops provide a hands-on learning experience in which participants use Microsoft products in a safe and collaborative environment based on real-world scenarios. Workshops are the learning products where students learn by doing through scenario and through troubleshooting hands-on labs, targeted reviews, information resources, and best practices, with instructor facilitation.

- Microsoft Official Clinics are for IT professionals, developers and technical decision makers. Clinics offer a detailed "how to" presentation that describes the features and functionality of an existing or new Microsoft product or technology, and that showcases product demonstrations and solutions. Clinics focus on how specific features will solve business problems.

- Microsoft Official Seminars are for business decision makers. Through featured business scenarios, case studies, and success stories, seminars provide a dynamic presentation of early and relevant information on Microsoft products and technology solutions that enable decision makers to make critical business decisions. Microsoft Official Seminars are concise, engaging, direct-from-the-source learning products that show how emerging Microsoft products and technologies help our customers serve their customers.

Microsoft Certified Professional Program

Exam number and title	Core exam for the following track	Elective exam for the following track
70-291: *Implementing, Managing, and Maintaining a Microsoft Windows Server 2003 Network Infrastructure*	MCSA	n/a

http://www.microsoft.com/learning/

Microsoft CERTIFIED Professional

Microsoft Learning offers a variety of certification credentials for developers and IT professionals. The Microsoft Certified Professional (MCP) program is the leading certification program for validating your experience and skills, keeping you competitive in today's changing business environment.

Related certification exams

This course helps students to prepare for Exam 70-291: *Implementing, Managing, and Maintaining a Microsoft Windows Server 2003 Network Infrastructure*.

Exam 70-291 is the core exam for the Windows Server 2003 Microsoft Certified Systems Administrator (MCSA) certification.

MCP certifications

The MCP program includes the following certifications:

- MCDST on Windows XP

  The Microsoft Certified Desktop Support Technician (MCDST) certification is designed for professionals who successfully support and educate end users and troubleshoot operating system and application issues on desktop computers running the Windows operating system.

- MCSA on Microsoft Windows Server 2003

  The Microsoft Certified Systems Administrator (MCSA) certification is designed for professionals who implement, manage, and troubleshoot existing network and system environments based on the Windows Server 2003 platform. Implementation responsibilities include installing and configuring parts of systems. Management responsibilities include administering and supporting systems.

- MCSE on Windows Server 2003

  The Microsoft Certified Systems Engineer (MCSE) credential is the premier certification for professionals who analyze business requirements and design and implement infrastructure for business solutions based on the Windows Server 2003 platform. Implementation responsibilities include installing, configuring, and troubleshooting network systems.

- MCAD

    The Microsoft Certified Application Developer (MCAD) for Microsoft .NET credential is appropriate for professionals who use Microsoft technologies to develop and maintain department-level applications, components, Web or desktop clients, or back-end data services, or who work in teams developing enterprise applications. The credential covers job tasks ranging from developing to deploying and maintaining these solutions.

- MCSD

    The Microsoft Certified Solution Developer (MCSD) credential is the premier certification for professionals who design and develop leading-edge business solutions with Microsoft development tools, technologies, platforms, and the Microsoft Windows DNA architecture. The types of applications MCSDs can develop include desktop applications and multi-user, Web-based, N-tier, and transaction-based applications. The credential covers job tasks ranging from analyzing business requirements to maintaining solutions.

- MCDBA on Microsoft SQL Server™ 2000

    The Microsoft Certified Database Administrator (MCDBA) credential is the premier certification for professionals who implement and administer SQL Server databases. The certification is appropriate for individuals who derive physical database designs, develop logical data models, create physical databases, use Transact-SQL to create data services, manage and maintain databases, configure and manage security, monitor and optimize databases, and install and configure SQL Server.

- MCP

    The Microsoft Certified Professional (MCP) credential is for individuals who have the skills to successfully implement a Microsoft product or technology as part of a business solution in an organization. Hands-on experience with the product is necessary to successfully achieve certification.

- MCT

    Microsoft Certified Trainers (MCTs) demonstrate the instructional and technical skills that qualify them to deliver Official Microsoft Learning Products through a Microsoft Certified Partner for Learning Solutions.

Certification requirements

Requirements differ for each certification category and are specific to the products and job functions addressed by the certification. To become a Microsoft Certified Professional, you must pass rigorous certification exams that provide a valid and reliable measure of technical proficiency and expertise.

For More Information See the Microsoft Learning Web site at http://www.microsoft.com/learning/.

You can also send e-mail to mcphelp@microsoft.com if you have specific certification questions.

Acquiring the skills tested by an MCP exam

Official Microsoft Learning Products can help you develop the skills that you need to do your job. They also complement the experience that you gain while working with Microsoft products and technologies. However, no one-to-one correlation exists between Official Microsoft Learning Products and MCP exams. Microsoft does not expect or intend for the courses to be the sole preparation method for passing MCP exams. Practical product knowledge and experience is also necessary to pass MCP exams.

To help prepare for MCP exams, use the preparation guides are available for each exam. Each Exam Preparation Guide contains exam-specific information such as a list of topics on which you will be tested. These guides are available on the Microsoft Learning Web site at http://www.microsoft.com/learning/.

Multimedia: Job Roles in Today's Information Systems Environment

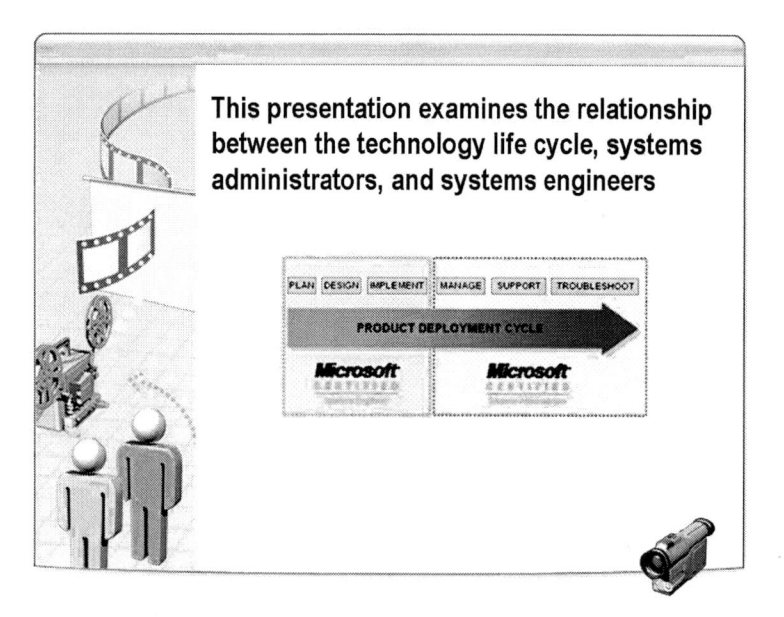

File location

To view the *Job Roles in Today's Information Systems Environment* presentation, open the Web page on the Student Materials compact disc, click **Multimedia**, and then click the title of the presentation. Do not open this presentation unless your instructor tells you to do so.

Facilities

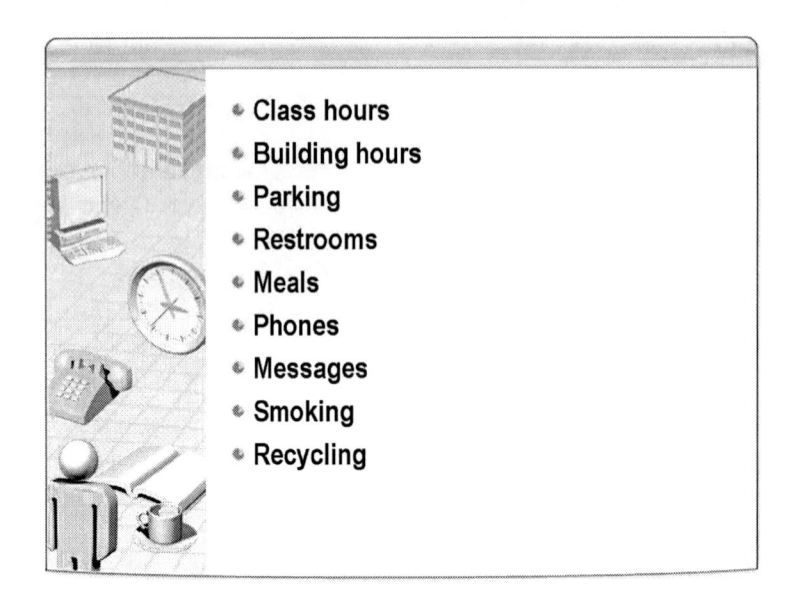

- Class hours
- Building hours
- Parking
- Restrooms
- Meals
- Phones
- Messages
- Smoking
- Recycling

Module 1: Reviewing the Suite of TCP/IP Protocols

Contents

Overview	1
Lesson: Overview of the OSI Model	2
Lesson: Overview of the TCP/IP Protocol Suite	10
Lesson: Viewing Frames by Using Network Monitor	21

Information in this document, including URL and other Internet Web site references, is subject to change without notice. Unless otherwise noted, the example companies, organizations, products, domain names, e-mail addresses, logos, people, places, and events depicted herein are fictitious, and no association with any real company, organization, product, domain name, e-mail address, logo, person, place or event is intended or should be inferred. Complying with all applicable copyright laws is the responsibility of the user. Without limiting the rights under copyright, no part of this document may be reproduced, stored in or introduced into a retrieval system, or transmitted in any form or by any means (electronic, mechanical, photocopying, recording, or otherwise), or for any purpose, without the express written permission of Microsoft Corporation.

The names of manufacturers, products, or URLs are provided for informational purposes only and Microsoft makes no representations and warranties, either expressed, implied, or statutory, regarding these manufacturers or the use of the products with any Microsoft technologies. The inclusion of a manufacturer or product does not imply endorsement of Microsoft of the manufacturer or product. Links are provided to third party sites. Such sites are not under the control of Microsoft and Microsoft is not responsible for the contents of any linked site or any link contained in a linked site, or any changes or updates to such sites. Microsoft is not responsible for webcasting or any other form of transmission received from any linked site. Microsoft is providing these links to you only as a convenience, and the inclusion of any link does not imply endorsement of Microsoft of the site or the products contained therein.

Microsoft may have patents, patent applications, trademarks, copyrights, or other intellectual property rights covering subject matter in this document. Except as expressly provided in any written license agreement from Microsoft, the furnishing of this document does not give you any license to these patents, trademarks, copyrights, or other intellectual property.

© 2005 Microsoft Corporation. All rights reserved.

Microsoft, Active Directory, Excel, MS-DOS, PowerPoint, Windows, Windows Media, Windows NT, and Windows Server are either registered trademarks or trademarks of Microsoft Corporation in the United States and/or other countries.

All other trademarks are property of their respective owners.

Overview

- Overview of the OSI Model
- Overview of the TCP/IP Protocol Suite
- Viewing Frames by Using Network Monitor

Introduction

This module provides you with a review of the Open Systems Interconnection (OSI) reference model and the Transmission Control Protocol/Internet Protocol (TCP/IP) suite. Understanding the protocols in the TCP/IP protocol suite enables you to determine whether a host on a network running Microsoft® Windows Server™ 2003 can communicate with other hosts in the network. Knowing the function of each protocol in the TCP/IP protocol suite and how the protocols relate to each other and to the OSI model provides you with the fundamental knowledge to perform common network administration tasks.

Objectives

After completing this module, you will be able to:

- Describe the architecture of the OSI model and the function of each layer.
- Describe the four layers of the TCP/IP suite.
- Capture and view frames by using Network Monitor.

Lesson: Overview of the OSI Model

- What Is the OSI Model?
- Multimedia: The Layers of the OSI Model
- OSI Network Communication
- The OSI Model and Network Devices

Introduction

To understand how the protocols in the TCP/IP protocol suite enable network communication, you must understand the concepts behind network communication. The OSI model is a conceptual model that is commonly used as a reference for understanding network communication.

Lesson objectives

After completing this lesson, you will be able to:

- Describe the architecture of the OSI model.
- Describe the function of each layer of the OSI model.
- Explain how data moves across a network by using the OSI model.
- Describe how the functionality of network devices relates to the OSI model.

What Is the OSI Model?

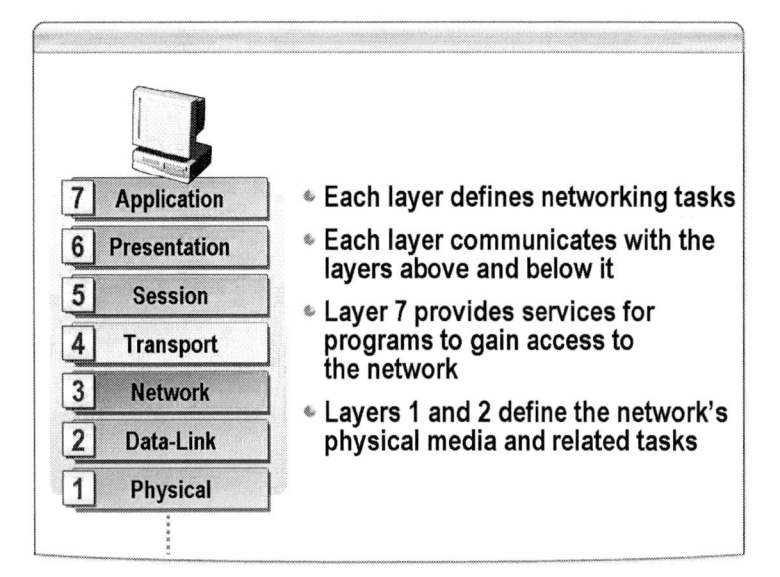

- Each layer defines networking tasks
- Each layer communicates with the layers above and below it
- Layer 7 provides services for programs to gain access to the network
- Layers 1 and 2 define the network's physical media and related tasks

7 Application
6 Presentation
5 Session
4 Transport
3 Network
2 Data-Link
1 Physical

Definition

The OSI model is an architectural model that represents networking communications. It was introduced in 1978 by the International Organization for Standardization (ISO) to standardize the levels of services and types of interactions for computers communicating over a network.

What does the OSI model do?

The OSI model defines the generic tasks that are performed for network communication. You can think of each layer of the OSI model as a piece of software that performs specific tasks for that layer. Each layer communicates with the layer below and the layer above. Data that is transmitted over the network must pass through all seven layers.

How to use the OSI model

The OSI model is used as a common reference point when comparing the function of different protocols and types of network hardware. Understanding the OSI model is important for comparing different products. For example, many switch vendors will refer to their products as layer-2 switches or layer-3 switches. The layers to which they refer are the layers of the OSI model.

Note For more information about the ISO, see the International Organization for Standardization Web site.

The architecture of the OSI model

The OSI model divides network communications into seven layers. Each layer has a defined networking function, as described in the following table.

Layer	Function
Application	Layer 7. Provides an entrance point for programs such as Web browsers and e-mail systems to gain access to network services. This layer does not represent programs such as Microsoft Office Word or Microsoft Office Excel®. This layer represents application programming interfaces (APIs) that developers can use to perform network functions when building applications.

(*continued*)

Layer	Function
Presentation	Layer 6. Translates data between different computing systems on a network. The presentation layer translates the data generated by the application layer from its own syntax into a common transport syntax suitable for transmission over a network. When the data arrives at the receiving computer, the presentation layer on the receiving computer translates the syntax into the computer's own syntax.
Session	Layer 5. Enables two applications to create a persistent communication connection. This layer ensures that both the sender and the receiver are ready to communicate. The session layer can also set checkpoints in the communication process to ensure that it can be restarted if communication is interrupted.
Transport	Layer 4. Ensures that packets are delivered in the order in which they are sent and without loss or duplication. On the sending side, this layer is responsible for breaking down larger messages into smaller packets for transmission on the network. On the receiving side, this layer is responsible for reassembling the packets into a single message to pass up to the session layer. In the context of the OSI reference model, a *packet* is an electronic envelope containing information formed from the session layer to the physical layer of the OSI model.
Network	Layer 3. Determines the physical path of the data to be transmitted based on the network conditions, the priority of service, and other factors. This is the only layer of the OSI model that uses logical networking and can move packets between different networks.
Data-link	Layer 2. Provides error-free transfer of data frames from one computer to another over the physical layer. The media access control (MAC) address of a network card exists at this layer and is added to the packet to create a frame. In the context of the OSI reference model, a *frame* is an electronic envelope of information that includes the packet and other information that is added by the seven layers of the OSI model. The data-link layer is responsible for determining when the frame will be sent on the network and then passing the data to the physical layer. Data is passed from the data-link layer to the physical layer as a stream of 1s and 0s.
Physical	Layer 1. Establishes the physical interface and mechanisms for placing a raw stream of data bits on the network cabling. As each bit of information is received from the data-link layer, the physical layer converts it to an appropriate format and transmits it on the network. On a wired network, each bit is translated into an electrical signal. On a fiber optic network, each bit is translated into a light signal.

Note Protocols operating at different layers of the OSI model use different names for the units of data that they create. At the data-link layer, the term *frame* is used. At the network layer, the term *datagram* is used. The more generic term *packet* is used to describe the unit of data created at any layer of the OSI model.

Multimedia: The Layers of the OSI Model

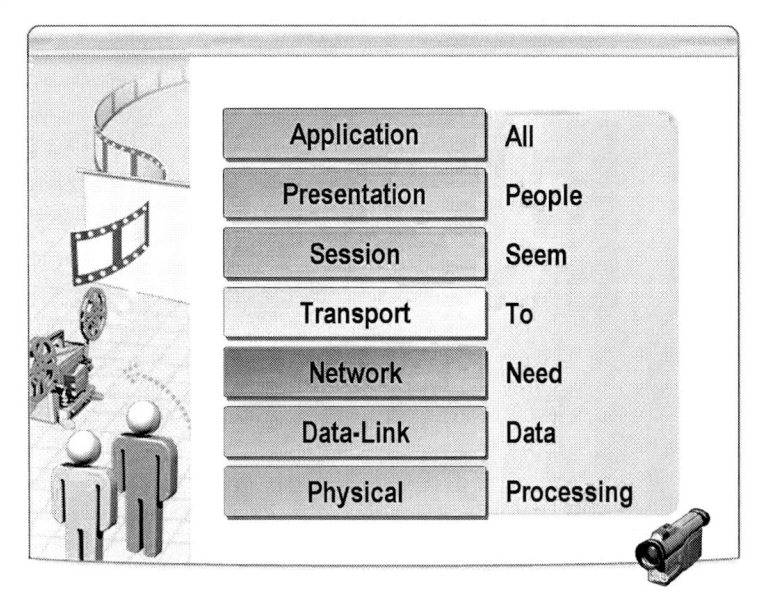

Layer	Mnemonic
Application	All
Presentation	People
Session	Seem
Transport	To
Network	Need
Data-Link	Data
Physical	Processing

File location To view the multimedia presentation, *The Layers of the OSI Model*, open the Web page on the Student Materials compact disc, click **Multimedia**, and then click the title of the presentation.

Objective At the end of this presentation, you will be able to name the OSI layers in order and describe each layer's functionality.

OSI Network Communication

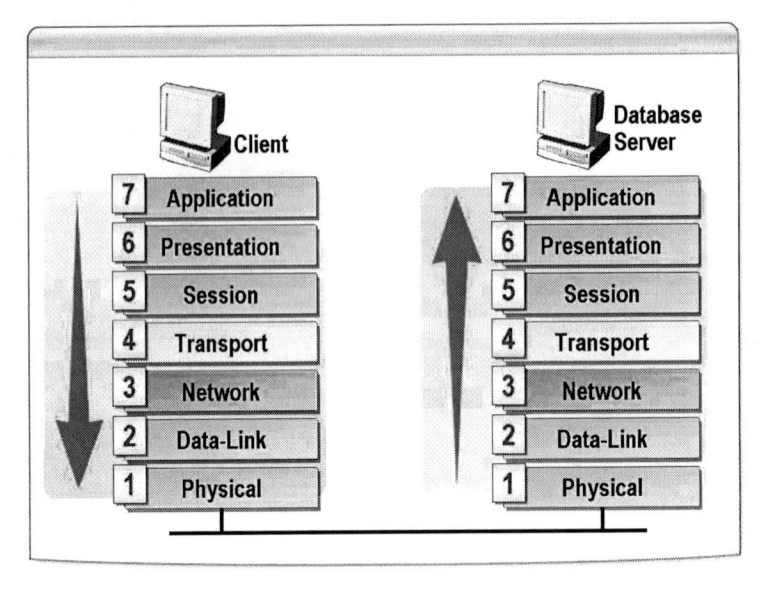

Introduction

To further understand what occurs at each layer of the OSI model, it is useful to look at a specific example of network communication using the OSI model. The following example is for a client/server application. The sender is the client, and the receiver is the database server.

The sending process

The sending process prepares and transmits data over the network as seen in the following table.

Layer	Function
Application	The application layer of the OSI model receives data from the client-side application and passes it to the presentation layer.
Presentation	The presentation layer performs any necessary formatting for the data to be placed on the network. Formatting can include encryption or compression. In this example, the data is compressed.
Session	The session layer confirms that the destination computer is ready to receive data. A connection to the destination is created.
Transport	The transport layer breaks the data into smaller packets for transmission on the network. The packets are also labeled so that they can put back together in their proper order at the destination.
Network	The network layer adds logical addressing information to each packet to ensure that the packets arrive at the correct location.

(*continued*)

Layer	Function
Data-link	The data-link layer adds physical address information to the packets. The data-link layer also adds a cyclical redundancy check (CRC) to each packet. The CRC is a checksum used ensure that there are no errors in delivery.
	In addition, the data-link layer monitors the network and determines when it is appropriate to send data. The data is converted to a stream of 1s and 0s and passed to the physical layer.
Physical	As each bit of information is received from the data-link layer, the physical layer converts it to an appropriate format and transmits it on the network. On a wired network, each bit is translated into an electrical signal. On a fiber optic network, each bit is translated into a light signal.

The receiving process

The receiving process accepts incoming signals from the network, converts them to data, and passes the data to an application. In this example, the application is a database. The process is shown in the following table.

Layer	Function
Physical	The physical layer receives electrical signals or light signals from the cabling and converts the signals to 1s and 0s. Each bit is then passed to the data-link layer.
Data-link	The data-link layer organizes the bits into frames. The CRC on each frame is verified to ensure that there were no errors in delivery. If there were errors, the data-link layer requests that the packet be resent. After the CRC is verified, it is removed from the packet.
	In addition, the data-link layer verifies that the physical address is the receiving computer. If it is, the physical address information is removed from each packet, and the packets are passed to the network layer. If the physical address is not the receiving computer, the packet is dropped.
Network	The network layer confirms that the logical address is the receiving computer. If it is, the logical address information is removed from the packets, and they are passed to the transport layer. If the logical address is not the receiving computer, the packet is dropped.
Transport	The transport layer organizes all the packets back into a single chunk of data and passes the data to the session layer.
Session	When the data transmission is complete, the session layer closes the connection between the sender and receiver.
Presentation	The presentation layer undoes the formatting performed by the sender. In this case, the data is uncompressed and passed to the application layer.
Application	The application layer receives data from the presentation layer and passes it to the appropriate application or service. In this case, the data is passed to the database service running on the server.

The OSI Model and Network Devices

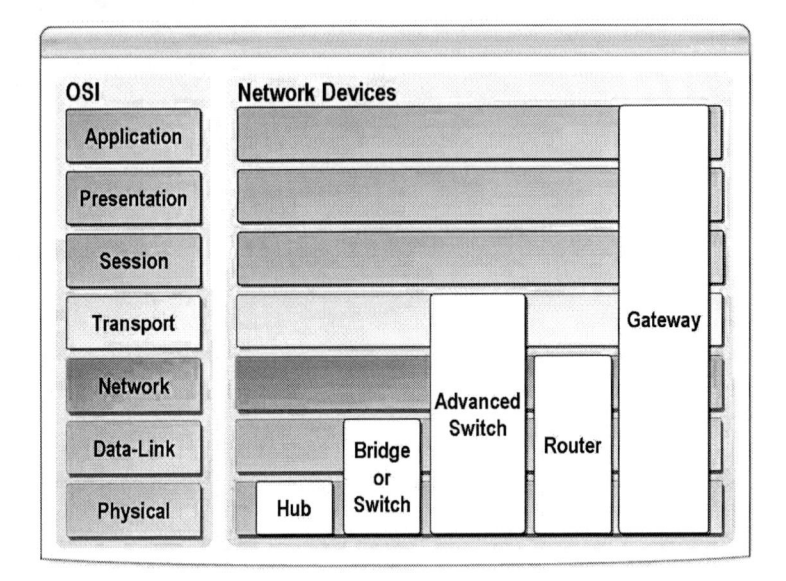

Introduction

One of the common uses of the OSI model is comparing the function of different network devices such as hubs, bridges, switches, routers, and gateways. If you understand the OSI model, you will understand how these devices operate differently and the benefits of each device.

Hubs

Hubs operate at the physical layer (layer 1) of the OSI model. As a result, hubs can only perform tasks with the electrical signal on the network cabling. Hubs regenerate 1s and 0s on network cabling. This allows the signals to be transmitted farther than would be possible without a hub.

Hubs are unable to make decisions about where the regenerated signal should be sent because they function only at the physical layer of the OSI model. Hubs send the regenerated signal out to all ports except the port on which the signal was received.

Note Repeaters have the same function as hubs. The term *multiport repeater* is sometimes used instead of *hub*.

Bridges

Bridges operate at the data-link layer (layer 2) of the OSI model. Bridges are able to control network traffic based on MAC addresses. This is useful for limiting traffic across small wide-area networks (WANs).

In a network with two locations, a bridge is used to separate the two locations and controls the packets transmitted between the two locations. The bridges automatically determine the location of computers by monitoring packets on the network and looking at the source MAC address in the packets. After the bridges have determined the location of the computers, they prevent local network traffic from being transmitted over the WAN.

Bridges are most often used over wireless links between buildings or locations.

Switches

The earliest switches and today's cheaper switches have the same functionality as a bridge and operate at the data-link layer of the OSI model. This functionality allows switches to control network traffic based on MAC addresses. Over time, switches create a table that lists the port location of each computer and direct packets to only the destination computer. This is in contrast to a hub, which propagates packets to all computers on the network. Directing the packets to the proper destination reduces the overall load on the network.

Many midrange and enterprise-level switches now have functionality that extends to layer 3 or layer 4 of the OSI model. Layer-3 switches can perform routing functions similar to a router. Layer-4 switches are application-aware and can give packets different priority levels based on the application that generated the packet.

Routers

Routers operate at the network layer (layer 3) of the OSI model. They are capable of moving packets from one logical network to another. This capability is required for larger local area networks (LANs) and WANs.

Large networks are sometimes divided into separate smaller networks to control communications between computers. An example of this would be a company with several different departments. Each department would have a small network that was a part of the larger company network. A router would be required to move packets from a computer in one department to a computer in a different department.

Gateways

A gateway is a device that converts one protocol to another. A gateway can operate at any layer of the OSI model, depending on which protocol is being converted.

One of the common gateway types in large organizations is a Systems Network Architecture (SNA) gateway. SNA is a protocol used for communication with mainframe computers. An SNA gateway allows computers on a TCP/IP network to communicate with mainframes by translating the TCP/IP communication into SNA communications. This is required to allow current computers to access older applications running on the mainframe.

Lesson: Overview of the TCP/IP Protocol Suite

- Multimedia: Why Do I Need to Know About TCP/IP?
- What Is the Architecture of the TCP/IP Protocol Suite?
- What Is an RFC?
- How Does the TCP/IP Model Relate to the OSI Model?
- Multimedia: Network Communication Using the TCP/IP Protocol Suite
- TCP/IP Network Communication
- Practice: Overview of the TCP/IP Protocol Suite

Introduction

The protocols in the TCP/IP protocol suite enable computers using different hardware and software to communicate over a network. TCP/IP for Windows Server 2003 provides a standard, routable, enterprise networking protocol to enable users to gain access to the World Wide Web and to send and receive e-mail. This lesson describes the four-layer conceptual model of the TCP/IP suite of protocols and how it maps to the OSI model. In addition, the lesson includes a depiction of a packet moving through the TCP/IP layers.

Note For more information about the TCP/IP protocol suite, see RFC 1180 under **Additional Reading** on the Student Materials compact disc.

Lesson objectives

After completing this lesson, you will be able to:

- Recognize why TCP/IP is important.
- Describe the architecture of the TCP/IP protocol suite.
- Describe what an RFC is.
- Associate the protocols of the TCP/IP protocol suite with those of the OSI model.
- Describe the function of the protocols at each layer of the TCP/IP protocol suite.
- Explain how data moves across a network by using the TCP/IP protocol suite.
- Match protocols to the layers of the TCP/IP protocol suite.

Multimedia: Why Do I Need to Know About TCP/IP?

- To understand the addressing scheme of your network to correctly configure client computers
- To know where to enter the TCP/IP information
- To find the TCP/IP information used to configure client computers

File location   To view the multimedia presentation *Why Do I Need to Know About TCP/IP?*, open the Web page on the Student Materials compact disc, click **Multimedia**, and then click the title of the presentation.

Objective   After you have completed this presentation, you will be able to explain the importance of understanding client computer addressing schemes and where to configure TCP/IP options on a client computer running a Microsoft Windows® operating system.

What Is the Architecture of the TCP/IP Protocol Suite?

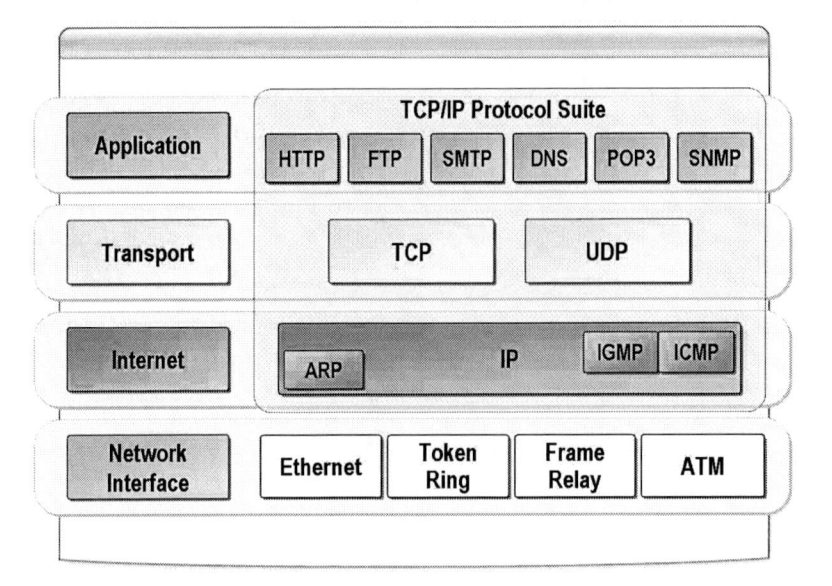

	TCP/IP Protocol Suite
Application	HTTP, FTP, SMTP, DNS, POP3, SNMP
Transport	TCP, UDP
Internet	ARP, IP, IGMP, ICMP
Network Interface	Ethernet, Token Ring, Frame Relay, ATM

Introduction

TCP/IP is an industry-standard suite of protocols that provides communication in a heterogeneous environment. The tasks that are involved in using TCP/IP in the communication process are distributed between protocols that are organized into four distinct layers of the TCP/IP stack.

Four layers of the TCP/IP stack

The four layers of the TCP/IP protocol stack are:

- The application layer.
- The transport layer.
- The Internet layer.
- The network interface layer.

Benefits of TCP/IP

Dividing the network functions into a stack of separate protocols, rather than creating a single protocol, provides several benefits:

- Separate protocols make it easier to support a variety of computing platforms. Creating or modifying protocols to support new standards does not require modification of the entire protocol stack.

- Having multiple protocols operating at the same layer makes it possible for applications to select the protocols that provide only the level of service required.

- Because the stack is split into layers, the development of the various protocols can proceed simultaneously, using personnel who are uniquely qualified in the operations of the particular layers.

Note For more information about the TCP/IP application layer and support protocols, see RFC 1123 under **Additional Reading** on the Student Materials compact disc. For more information about the transport, Internet, and network interface layers, see RFC 1122 under **Additional Reading** on the Student Materials compact disc.

What Is an RFC?

> An RFC is:
> - A description of Internet functionality
> - Categorized by status
> - Categorized by maturity
> - Never modified

Definition

The standards for TCP/IP are published in a series of documents called requests for comments (RFCs). RFCs describe the internal workings of the Internet. Some RFCs describe network services or protocols and their implementations, whereas others summarize policies. TCP/IP standards are always published as RFCs, although not all RFCs specify standards.

RFC status

TCP/IP standards are not developed by a committee, but rather by consensus. Anyone can submit a document for publication as an RFC. Documents are reviewed by a technical expert, a task force, or the RFC editor and are then assigned a status. The status specifies whether a document is being considered as a standard. The various status levels are listed in the following table.

Status	Description
Required	Must be implemented on all TCP/IP-based hosts and gateways.
Recommended	Encouraged that all TCP/IP-based hosts and gateways implement the RFC specification. Recommended RFCs are usually implemented.
Elective	Implementation is optional. Its application has been agreed to but is not a requirement
Limited Use	Not intended for general use.
Not Recommended	Not recommended for implementation.

RFC maturity

If a document is being considered as a standard, it goes through stages of development, testing, and acceptance known as the *Internet Standards process*. These stages, which are formally labeled *maturity levels*, are applied in addition to the RFC status. The possible maturity levels are listed in the following table.

Maturity level	Description
Proposed Standard	A Proposed Standard specification is generally stable, has resolved known design choices, is believed to be well understood, has received significant community review, and appears to enjoy enough community interest to be considered valuable.
Draft Standard	A Draft Standard must be well understood and known to be quite stable, both in its semantics and as a basis for developing an implementation.
Internet Standard	The Internet Standard specification (which might simply be referred to as a Standard) is characterized by a high degree of technical maturity and by a generally held belief that the specified protocol or service provides significant benefit to the Internet community.

RFC numbers

When a document is published, it is assigned an RFC number. The original RFC is never updated. Each time an RFC is revised and moves through the maturity levels, a new RFC is published with a new number. Therefore, it is important to verify that you have the most recent RFC on a particular topic.

Note More information about RFCs, including a complete list of RFCs, can be found at the IETF Web site. Also, RFC 2026 contains detailed information about the RFC approval process.

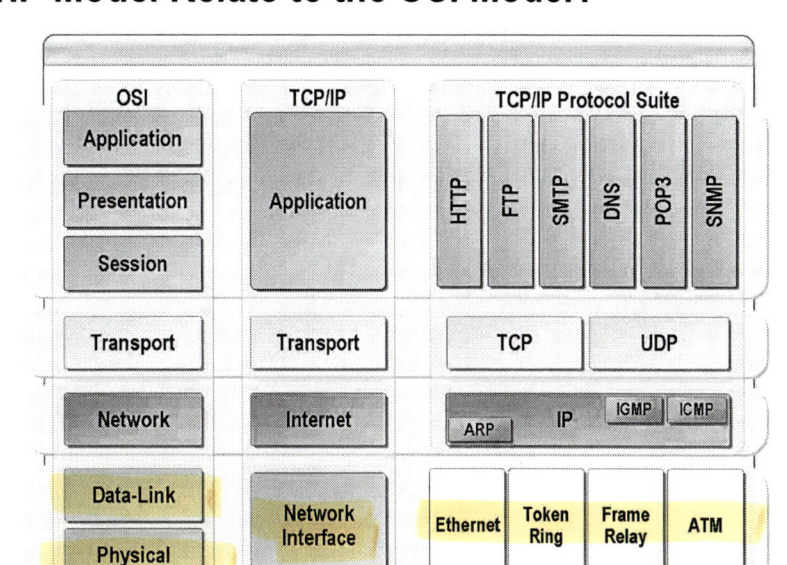

How Does the TCP/IP Model Relate to the OSI Model?

Introduction

The OSI model defines distinct layers related to packaging, sending, and receiving data transmissions in a network. The layered suite of protocols that form the TCP/IP stack carry out these functions.

Application layer

The application layer corresponds to the application, presentation, and session layers of the OSI model. This layer provides services and utilities that enable applications to access network resources.

On a computer running Windows Server, applications can request network services by using Windows Sockets or network basic input/output systems (NetBIOS). Windows Sockets is used by Internet applications and most other applications. NetBIOS is used for file sharing by clients running Microsoft Windows 98 and earlier, and by many older Windows applications. The developer of the application specifies whether an application will use Windows Sockets or NetBIOS.

Some application-layer protocols are described in the following table.

Protocol	Description
HTTP	Hypertext Transfer Protocol. Specifies the client/server interaction processes between Web browsers and Web servers.
FTP	File Transfer Protocol. Performs file transfers and basic file management tasks on remote computers.
SMTP	Simple Mail Transfer Protocol. Carries e-mail messages between servers and from clients to servers.
DNS	Domain Name System. Resolves Internet host names to IP addresses for network communications.
POP3	Post Office Protocol version 3. Used by mail clients for reading e-mail.
SNMP	Simple Network Management Protocol. Enables you to collect information about network devices such as hubs, routers, and bridges. Each piece of information to be collected about a device is defined in a Management Information Base (MIB).

Transport layer

The transport layer corresponds to the transport layer of the OSI model and is responsible for guaranteed delivery and end-to-end communication using one of two protocols described in the following table.

Protocol	Description
TCP	Transmission Control Protocol. Provides connection-oriented reliable communications for applications. Connection-oriented communication confirms that the destination is ready to receive data before sending. TCP confirms that all packets are received to make communication reliable.
	Reliable communication is desired in most cases and is used by most applications. Web servers, FTP clients, and other applications that move large amounts of data use TCP.
UDP	User Datagram Protocol. Provides connectionless and unreliable communication. Reliable delivery is the responsibility of the application when UDP is used. Applications use UDP for faster communication with less overhead than TCP.
	Applications such as streaming audio and video use UDP so that a single missing packet will not delay playback. UDP is also used by applications that send small amounts of data, such as DNS name lookups.

Internet layer

The Internet layer corresponds to the network layer of the OSI model. The protocols at this layer encapsulate transport-layer data into units called *datagrams*, address them, and route them to their destinations.

There are four protocols at the Internet layer, as described in the following table.

Protocol	Description
IP	Internet Protocol. Addresses and routes packets between hosts and networks.
ARP	Address Resolution Protocol. Obtains hardware addresses of hosts located on the same physical network.
IGMP	Internet Group Management Protocol. Manages host membership in IP multicast groups.
ICMP	Internet Control Message Protocol. Sends messages and reports errors regarding the delivery of a packet.

Network interface layer

The network interface layer (sometimes referred to as the link layer or data-link layer) corresponds to the data-link and physical layers of the OSI model. This layer specifies the requirements for sending and receiving packets on the network media. This layer is often not formally considered part of the TCP/IP protocol suite because the tasks are performed by the combination of the network card driver and the network card.

Multimedia: Network Communication Using the TCP/IP Protocol Suite

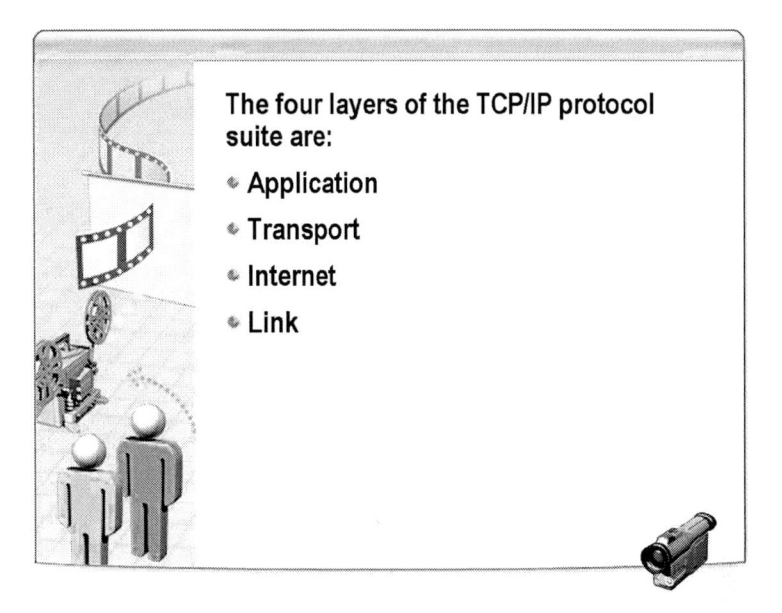

File location

To view the multimedia presentation *Network Communication Using the TCP/IP Protocol Suite*, open the Web page on the Student Materials compact disc, click **Multimedia**, and then click the title of the presentation.

Objective

After completing this presentation, you will be able to explain the role of each layer in the TCP/IP protocol stack and how an IP packet is sent and received by each layer.

TCP/IP Network Communication

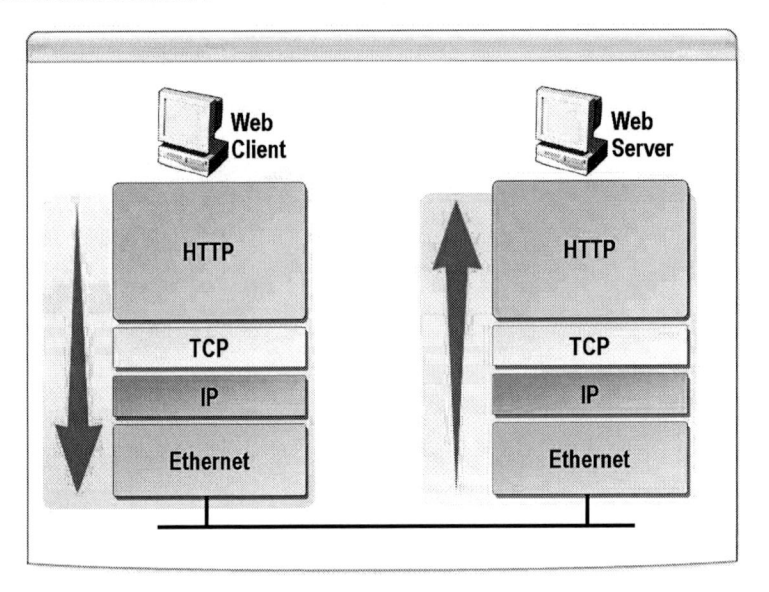

Introduction

To further understand what occurs at each layer of the TCP/IP protocol suite, it is useful to look at a specific example of network communication using the TCP/IP protocol suite. The following example is for a Web client communicating with a Web server.

The sending process

The sending process prepares and transmits data over the network, as described in the following table.

Layer	Function
Application	The Web browser software uses HTTP to build a request for the Web server and passes the request to TCP.
Transport	TCP initiates a session with the Web server that confirms details such as maximum packet size. If the request is large enough, TCP will also break the request into multiple packets. Packets are passed to IP.
Network	IP adds the source and destination IP addresses to the packets and passes them to the network card driver.
Network interface	Ethernet is a combination of functionality in the network card driver and the network card hardware. It is responsible for adding a source and destination MAC address and a CRC check to the packets. Ethernet is also responsible for placing the packets on the network media for delivery to the destination Web server.

The receiving process

The receiving process accepts data from the network and passes it to the Web server, as described in the following table.

Layer	Function
Network interface	Ethernet receives the signals from the network and converts them to a frame, and the CRC check on the frame is verified. The destination MAC addresses on the packets are verified, and the packets are passed up to IP.
Network	IP verifies the destination IP address and passes the packets to TCP.
Transport	TCP confirms that all of the packets have arrived and recombines them into a single request. TCP then passes the request to HTTP. The session initiated by TCP on the client side stays open until the entire communication process is complete.
Application	HTTP is used by the Web server to interpret the request. The Web server then sends a response back to the Web client. This response is typically the contents of a Web page, but it can also be an error message.

Practice: Overview of the TCP/IP Protocol Suite

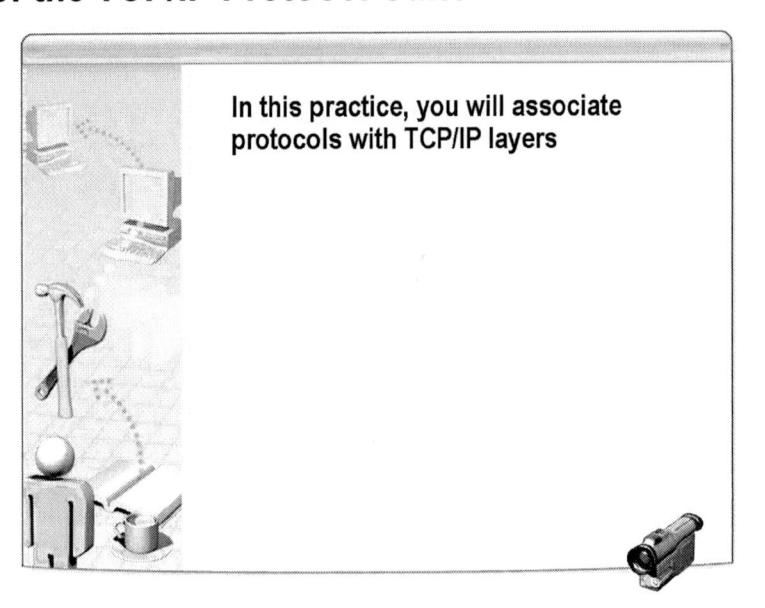

Objectives In this practice, you will associate protocols with TCP/IP layers.

Instructions No virtual machines are required for this practice.

Practice

▶ **Associate protocols with TCP/IP layers**

1. Insert the Student Materials compact disc.
2. If necessary, click **Start**, click **Run**, type *X*:**\StartCD.exe**, and then click **OK**.

   Note *X* represents the drive where the Student CD is located.

3. Click **Yes** to allow active content.
4. Click **Multimedia**.
5. Under **Module 1: Reviewing the Suite of TCP/IP Protocols**, click **Practice: Associating Protocols of an IP Address**.

▶ **Prepare for the next practice**

1. Start the DEN-DC1 virtual machine.
2. Start the DEN-SRV1 virtual machine.
3. Start the DEN-CL1 virtual machine.

Lesson: Viewing Frames by Using Network Monitor

- What Is Ping?
- What Is ARP?
- How ARP Resolves IP Addresses to MAC Addresses
- What Is Network Monitor?
- Captured Network Traffic
- Practice: Viewing Frames by Using Network Monitor

Introduction

Microsoft Network Monitor is a protocol analyzer that you can use to analyze and monitor network communications. Network Monitor simplifies your task of isolating complex network problems by performing real-time network traffic analysis and capturing packets for decoding and analysis.

In this lesson, you will use the Ping utility (Ping) to generate traffic for analysis.

Lesson objectives

After completing this lesson, you will be able to:

- Describe the Ping utility.
- Describe ARP.
- Describe how ARP resolves IP addresses to MAC addresses.
- Describe Network Monitor.
- Describe captured network traffic.
- View frames by using Network Monitor.

What Is Ping?

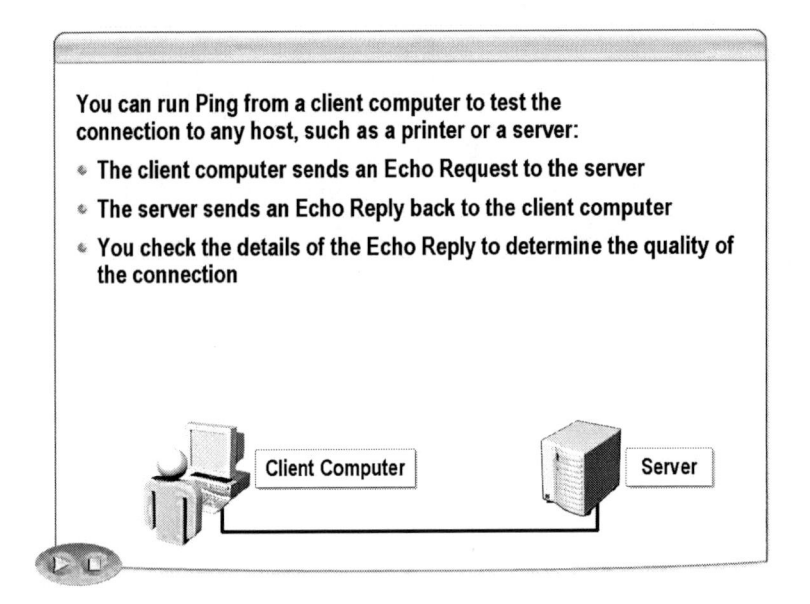

> You can run Ping from a client computer to test the connection to any host, such as a printer or a server:
> - The client computer sends an Echo Request to the server
> - The server sends an Echo Reply back to the client computer
> - You check the details of the Echo Reply to determine the quality of the connection

Definition

TCP/IP implementations include a basic network utility named Ping. You use Ping to test whether a target computer's networking hardware and protocols are functioning correctly, at least up to the network layer of the OSI model. When you use Ping, you generate network traffic. You can then use Network Monitor to analyze this traffic.

Example of using Ping

You run Ping by using the syntax ping *target*, where *target* is the computer name or IP address of the target computer. For example, in the slide:

1. The client computer is running the **ping** command, specifying the server as the target computer.
2. Ping generates a series of Echo messages using ICMP and transmits the Echo messages to the server.
3. The server sends Echo Reply messages back to the client computer.
4. When the originating computer receives the Echo Reply messages, it produces output.

Example of Ping output

When the originating computer receives the Echo Reply messages from the target computer, it produces a display similar to the following:

```
Pinging DEN-DC1 (10.10.0.2) with 32 bytes of data:
Reply from 10.10.0.2: bytes=32 time<10ms TTL=128
Reply from 10.10.0.2: bytes=32 time<10ms TTL=128
Reply from 10.10.0.2: bytes=32 time<10ms TTL=128
Reply from 10.10.0.2: bytes=32 time<10ms TTL=128
Ping statistics for 10.10.0.2:
Packets: Sent = 4, Received = 4, Lost = 0 (0% loss),
Approximate round trip times in milli-seconds:
Minimum = 0ms, Maximum = 0ms, Average = 0ms
```

This display shows the echo replies from the target computer. Information displayed includes the IP address of the target computer, the number of bytes of data included with each request, the elapsed time between the transmission of each request and the receipt of each reply, and the value of the Time to Live (TTL) field in the IP header. In this particular example, the target computer is on the same LAN, so the time measurement is very short—less than 10 milliseconds.

Responses to Ping requests

When you submit a Ping request to, or *ping*, a computer on the Internet, the interval is likely to be longer than when you ping a computer on your local network. A reply from the target computer indicates that its networking hardware and protocols are functioning correctly, at least as high as the network layer of the OSI model. Be careful not to assume that simply because a host did not respond to an echo request it is offline or that you are not properly connected to the network. Inability to obtain a reply to a ping can be an indication of network trouble.

Note Because of security issues such as the Ping of Death, in which a remote host sends an oversized packet to interrupt service in another system or to prevent outsiders from gaining network configuration information, it is not uncommon for network administrators to prevent external systems from responding to a Ping request.

What Is ARP?

- Resolves IP addresses to MAC addresses
- Provides MAC address for IP frames
- Dynamically stores MAC addresses in ARP cache
- Allows static entries in ARP cache

Definition

The destination MAC address in an IP frame is critical to the proper delivery of IP frames on a network. ARP is used to resolve IP addresses to MAC addresses. A MAC address is a 6-byte (48-bit) number that is used to uniquely identify network devices. The MAC address for a network card or network device is configured by the manufacturer of the device. The conversion of IP addresses to MAC addresses is done by computers as IP frames are built.

Why is ARP required?

When IP frames are delivered on a network, the network cards and network devices use MAC addresses to filter out packets that are not addressed to them. When an IP frame is received by a network card, the network card will verify whether the destination MAC address in the frame matches the MAC address of the network card. If the destination MAC address in the frame matches the MAC address of the network card, the frame is accepted and passed up to the IP. However, if the destination MAC address does not match the MAC address of the network card, the IP frame is dropped.

Note Some network cards support *promiscuous mode*. A network card that is placed in promiscuous mode does not filter packets based on the destination MAC address and will accept all packets that are received. This mode is used by network-sniffing software such as Network Monitor.

The ARP cache

To minimize the amount of broadcast network traffic that ARP generates, the computer stores recently resolved IP addresses and their corresponding MAC addresses in a cache. Entries automatically added to the ARP are called *dynamic entries*. TCP/IP checks the cache before sending out a broadcast request to obtain a MAC address.

Dynamic entries in the ARP cache have a time-out value of two minutes. If a dynamic ARP cache entry is not used within two minutes, it is removed from the ARP cache. If a dynamic ARP cache entry is used within two minutes, the time-out for the entry is increased to 10 minutes.

Static cache entries

You can place static entries directly into the ARP cache by using the Arp.exe utility. However, this is not recommended, as it will cause problems when IP addresses are changed or a network card is replaced. The amount of network traffic generated by ARP requests is unlikely to degrade network performance.

Note Static entries in the ARP cache are erased when the system is restarted.

How to use ARP to isolate connection issues

You can use the ARP tool to isolate connection issues. For example, if two computers on the same subnet cannot communicate with each other, you can use ARP to determine whether the correct MAC addresses are listed. To verify that the MAC addresses are correctly listed in the ARP cache, you run the **arp -a** command on each computer. This displays the IP and MAC addresses listed in the ARP cache for each computer. You verify that the MAC address listed in the ARP cache is the same as the actual MAC address for the destination computer by using Ipconfig.exe.

Example of output from the arp –a command

The following example shows the output for the **arp -a** command, which displays the ARP cache tables for all network interfaces:

```
C:\>arp -a
Interface: 10.10.0.2 ---  0x2
Internet address      Physical address        Type
10.10.0.1             00-e0-34-c0-a1-40       dynamic
10.10.1.231           00-00-f8-03-6d-65       dynamic
10.10.3.34            08-00-09-dc-82-4a       dynamic
10.10.4.53            00-c0-4f-79-49-2b       dynamic
10.10.5.102           00-00-f8-03-6c-30       dynamic
```

ARP syntax and parameters

ARP uses the following syntax:

arp [**-a** [*InetAddr*] [**-N** [*IfaceAddr*]] [**-g** [*InetAddr*] [**-N** [*IfaceAddr*]] [**-d** *InetAddr* [*IfaceAddr*]] [**-s** *InetAddr* *EtherAddr* [*IfaceAddr*]]

The following table describes the function of the ARP parameters.

Parameter	Function
-a	Displays current ARP cache entries for all interfaces. To display the ARP cache entry for a specific IP address, type **arp -a** *InetAddr*, where *InetAddr* is an IP address.
-N	Lists ARP entries for the interface specified by **-N** *IfaceAddr*, where *IfaceAddr* is the IP address assigned to the interface. The **-N** parameter is case-sensitive.
-g	Same as **-a**.
-d	Removes an entry specified by its IP address (*InetAddr*) from the ARP cache. To remove an entry for a specific interface, type **arp -d** *IfaceAddr*, where *IfaceAddr* is the IP address assigned to that interface. To delete all entries, use the asterisk (*) wildcard in place of *InetAddr*.
-s	Adds a static entry to the ARP cache that resolves the specified IP address (*InetAddr*) to the MAC address (*EtherAddr*). To add a static ARP cache entry to the table for a specific interface, type **arp -s** *IfaceAddr*, where *IfaceAddr* is the IP address assigned to that interface.
/?	Displays ARP parameters.

How ARP Resolves IP Addresses to MAC Addresses

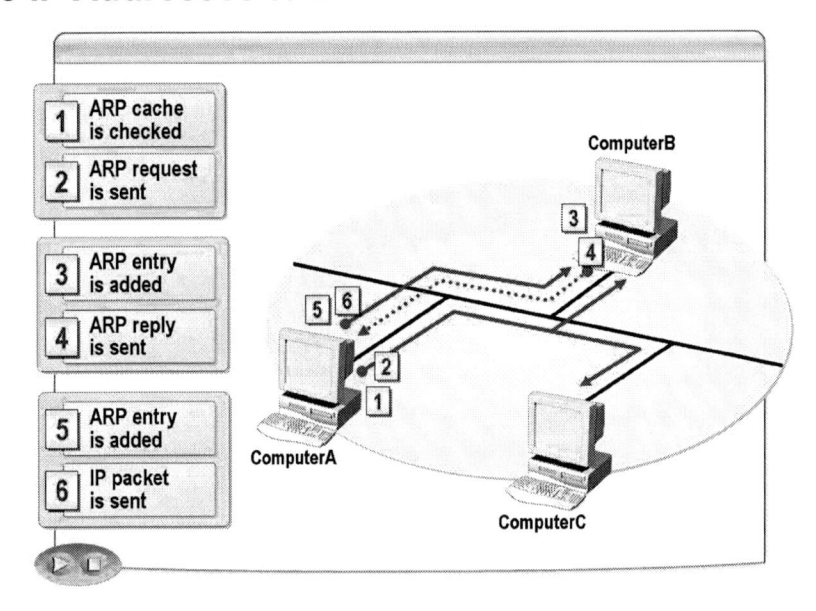

Introduction

Before transmitting an IP packet, TCP/IP clients must resolve the forwarding, or next-hop, IP address to its corresponding MAC address. If the MAC address for the next-hop is not in the ARP cache, the client will broadcast an ARP request frame to obtain the MAC address. The computer using that IP address responds with an ARP reply message containing its MAC address. With the information in the reply message, the computer can encapsulate the IP packet in the appropriate frame and transmit it to the next-hop.

The ARP process

In the preceding illustration, ComputerA is broadcasting an ARP request to ComputerB and ComputerC. The following steps describe the process:

1. On ComputerA, ARP consults its own ARP cache for an entry for the destination IP address. If an entry is found, ARP proceeds to step 6.

2. If an entry is not found, ARP on ComputerA builds an ARP request frame containing its own MAC address and IP address and the destination IP address. ARP then broadcasts the ARP request.

3. ComputerB and ComputerC receive the broadcasted frame and the ARP request is processed. If the receiving computer's IP address matches the requested IP address (the destination IP address), its ARP cache is updated with the address of the sender of the ARP request, ComputerA.

   If the receiving host's IP address does not match the requested IP address, as in the case of ComputerC, the ARP request is discarded.

4. ComputerB formulates an ARP reply containing its own MAC address and sends it directly to ComputerA.

5. When ComputerA receives the ARP reply from ComputerB, it updates its ARP cache with the IP address and MAC address.

   ComputerA and ComputerB now have each other's IP to MAC address mappings in their ARP caches.

6. ComputerA sends the IP packet to ComputerB.

What Is Network Monitor?

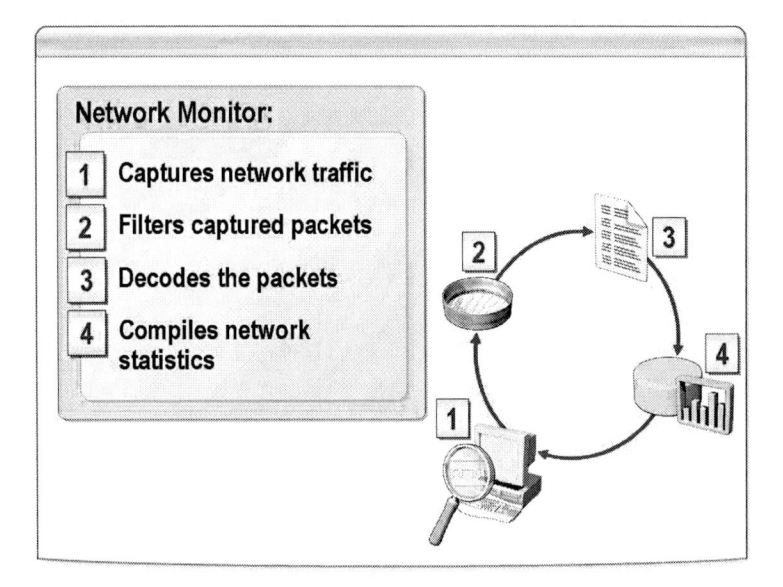

Network Monitor:
1. Captures network traffic
2. Filters captured packets
3. Decodes the packets
4. Compiles network statistics

Definition

Network Monitor is a utility included in Windows Server 2003, in Windows 2000 Server products, and in Microsoft Systems Management Server. The version that is included in Windows Server is capable of capturing only network traffic that is addressed to the server. The version of Network Monitor in Microsoft Systems Management Server operates in promiscuous mode and can capture all network traffic.

Uses of Network Monitor

You can use Network Monitor to:

- Locate client-to-server connection problems.
- Identify computers that make a disproportionate number of service requests.
- Capture frames (packets) directly from the network.
- Display and filter captured frames.

How Network Monitor works

To monitor network traffic, Network Monitor:

1. Captures a snapshot of network traffic.
2. Uses filters to select or highlight specific packets.
3. Decodes the packets in a language of the individual protocols.
4. Compiles network statistics.

Captured Network Traffic

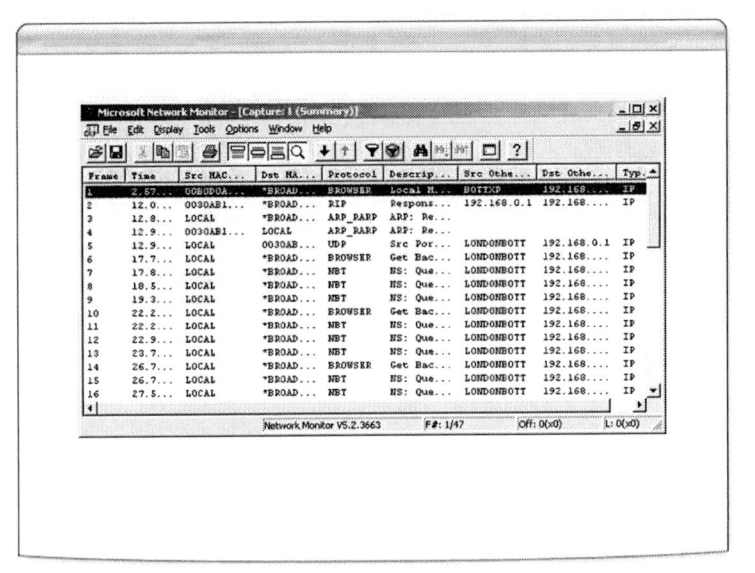

Introduction

When you capture a sample of network traffic, the Network Monitor Capture Summary window displays a chronological list of the frames in your sample.

The following table describes the fields that are displayed for each frame in your sample.

Field	Description
Frame	Shows the number of the frame in the sample.
Time	Indicates the time (in seconds) at which the frame was captured, measured from the beginning of the sample.
Src MAC Addr	Gives the hardware address of the network interface in the computer that transmitted the frame. For computers that the analyzer recognizes by a friendly name, such as a NetBIOS name, this field contains that name instead of the address. The computer on which the analyzer is running is identified as LOCAL.
Dst MAC Addr	Gives the hardware address of the network interface in the computer that received the frame. Friendly names are substituted if available. By compiling an address book of the computers on your network, you can eventually have frame captures that use only friendly names.
Protocol	Shows the dominant protocol in the frame. Each frame contains information generated by protocols running at several different layers of the OSI model.
Description	Indicates the function of the frame, using information specific to the protocol referenced in the Protocol field.
Src Other Addr	Specifies another address used to identify the computer that transmitted the frame.

(*continued*)

Field	Description
Dst Other Addr	Specifies another address (such as an IP address) used to identify the computer that received the frame.
Type Other Addr	Specifies the type of address used in the Src Other Addr and Dst Other Addr fields.

Tip To work with large capture files, increase the size of the Windows page file, and save large capture files before viewing them.

Practice: Viewing Frames by Using Network Monitor

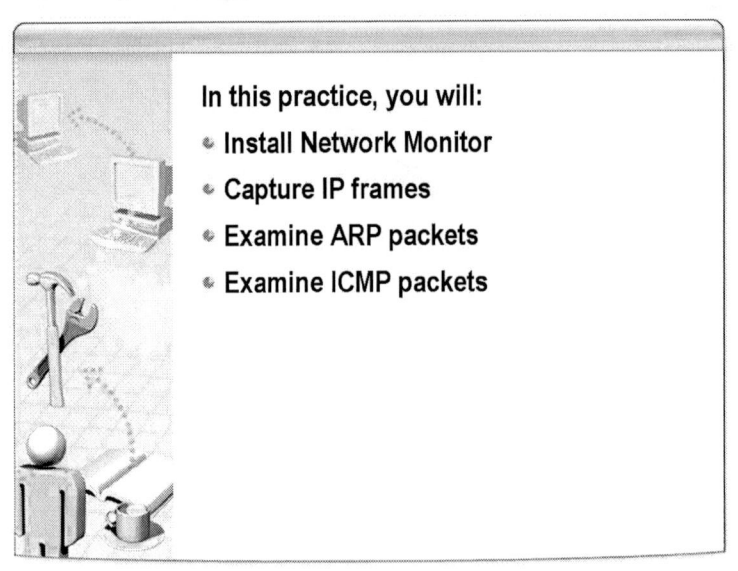

In this practice, you will:
- Install Network Monitor
- Capture IP frames
- Examine ARP packets
- Examine ICMP packets

Objectives

In this practice, you will:

- Install Network Monitor.
- Capture IP frames.
- Examine ARP packets.
- Examine ICMP packets.

Instructions

Ensure that the DEN-DC1, DEN-SRV1, and DEN-CL1 virtual machines are running.

Note Microsoft recommends that you log on using a standard user account and use the **Run As** command to perform administrative tasks. In this practice, you will log on as Administrator for convenience.

Practice

▶ **Install Network Monitor**

1. On DEN-SRV1, log on to the **Contoso** domain as **Administrator**, with a password of **Pa$$w0rd**.
2. Click **Start**, point to **Control Panel**, and then click **Add or Remove Programs**.
3. Click **Add/Remove Windows Components**.
4. In the **Windows Components Wizard** dialog box, click **Management and Monitoring Tools**, and then click **Details**.
5. Select the check box next to **Network Monitor Tools**, click **OK**, and then click **Next**.
6. Click **Finish**.
7. Close **Add or Remove Programs**.

▶ Capture IP frames

1. On DEN-DC1, log on as **Administrator**, with a password of **Pa$$w0rd**.
2. Click **Start**, point to **Administrative Tools**, and then click **Network Monitor**.
3. Click **OK** to begin selecting the network on which you want to capture data.
4. Expand **Local Computer**, click **Local Area Connection**, and then click **OK**. Maximize the Microsoft Network Monitor window.
5. On DEN-CL1, log on to the **Contoso** domain as **Paul**, with a password of **Pa$$w0rd**.
6. Click **Start**, click **Run**, type **cmd**, and then click **OK**.
7. Type **arp –d *** and then press ENTER to delete all entries in the ARP cache.
8. On DEN-DC1, on the **Capture** menu, click **Start**.
9. On DEN-CL1, type **ping 10.10.0.2**, and then press ENTER.
10. Wait for the **Ping** command to complete on DEN-CL1.
11. On DEN-DC1, on the **Capture** menu, click **Stop**.
12. On the **Capture** menu, click **Display Captured Data**.

▶ Examine ARP packets

1. On DEN-DC1, on the **Display** menu, click **Filter**.
2. Double-click **Protocol==Any**.
3. Click **Disable All**.
4. Under **Disabled Protocols**, double-click **ARP_RARP:** and then click **OK**.
5. Click **OK**. Notice that only two frames are visible now. These are the two ARP packets.
6. Read the description of the two frames that are listed. Notice that the first is an ARP request for the IP address 10.10.0.2 and the second is the ARP reply.
7. Double-click the first frame to display more detailed information about the packet. The middle pane shows the decoded information about the frame. The bottom pane shows the packet displayed as hex values and ASCII.
8. In the middle pane, expand **ARP_RARP: ARP: Request, Target IP: 10.10.0.2** to display detailed information about the ARP request, including the MAC address and IP address of the sender.

▶ **Examine ICMP packets**

1. On the **Display** menu, click **Disable Filter**.
2. On the **Display** menu, click **Colors**.
3. In the **Protocol Colors** dialog box, click **ICMP**.
4. Under **Colors**, set the foreground to red, and then click **OK**. This displays all ICMP packets in red.
5. Click the first red frame to display the details of the ICMP ECHO from 10.10.0.20 (DEN-CL1) to 10.10.0.2 (DEN-DC1).
6. In the middle pane, expand **FRAME: Base frame properties** to display general information about the frame.
7. Expand **ETHERNET: EType = Internet IP (IPv4)** to display the source and destination MAC addresses.
8. Expand **IP: Protocol = ICMP – Internet Control Message** to display the source and destination IP addresses as well as other IP information.
9. Expand **ICMP: Echo: From 10.10.00.20 to 10.10.00.02** to display detailed information about the ICMP protocol. Notice that the ICMP packet type is **Echo**.
10. Click **ICMP: Packet Type = Echo**. Notice that the hexadecimal value that corresponds to this information is selected in the bottom pane. The hexadecimal value is **08**.
11. In the top pane, click the second red frame.
12. If necessary, in the middle pane, expand **ICMP: Echo Reply: to 10.10.00.20 From 10.10.00.02**. Notice that the packet type is **Echo Reply**.
13. Close Network Monitor. Do not save the frame capture.

Important When you have finished the practice, shut down all the virtual machines without saving changes.

Module 2: Assigning IP Addresses in a Multiple-Subnet Network

Contents

Overview	1
Lesson: Configuring IP Addressing for Simple Networks	2
Lesson: Configuring IP Addressing for Complex Networks	13
Lesson: Using IP Routing Tables	25
Lesson: Overcoming the Limitations of the IP Addressing Scheme	35
Lab: Assigning IP Addresses in a Multiple-Subnet Network	47

Information in this document, including URL and other Internet Web site references, is subject to change without notice. Unless otherwise noted, the example companies, organizations, products, domain names, e-mail addresses, logos, people, places, and events depicted herein are fictitious, and no association with any real company, organization, product, domain name, e-mail address, logo, person, place or event is intended or should be inferred. Complying with all applicable copyright laws is the responsibility of the user. Without limiting the rights under copyright, no part of this document may be reproduced, stored in or introduced into a retrieval system, or transmitted in any form or by any means (electronic, mechanical, photocopying, recording, or otherwise), or for any purpose, without the express written permission of Microsoft Corporation.

The names of manufacturers, products, or URLs are provided for informational purposes only and Microsoft makes no representations and warranties, either expressed, implied, or statutory, regarding these manufacturers or the use of the products with any Microsoft technologies. The inclusion of a manufacturer or product does not imply endorsement of Microsoft of the manufacturer or product. Links are provided to third party sites. Such sites are not under the control of Microsoft and Microsoft is not responsible for the contents of any linked site or any link contained in a linked site, or any changes or updates to such sites. Microsoft is not responsible for webcasting or any other form of transmission received from any linked site. Microsoft is providing these links to you only as a convenience, and the inclusion of any link does not imply endorsement of Microsoft of the site or the products contained therein.

Microsoft may have patents, patent applications, trademarks, copyrights, or other intellectual property rights covering subject matter in this document. Except as expressly provided in any written license agreement from Microsoft, the furnishing of this document does not give you any license to these patents, trademarks, copyrights, or other intellectual property.

© 2005 Microsoft Corporation. All rights reserved.

Microsoft, Active Directory, Excel, MS-DOS, PowerPoint, Windows, Windows Media, Windows NT, and Windows Server are either registered trademarks or trademarks of Microsoft Corporation in the United States and/or other countries.

All other trademarks are property of their respective owners.

Overview

- Configuring IP Addressing for Simple Networks
- Configuring IP Addressing for Complex Networks
- Using IP Routing Tables
- Overcoming the Limitations of the IP Addressing Scheme

Introduction

This module describes how to construct and assign an Internet Protocol (IP) address to host computers on a network that is running the suite of Transmission Control Protocol/Internet Protocol (TCP/IP) protocols. IP addresses enable computers running any operating system on any platform to communicate by providing unique identifiers. To send data between multiple subnets, IP must select a route. Understanding the IP routing procedures will assist you in constructing and assigning the appropriate IP addresses for hosts on your network.

Note In this module, the term *host* refers to any device on the network that has an IP address. The term *client* refers to a computer running a Microsoft® Windows® operating system on a network running TCP/IP.

Objectives

After completing this module, you will be able to:

- Explain how to configure IP addressing for simple TCP/IP-based networks.
- Explain how to configure IP addressing for complex TCP/IP-based networks.
- Describe how routing tables are used.
- Overcome limitations that are caused by class-based routing.

Lesson: Configuring IP Addressing for Simple Networks

- Multimedia: The Components of an IP Address
- What Is a Subnet Mask?
- Multimedia: The Role of Routing in the Network Infrastructure
- What Is a Default Gateway?
- What Are the Classes of IP Addresses?
- How IP Communication Within a Single Network Works
- How IP Communication Between Networks Works
- Practice: Configuring IP Addressing for Simple Networks

Introduction

The primary function of IP is to add address information to data packets and route them across the network. To understand how IP accomplishes this, it is necessary for you to be familiar with the concepts that determine the intermediate and final destination addresses of data packets. Understanding how IP uses address information will enable you to ensure that IP routes data to the correct destination.

A simple network is one in which IP networks are based on full octets. Basing networks on full octets allows a simple subnet mask composed of only 255s and 0s.

Lesson objectives

After completing this lesson, you will be able to:

- Describe the components of an IP address.
- Describe what a subnet mask is and its purpose.
- Explain how routers are used to move packets between networks.
- Explain what a default gateway is.
- Describe the classes of IP addresses and their characteristics.
- Describe the communication process within a single IP network.
- Describe the communication process between IP networks.
- Perform the calculations that are used in routing between simple networks.

Multimedia: The Components of an IP Address

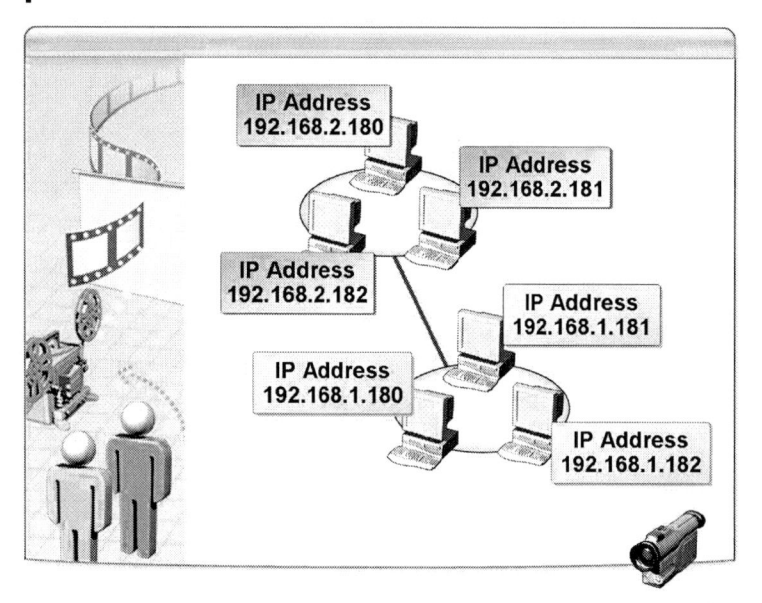

File location

To view the multimedia presentation *The Components of an IP Address*, open the Web page on the Student Materials compact disc, click **Multimedia**, and then click the title of the presentation.

Objective

After this presentation, you will be able to describe how the numbers in an IP address are grouped to designate network and host addresses.

What Is a Subnet Mask?

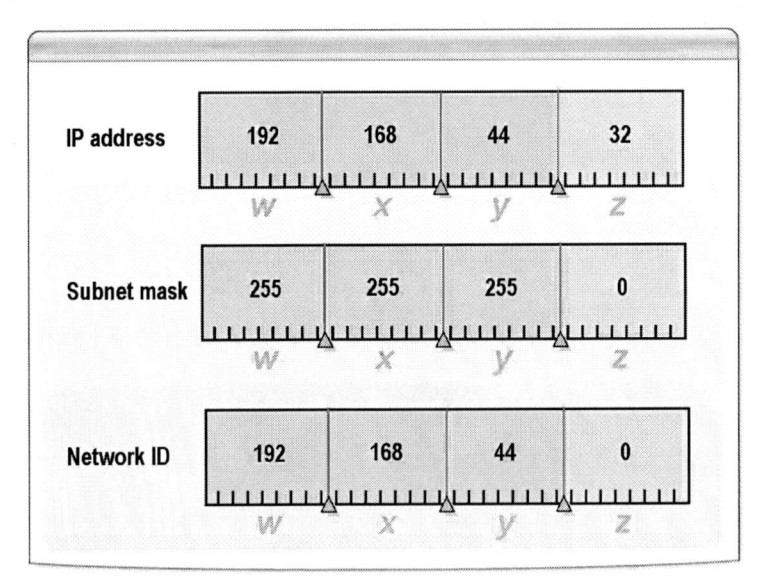

[Diagram showing:
- IP address: 192.168.44.32 with octets labeled w, x, y, z
- Subnet mask: 255.255.255.0 with octets labeled w, x, y, z
- Network ID: 192.168.44.0 with octets labeled w, x, y, z]

Definition

A *subnet mask* defines the part of an IP address that is the network ID and the part of an IP address that is the host ID. A subnet mask is composed of four octets, similar to an IP address.

In simple IP networks, the subnet mask defines full octets as part of the network ID and host ID. A 255 represents an octet that is part of the network ID, and a 0 represents an octet that is part of the host ID. In complex IP networks, octets can be subdivided.

Why a subnet mask is required

When a computer delivers an IP packet, it uses the subnet mask to validate whether the destination is on the same network or on a remote network. If the destination is on the same network, the packet can be delivered by the computer. If the destination is on a different network, the computer must send the packet to a router for delivery.

Valid subnet masks

In a simple IP network, a subnet mask is composed of only 255s and 0s. Other values are not used. In addition, 255s appear at the beginning of the subnet mask and 0s appear at the end. In a valid subnet mask, 0s cannot be interspersed with 255s. Examples of valid and invalid subnet masks are shown in the following table.

Valid subnet masks	Invalid subnet masks
255.0.0.0	0.0.255.255
255.255.0.0	255.0.255.0
255.255.255.0	0.255.255.0

Calculating the network ID of an IP address

To calculate the network ID of an IP address, the address must be compared to the subnet mask configured on that host. For each octet in the subnet mask that has a value of 255, the corresponding octet of the IP address is part of the network ID. Several examples are shown in the following table.

Description	Example 1	Example 2
IP address	192.168.44.32	172.31.99.220
Subnet mask	255.255.255.0	255.255.0.0
Network ID	192.168.44.0	172.31.0.0
Host ID	0.0.0.32	0.0.99.220

Multimedia: The Role of Routing in the Network Infrastructure

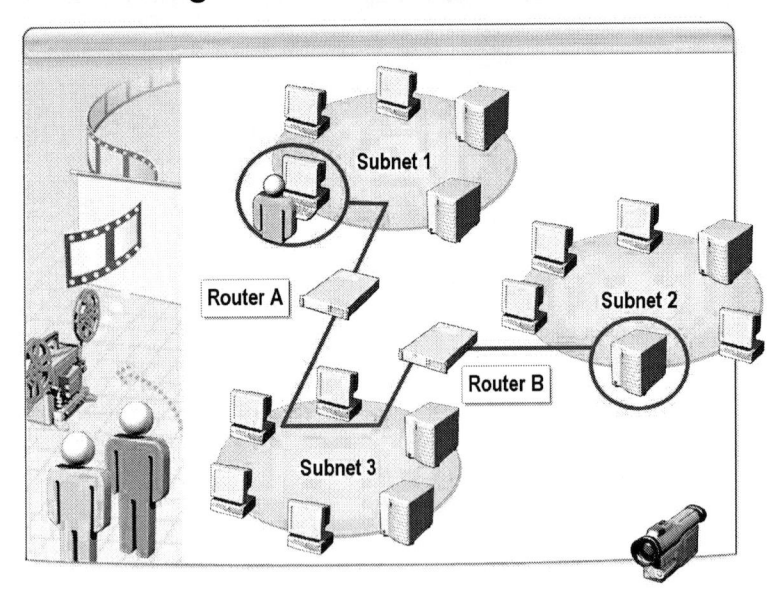

File location	To view the multimedia presentation *The Role of Routing in the Network Infrastructure*, open the Web page on the Student Materials compact disc, click **Multimedia**, and then click the title of the presentation.
Objective	After this presentation, you will be able to describe how IP addresses are used by routers to pass data between networks and subnetworks.

What Is a Default Gateway?

> **The default gateway:**
> - Is used to route packets to other networks
> - Is used when the internal routing table on the host has no information about the destination subnet
>
> Use DHCP to automatically deliver the IP address for the default gateway to the client

Definition

A *default gateway* is a device, usually a router, on a TCP/IP internetwork that can forward IP packets to other networks. An *internetwork* is a group of networks that are connected by routers. When a host does not have enough information to deliver an IP packet, the host delivers the packet to a default gateway. The default gateway is then responsible for delivering the packet to the destination.

The role of the default gateway

In an internetwork, any given subnet might have several routers that connect it to other subnets, both local and remote. At least one of the routers is configured as the default gateway for the subnet. When a host on the network uses IP to send a packet to a destination subnet, IP consults the internal routing table to determine the appropriate router for the packet to reach the destination subnet. If the routing table does not contain any routing information about the destination subnet, the packet is forwarded to the default gateway. The host assumes that the default gateway contains the required routing information.

How to configure the client for the default gateway

In most cases, the Dynamic Host Configuration Protocol (DHCP) is used to automatically assign a default gateway to a DHCP client. In the event that you need to assign the default gateway manually on clients running Microsoft Windows Server™ 2003, Windows 2000, Windows 98, or Windows 95, you configure the Default Gateway Address property on the General tab in the Network Connections Properties dialog box.

What Are the Classes of IP Addresses?

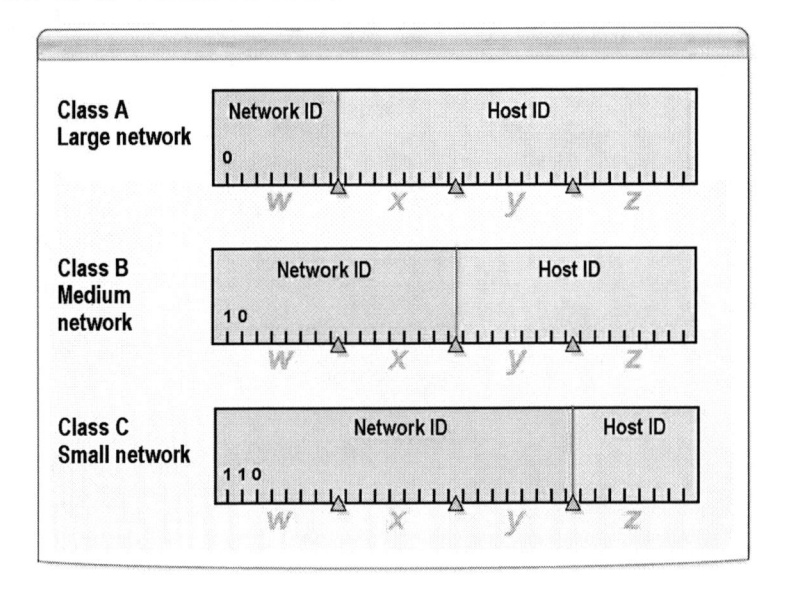

Introduction

IP addresses are organized into classes. You obtain registered addresses through an Internet service provider (ISP). Your ISP obtains addresses from a Regional Internet Registry. The number of hosts on the network determines the class of addresses that are required.

IP address classes

The IP address classes are named Class A through Class E. Classes A, B, and C are IP addresses that can be assigned to hosts as unique IP addresses. Class D is used for multicasting, and Class E is reserved for experimental use. Packet delivery to Class A, B, and C addresses is referred to as a *unicast*, because the packets are delivered to a single host.

Class A, B, and C networks have a default subnet mask associated with them. This subnet mask defines the portion of the IP address that is used for the host ID. The portion of the address that is used for the host ID determines the number of hosts on a network. The following table lists the characteristics of each IP address class.

Class	First octet	Default subnet mask	Number of networks	Number of hosts per network
A	1–127	255.0.0.0	126	16,777,214
B	128–191	255.255.0.0	16,384	65,534
C	192–223	255.255.255.0	2,097,152	254
D	224–239	n/a	n/a	n/a
E	240–255	n/a	n/a	n/a

Class A

Any IP address in which the first octet has a value between 1 and 127 is a part of a Class A network. There are only 126 available Class A networks, each with up to 16,777,214 hosts.

Because Class A networks are very large, they are allocated to very large organizations. It is no longer possible for individual companies to obtain Class A networks.

Note All IP addresses on the network 127.0.0.0 refer to the local host. The IP addresses on this network are used for diagnostics only.

Class B

An IP address in which the first octet has a value between 128 and 191 is part of a Class B network. There are 16,384 Class B networks, each with up to 65,534 hosts.

Class B networks are assigned to a variety of large companies and universities. For example, the 131.107.0.0 network is allocated to Microsoft Corporation.

Class C

An IP address in which the first octet has a value between 192 and 223 is part of a Class C network. There are 2,097,152 Class C networks, each with up to 254 hosts.

Class C addresses are assigned to many small and medium-size organizations. In some cases, companies are assigned a Class C network for each of their locations.

Class D

Class D addresses are not assigned to individual hosts. Class D addresses are assigned to groups of computers called multicast groups. Using multicast groups is an efficient way to deliver information on a network when multiple hosts need the same information at the same time.

If six computers were receiving a video at the same time, the video would need to be transmitted over the network six times using Class A, B, or C addresses. When multicasting is used, the video is transmitted to the multicast address and received by all six computers in a single transfer.

Multicast addresses are typically selected by application developers. The applications use a consistent multicast address each time, and all computers running the application use the same multicast address.

Class E

Class E addresses are reserved for experimental use and are never used on TCP/IP networks except for the broadcast address. The address 255.255.255.255 is a broadcast. Packets addressed to this IP address are delivered to all hosts on the local network.

Broadcasts are used when applications are not configured with the IP address of the host that they should be contacting. For example, DHCP clients use broadcasts to communicate with a DHCP server and obtain an IP address.

How IP Communication Within a Single Network Works

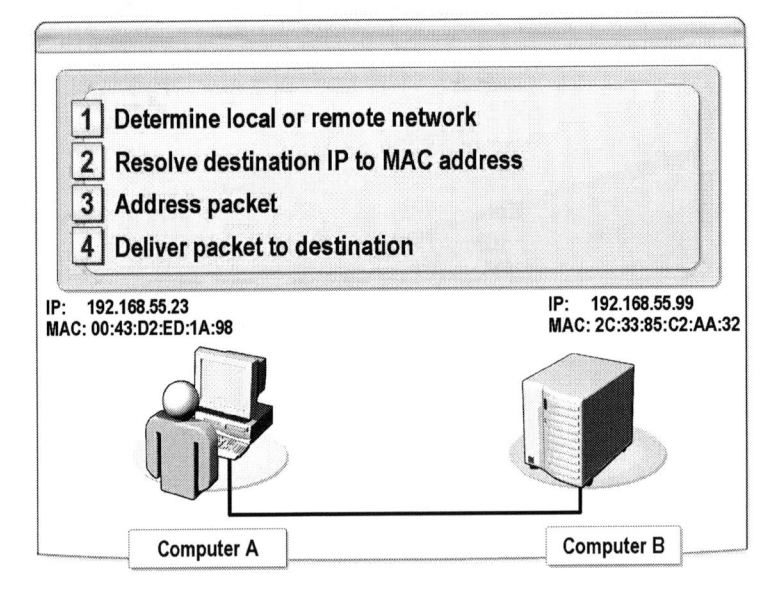

> 1. Determine local or remote network
> 2. Resolve destination IP to MAC address
> 3. Address packet
> 4. Deliver packet to destination
>
> IP: 192.168.55.23
> MAC: 00:43:D2:ED:1A:98
>
> IP: 192.168.55.99
> MAC: 2C:33:85:C2:AA:32
>
> Computer A — Computer B

Introduction

On a single network, each computer can deliver packets to the destination by itself. There is no need for a router to help with packet delivery. The sending computer resolves the destination IP address to a media access control (MAC) address and sends the packet on to the network.

Packet delivery within a single network

The following steps describe how IP communication within a single network works:

1. Computer A uses its own subnet mask to determine that it is on the same network as Computer B.

2. Computer A uses the Address Resolution Protocol (ARP) to resolve the IP address of Computer B to a MAC address.

3. The packet is addressed with the source IP address of Computer A, destination IP address of Computer B, source MAC address of Computer A, and destination MAC address of Computer B.

4. The packet is delivered to Computer B.

How IP Communication Between Networks Works

```
1  Determine local or remote network
2  Resolve default gateway IP to MAC address
3  Address and deliver packet to default gateway
4  Resolve destination IP to MAC address
5  Address and deliver packet to destination
```

IP: 192.168.55.23
MAC: 00:43:D2:ED:1A:98

IP: 192.168.37.1
MAC: 6B:11:43:75:CB:12

IP: 192.168.55.1
MAC: 6B:11:43:75:CB:12

IP: 192.168.37.99
MAC: 2C:33:85:C2:AA:32

Computer A   Computer B

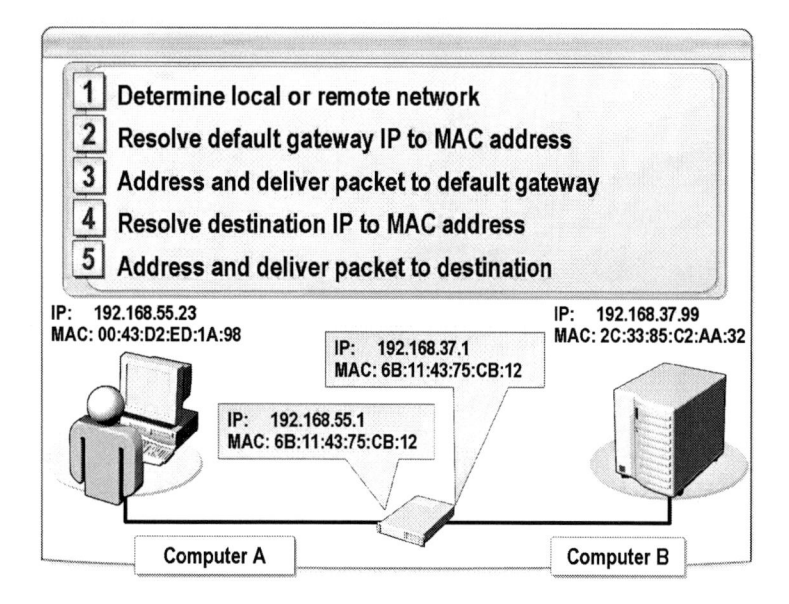

Introduction

Packets delivered between networks use a default gateway. The default gateway moves packets from one network to another. The sending computer delivers packets to the default gateway, and the default gateway delivers the packets to the destination.

Packet delivery between networks

The following steps describe how IP communication between networks works:

1. Computer A uses its own subnet mask to determine that it is on a different network than Computer B.

2. Computer A uses ARP to resolve the default gateway IP address to a MAC address.

3. The packet is addressed with the source IP address of Computer A, destination IP address of Computer B, source MAC address of Computer A, and destination MAC address of the default gateway. The packet is delivered to the default gateway.

4. The default gateway uses ARP to resolve the IP address of Computer B to a MAC address.

5. The packet is addressed with the source IP address of Computer A, destination IP address of Computer B, source MAC address of the default gateway, and destination MAC address of Computer B. The packet is delivered to Computer B.

Practice: Configuring IP Addressing for Simple Networks

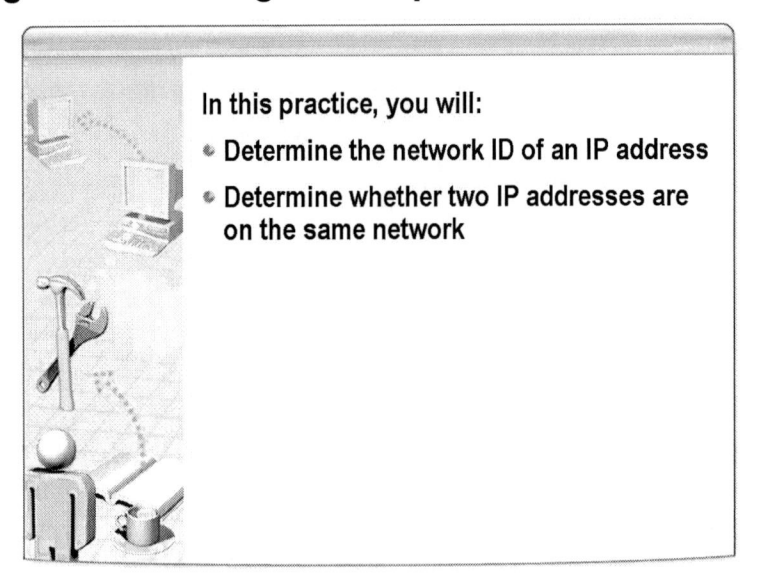

Objectives

In this practice, you will:

- Determine the network ID of an IP address.
- Determine whether two IP addresses are on the same network.

Instructions

No virtual machines are required for this practice.

Practice

▶ **Determine the network ID of an IP address**

Enter the address class and default subnet mask, and then determine the network ID of the address.

IP address	Address class	Subnet mask	Network ID
10.50.43.222			
206.73.118.92			
172.29.78.133			
239.192.10.5			
157.54.255.2			
192.168.200.200			

▶ **Determine whether two IP addresses are on the same network**

IP address #1	Subnet mask	IP address #2	Same (Y/N)
192.168.22.65	255.255.255.0	192.168.25.200	
10.38.99.10	255.0.0.0	10.208.99.10	
192.168.199.208	255.255.255.0	192.168.199.1	
172.18.165.36	255.255.0.0	172.31.218.118	

Lesson: Configuring IP Addressing for Complex Networks

- How Dotted Decimal Notation Relates to Binary Numbers
- What Is a Subnet?
- How Bits Are Used in a Subnet Mask
- How the Computer Determines Whether an IP Address Is a Local or Remote Address
- Guidelines for Choosing a Subnet Mask
- Practice: Configuring IP Addressing for Complex Networks

Introduction

Complex networks are often not able to use the default subnet mask assigned to Class A, B, or C networks. They must be subdivided into smaller networks, called subnets. This lesson describes how to convert dotted decimal notation to binary and calculate the subnet mask for subdivided networks.

Lesson objectives

After completing this lesson, you will be able to:

- Convert an IP address in dotted decimal notation to binary numbers.
- Describe what a subnet is.
- Explain how bits are used in a subnet mask.
- Describe how a computer determines whether an IP address is a local or remote address.
- Apply guidelines for choosing a subnet mask.
- Configure IP addressing for a complex network.

How Dotted Decimal Notation Relates to Binary Numbers

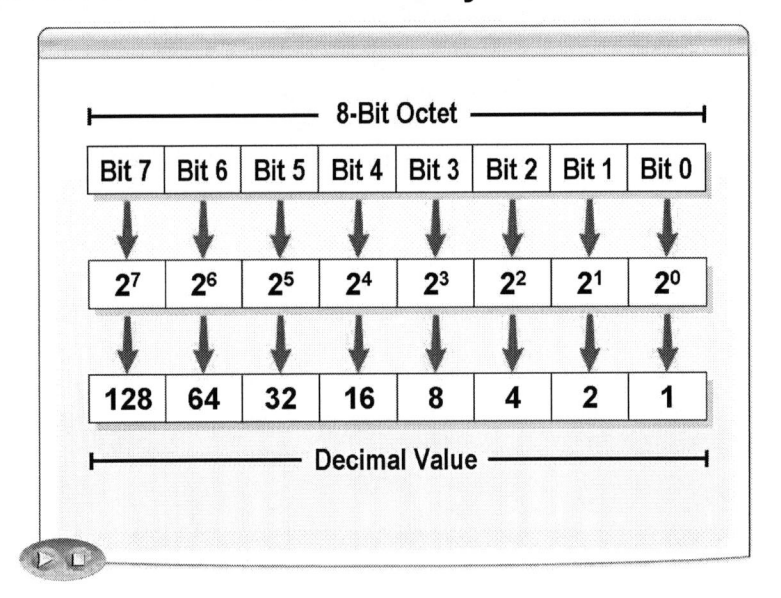

```
|---------------------- 8-Bit Octet ----------------------|
| Bit 7 | Bit 6 | Bit 5 | Bit 4 | Bit 3 | Bit 2 | Bit 1 | Bit 0 |
   ↓       ↓       ↓       ↓       ↓       ↓       ↓       ↓
|  2⁷   |  2⁶   |  2⁵   |  2⁴   |  2³   |  2²   |  2¹   |  2⁰   |
   ↓       ↓       ↓       ↓       ↓       ↓       ↓       ↓
|  128  |  64   |  32   |  16   |   8   |   4   |   2   |   1   |
|---------------------- Decimal Value ---------------------|
```

Introduction

When you assign IP addresses, you use dotted decimal notation, which is based on the decimal number system. However, in the background, computers use IP addresses in binary. To understand how to choose a subnet mask for complex networks, you must understand IP addresses in binary.

Within an 8-bit octet, each bit position has an assigned decimal value. A bit that is set to 0 always has a zero value. A bit that is set to 1 can be converted to a decimal value. The low-order bit, the rightmost bit in the octet, represents a decimal value of 1. The high-order bit, the leftmost bit in the octet, represents a decimal value of 128. The highest decimal value of an octet is 255—that is, all bits are set to 1.

Most of the time, you will use a calculator to convert decimal numbers to binary and vice versa. The Calculator application included in Windows is capable of performing decimal-to-binary conversions.

Example of an IP address in binary and dotted decimal formats

The following table shows the binary format and dotted decimal notation of an IP address.

Binary format	Dotted decimal notation
10000011 01101011 00000011 00011000	131.107.3.24

How to calculate the decimal value of a binary number

To calculate the decimal value of a binary representation:

1. Starting with the leftmost digit of the octet, multiply each number in the octet by decreasing powers of 2, beginning with 2^7.
2. Add these values to obtain the number.

   For example, for the number 10000011:

   $1 \times 2^7 = 1 \times 128 = 128$

   $0 \times 2^6 = 0 \times 64 = 0$

   $0 \times 2^5 = 0 \times 32 = 0$

   $0 \times 2^4 = 0 \times 16 = 0$

   $0 \times 2^3 = 0 \times 8 = 0$

   $0 \times 2^2 = 0 \times 4 = 0$

   $1 \times 2^1 = 1 \times 2 = 2$

   $1 \times 2^0 = 1 \times 1 = 1$

   $128+0+0+0+0+0+2+1 = 131$

Values for converting from binary to decimal

The following table shows the bit values and the decimal values for all the bits in one octet.

Binary format	Bit values	Decimal value
00000000	0	0
00000001	1	1
00000011	2+1	3
00000111	4+2+1	7
00001111	8+4+2+1	15
00011111	16+8+4+2+1	31
00111111	32+16+8+4+2+1	63
01111111	64+32+16+8+4+2+1	127
11111111	128+64+32+16+8+4+2+1	255

What Is a Subnet?

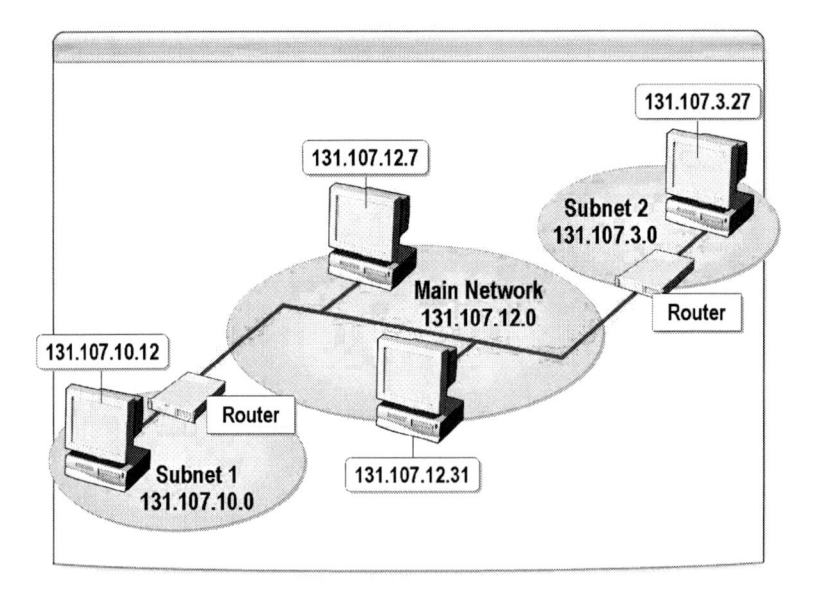

Definition

A *subnet* is a physical segment of a network that is separated from the rest of the network by a router or routers. When a Class A, B, or C network is assigned to your organization, it often must be subdivided to match the physical layout of your network or design specifications. A larger network is subdivided into subnets.

To create subnets, you must allocate some of the bits in the host ID to the network ID. This allows you to create more networks.

Subnet IP addresses

The IP address for each subnet is derived from the main network ID. When you divide a network into subnets, you must create a unique ID for each subnet. To create subnets, you must allocate some of the bits in the host ID to the network ID. This allows you to create more networks. The process of creating subnets is called *subnetting*.

Benefits of using a subnet

Using subnets allows you to:

- Use a single Class A, B, or C network across multiple physical locations.
- Reduce network congestion by segmenting traffic and reducing the number of broadcasts that are sent on each segment.
- Overcome limitations of current technologies, such as exceeding the maximum number of hosts allowed per segment. For example, Ethernet is limited to 1024 hosts on a network. Breaking the segment into further segments increases the total number of hosts allowed.

Considerations for creating a subnet

Before you implement subnetting, you must determine your current requirements and take into consideration future requirements so that you can allow for growth. To create a subnet:

1. Determine the number of physical segments on your network.

2. Determine the number of required host addresses for each physical segment. Each interface on the physical segment requires at least one IP address. Typical TCP/IP hosts have a single interface.

3. Based on your requirements as determined in steps 1 and 2, define:

    - One subnet mask for your entire network.

    - A unique subnet ID for each physical segment.

    - A range of host IDs for each subnet.

How Bits Are Used in a Subnet Mask

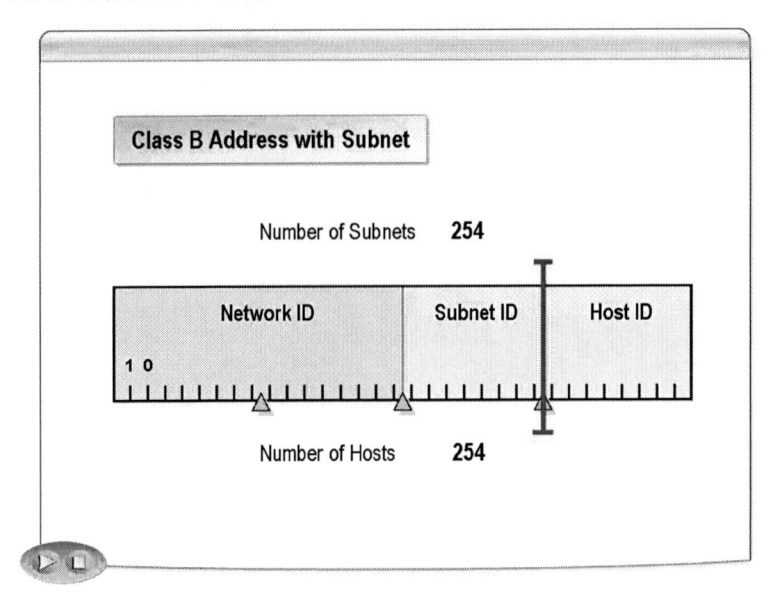

Class B Address with Subnet

Number of Subnets **254**

| Network ID | Subnet ID | Host ID |

1 0

Number of Hosts **254**

Introduction

Before you define a subnet mask, you must estimate the number of segments and hosts per segment that you are likely to require in the future. This will enable you to use the appropriate number of bits for the subnet mask.

Using bits in the subnet mask

In simple networks, subnet masks are composed of four octets, and each octet has a value of 255 or 0. If the octet is 255, that octet is part of the network ID. If the octet is 0, that octet is part of the host ID.

In complex networks, you must convert the subnet mask to binary and evaluate each bit in the subnet mask. A subnet mask is composed of contiguous 1s and 0s. The 1s start at the leftmost bit and continue uninterrupted until the bits change to all 0s.

The network ID of a subnet mask can be identified by the 1s. The host ID can be identified by the 0s. Any bits taken from the host ID and allocated to the network ID must be contiguous with the original network ID. For each bit that is 1, that bit is part of the network ID. For each bit that is 0, that bit is part of the host ID. The mathematical process used to compare an IP address and a subnet mask is called ANDing.

When more bits are used for the subnet mask, more subnets are available, but fewer hosts are available on each subnet. Using more bits than are needed will allow for growth in the number of subnets but will limit growth in the number of hosts. Using fewer bits than are needed will allow for growth in the number of hosts but will limit growth in the number of subnets.

Note For more information about subnetting, see Request for Comments (RFCs) 950 and 1860 under **Additional Reading** on the Student Materials compact disc.

How the Computer Determines Whether an IP Address Is a Local or Remote Address

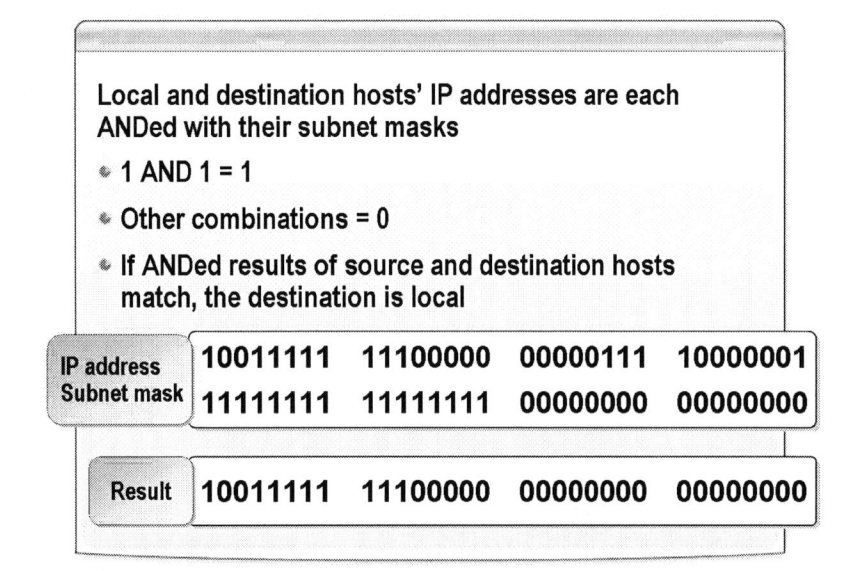

Local and destination hosts' IP addresses are each ANDed with their subnet masks
- 1 AND 1 = 1
- Other combinations = 0
- If ANDed results of source and destination hosts match, the destination is local

IP address	10011111	11100000	00000111	10000001
Subnet mask	11111111	11111111	00000000	00000000

Result	10011111	11100000	00000000	00000000

Introduction

When IP routes a data packet, it must determine whether the destination IP address is on the local network or on a remote network. Understanding how IP makes this determination provides you with the knowledge that you will need when you isolate issues associated with IP addressing.

What is ANDing?

ANDing is the internal process that IP uses to determine whether a packet is destined for a host on a local network or a remote network. It is also used to find routes that match the destination address of packets being sent or forwarded.

When IP forwards a packet to its destination, it must first AND the sending host's IP address with its subnet mask. Before the packet is sent, IP ANDs the destination IP address with the same subnet mask. If both results match, IP recognizes that the packet belongs to a host on the local network. If the results do not match, the packet is sent to an IP router.

How IP ANDs the IP address to a subnet mask

To AND the IP address to a subnet mask, IP compares each bit in the IP address to the corresponding bit in the subnet mask. If both bits are 1s, the resulting bit is 1. If there is any other combination, the resulting bit is 0.

Examples of bit combinations

For combinations of 1 and 0, the results are as follows:

- 1 AND 1 = 1
- 1 AND 0 = 0
- 0 AND 0 = 0
- 0 AND 1 = 0

Guidelines for Choosing a Subnet Mask

- Choose the number of subnet bits based on the number of subnets required
- Use 2^n-2 to determine the number of subnets available from *n* bits
- Calculate subnet IDs by using the value of the lowest high-order bit
- Use 2^n-2 to determine the number of hosts available from *n* bits

Introduction

The process for selecting a subnet mask might seem confusing and complex at first. However, if you understand the process in binary and follow a few simple guidelines, the process is quite easy.

To make the subnetting process even easier, you can use a subnet calculator. A subnet calculator takes the network address and the number of subnets required and creates a list of the appropriate subnets and the subnet mask. Many of these calculators can be found on the Internet by searching for *subnet calculator*.

Choosing the number of bits

The first step in subnetting is selecting the number of bits that must be taken from the host ID and allocated to the network ID. The number of bits in the subnet mask is determined by the number of subnets that are required and the number of hosts that are required on each subnet. It is typical to first calculate subnet bits based on the number of subnets that are required and then confirm that the number of hosts is sufficient. The following examples use this procedure; the procedure can also be used in reverse.

The formula 2^n-2 calculates the number of subnets that can be created with *n* bits. The value of 2^n calculates the number of combinations that *n* bits can create. Two combinations are removed because class-based networking environments cannot use subnet masks where the subnetted bits are all 1s or all 0s. However, most networking environments are not class-based, and the removal of two subnets is not required. The following table lists the number of subnets available from a given number of bits.

Subnet bits	Calculation	Number of subnets
3	2^3-2	8–2 = 6
5	2^5-2	32–2 = 30
7	2^7-2	128–2 = 126

Calculating subnet IDs

The subnet IDs are calculated by taking every combination of bits possible from the subnet bits and adding them to the original network ID. In the following table, the network 172.20.0.0 is being subnetted using three bits from the host ID. The bolded bits are the subnet bits.

Description	Binary	Decimal
Original network	10101100.00010100.00000000.00000000	172.20.0.0
Original subnet mask	11111111.11111111.00000000.00000000	255.255.0.0
New subnet mask	11111111.11111111.**111**00000.00000000	255.255.224.0
Subnet 1	10101100.00010100.**000**00000.00000000	172.20.0.0
Subnet 2	10101100.00010100.**001**00000.00000000	172.20.32.0
Subnet 3	10101100.00010100.**010**00000.00000000	172.20.64.0
Subnet 4	10101100.00010100.**011**00000.00000000	172.20.96.0
Subnet 5	10101100.00010100.**100**00000.00000000	172.20.128.0
Subnet 6	10101100.00010100.**101**00000.00000000	172.20.160.0
Subnet 7	10101100.00010100.**110**00000.00000000	172.20.192.0
Subnet 8	10101100.00010100.**111**00000.00000000	172.20.224.0

Shortcut to calculating subnet IDs

Using the preceding method is impractical when you are using more than 4 bits for your subnet mask because it requires listing and converting many bit combinations.

To define a range of subnet IDs:

1. List the number of bits in the high order used for the subnet ID. For example, if 3 bits are used for the subnet mask, the binary octet is 11100000.

2. Convert the bit with the lowest value to decimal format. This is the increment value used to determine each successive subnet ID. For example, if you use 3 bits, the lowest value is 32.

3. Starting with 0, increment the value for each successive subnet until you have enumerated the maximum number of subnets.

Determining valid IP addresses

To quickly calculate the number of hosts available on a subnet, you can use the formula 2^n-2, where n is the number of bits in the host ID. The following table lists the number of hosts available based on the number of bits allocated to the host ID.

Host ID bits	Calculation	Number of subnets
5	2^5-2	32–2 = 30
8	2^8-2	256–2 = 254
13	$2^{13}-2$	8192–2 = 8190

Within a subnet, not all combinations of host bits can be used. When all host bits are set to 0, the combination represents the subnet. When all host bits are set to 1, the combination represents a broadcast on that subnet. When the formula 2^n-2 is used to calculate the number of hosts on a subnet, the –2 represents removing the subnet address and the broadcast address.

The following table lists several subnets, the first host on each subnet, the last host on each subnet, and the broadcast address. The bolded bits are the subnet bits.

Description	Binary	Decimal
Original network	10101100.00010100.00000000.00000000	172.20.0.0
Original subnet mask	11111111.11111111.00000000.00000000	255.255.0.0
New subnet mask	11111111.11111111.**111**00000.00000000	255.255.224.0
Subnet 1	10101100.00010100.**000**00000.00000000	172.20.0.0
First host on subnet 1	10101100.00010100.**000**00000.00000001	172.20.0.1
Last host on subnet 1	10101100.00010100.**000**11111.11111110	172.20.31.254
Broadcast on subnet 1	10101100.00010100.**000**11111.11111111	172.20.31.255
Subnet 2	10101100.00010100.**001**00000.00000000	172.20.32.0
First host on subnet 2	10101100.00010100.**001**00000.00000001	172.20.32.1
Last host on subnet 2	10101100.00010100.**001**11111.11111110	172.20.63.254
Broadcast on subnet 2	10101100.00010100.**001**11111.11111111	172.20.63.255

Practice: Configuring IP Addressing for Complex Networks

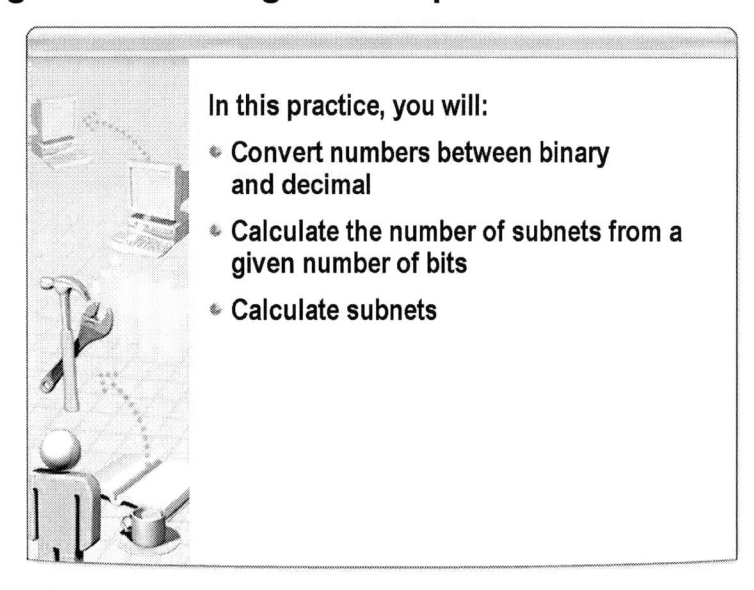

Objectives

In this practice, you will:

- Convert numbers between binary and decimal.
- Calculate the number of subnets from a given number of bits.
- Calculate subnets.

Instructions

No virtual machines are required for this practice.

Practice

▶ **Convert numbers between binary and decimal**

1. On your computer, click **Start**, point to **All Programs**, point to **Accessories**, and then click **Calculator**.
2. On the **View** menu, click **Scientific**.
3. If necessary, click **Dec**. This sets the Calculator to decimal mode.
4. Type **255**, and then click **Bin**. You now see the binary value of 255, which is 11111111. Be aware that if there are leading 0s, the Calculator does not display them.
5. Click **C** to clear the display.
6. Type **10011001**, and then click **Dec**. You now see the decimal value of 10011001, which is 153.

Module 2: Assigning IP Addresses in a Multiple-Subnet Network

▶ **Calculate the number of subnets from a given number of bits**

- Using the formula 2^n-2, fill in the following table.

Number of bits	Number of possible subnets
3	
4	
5	
8	

▶ **Calculate subnets**

- Fill in the following table and calculate the new subnets.

Description	Binary	Decimal
Original network	10101100.00011101.00000000.00000000	172.29.0.0
Original subnet mask	11111111.11111111.00000000.00000000	255.255.0.0
New subnet mask	11111111.11111111.**1111**0000.00000000	255.255.224.0
Subnet 1	10101100.00011101.**0000**0000.00000000	172.29.0.0
Subnet 2	10101100.00011101.**0001**0000.00000000	172.29.16.0
Subnet 3	10101100.00011101.**0010**0000.00000000	172.29.32.0
Subnet 4	10101100.00011101.	
Subnet 5	10101100.00011101.	
Subnet 6	10101100.00011101.	
Subnet 7	10101100.00011101.	
Subnet 8	10101100.00011101.	
Subnet 9	10101100.00011101.	
Subnet 10	10101100.00011101.	
Subnet 11	10101100.00011101.	
Subnet 12	10101100.00011101.	
Subnet 13	10101100.00011101.	
Subnet 14	10101100.00011101.	
Subnet 15	10101100.00011101.	
Subnet 16	10101100.00011101.	

▶ **Prepare for the next practice**

1. Start the DEN-DC1 virtual machine.
2. Start the DEN-CL1 virtual machine.

Lesson: Using IP Routing Tables

- What Is a Router?
- What Are Static and Dynamic Routing?
- How the IP Protocol Selects a Route
- How IP Uses the Routing Table
- Guidelines for Troubleshooting IP Routing by Using the Routing Table
- Practice: Using IP Routing

Introduction

In a multiple-subnet network, routers pass IP packets from one subnet to another. This process is known as *routing* and is a primary function of IP. To make routing decisions, IP consults a routing table. To troubleshoot communication problems, you must understand how routers use routing tables in an internetwork.

Lesson objectives

After completing this lesson, you will be able to:

- Describe what a router is and its role in the network.
- Describe static and dynamic routing.
- Describe how IP selects a route.
- Describe how IP uses the routing table.
- Apply guidelines for troubleshooting IP routing by using the routing table.
- View and configure the routing table.

What Is a Router?

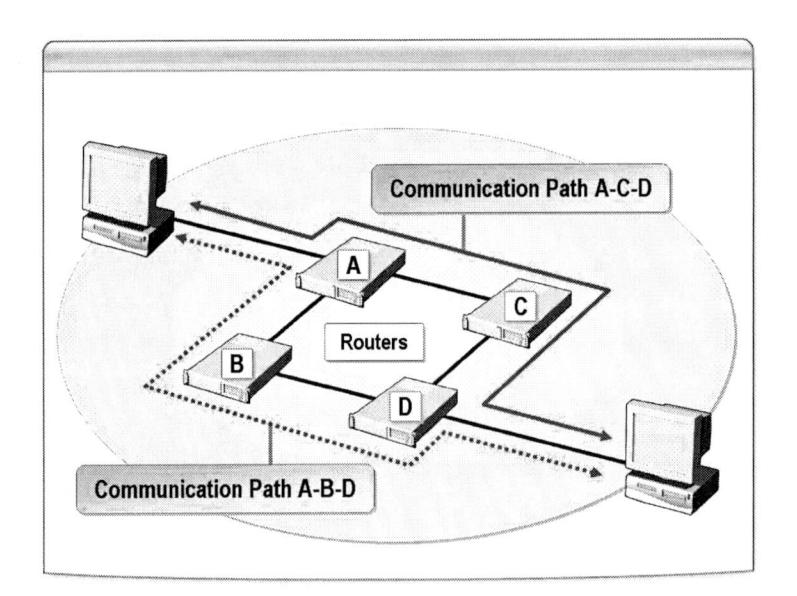

Definition

In an internetwork, a *router* connects subnets to each other and connects the internetwork to other networks. Knowing how the router forwards data packets to their destination IP addresses enables you to ensure that host computers on your network are correctly configured to transmit and receive data.

Routers operate at the network layer of the Open Systems Interconnection (OSI) reference model, so they can connect networks running different data-link layer protocols and different network media.

Example of a router on a small internetwork

On a small internetwork, such as a single location, a router's job can be quite simple. When two local area networks (LANs) are connected by one router, the router receives packets from one network and forwards only those destined for the other network.

Example of routers on a large internetwork

On a large internetwork, such as a 10-site wide area network (WAN), routers connect several different networks together, and in many cases, networks have more than one router connected to them. This enables packets to take different paths to a given destination. If one router on the network fails, packets can bypass it and still reach their destinations.

How routers select a path

In an internetwork, a router selects the most efficient route to a packet's destination. The most efficient route is the lowest-cost route. Usually, cost is based on hops. (Each time a packet passes through a router is called a *hop*.)

Routers share information about the networks to which they are attached with other routers in the immediate vicinity. As a result, a composite picture of the internetwork eventually develops. On a large internetwork, such as the Internet, no single router possesses the entire image. Instead, the routers work together by passing each packet from router to router, one hop at a time.

How a router moves packets between networks

Routers use the destination IP addresses in packets and routing tables to forward packets between networks. The routing table might contain all the network addresses and possible paths through the network, along with the cost of reaching each network. Routers route packets based on the available paths and their costs.

What Are Static and Dynamic Routing?

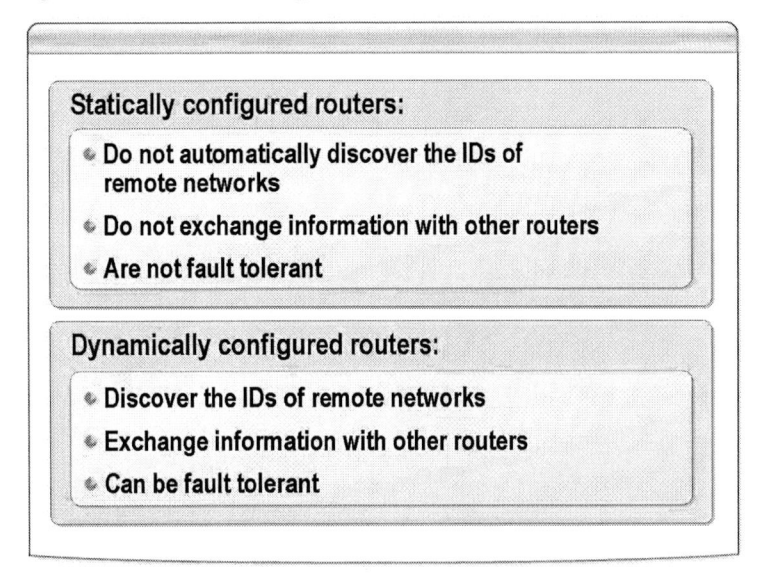

> **Statically configured routers:**
> - Do not automatically discover the IDs of remote networks
> - Do not exchange information with other routers
> - Are not fault tolerant
>
> **Dynamically configured routers:**
> - Discover the IDs of remote networks
> - Exchange information with other routers
> - Can be fault tolerant

Introduction

The process that routers use to obtain routing information differs based on whether the router performs static or dynamic IP routing. Understanding each of these routing methods will give you the information that you need to maintain routing tables so that IP can use the most efficient route to transmit data to its destination.

Static routing

Static routing uses fixed routing tables. Static routers require you to build and update tables manually.

Statically configured routers:

- Do not automatically discover the network IDs of remote networks. You must configure these network IDs manually.
- Do not inform each other of route changes.
- Do not exchange routes with dynamic routers.
- Are not fault tolerant. This means that when the router fails, neighboring routers do not sense the fault and so do not inform other routers.

Dynamic routing

Dynamic routing automatically updates the routing tables. Dynamic routing is a function of TCP/IP routing protocols, such as Routing Information Protocol (RIP) and Open Shortest Path First (OSPF).

Dynamically configured routers:

- Can automatically discover the network IDs of remote networks.
- Automatically inform other routers of route changes.
- Use routing protocols to periodically transmit or transmit on demand the contents of their routing tables to the other routers on the network.
- Are fault tolerant (in a multiple-path routing topology). When the router fails, the fault is detected by neighboring routers, which send the changed routing information to the other routers in the internetwork.

How the IP Protocol Selects a Route

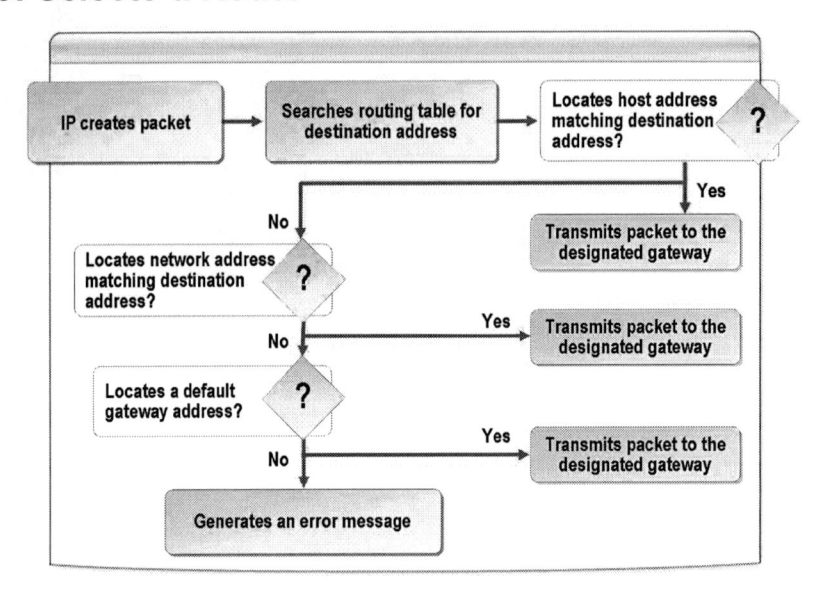

Introduction

To send data packets from one network to another, IP must select the appropriate path. When a router receives a packet, the network interface adapter passes the packet to IP. IP examines the destination address and compares it to a routing table. A routing table is a series of entries, called *routes*, that contain information about the location of the network IDs for the internetwork. IP then makes a decision as to how to forward the packet.

The routing procedure

The IP protocol selects a route by using the following procedure:

1. IP compares the destination IP address for the packet with the routing table entries, looking for a route. A host route in the routing table has the destination IP address in the Network Address column and the value 255.255.255.255 in the Netmask column.

2. If there is no host route for the destination, the system then scans the routing table Network Address and Netmask columns for a network route that matches the destination. If more than one entry in the routing table matches the destination, IP uses the entry with the greatest number of bits set to 1 in the Netmask column. If multiple matching entries in the routing table have the same number of bits set to 1 in the Netmask column, IP uses the entry with the lower value in the Metric column.

3. If there are no network routes to the destination, the system searches for a default gateway entry that has a value of 0.0.0.0 in the Network Address and Netmask columns.

4. If there is no default route, the system generates an error message. If the system transmitting the datagram is a router, it discards the packet and sends an Internet Control Message Protocol (ICMP) Destination Unreachable message back to the end system that originated the datagram. If the system transmitting the datagram is the source host, the error message gets passed back up to the application that generated the data.

5. When the system locates a viable routing table entry, IP passes the forwarding, or *next-hop*, IP address and interface to the ARP module. ARP consults the ARP cache or performs an ARP exchange to obtain the hardware address of the router.
6. After it has the router's hardware address, ARP passes the packet to the network adapter driver for transmission. The network adapter constructs a frame using the router's hardware address in its Destination Address field and transmits the packet.

How IP Uses the Routing Table

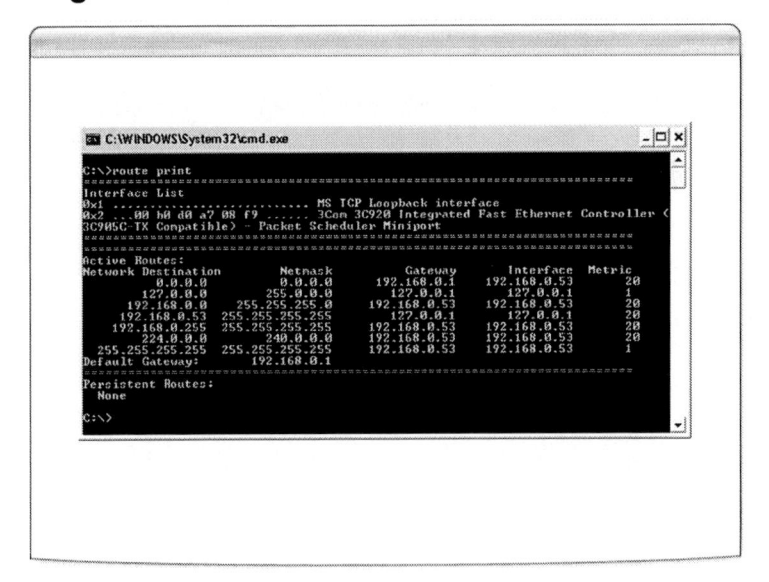

Introduction

To make IP routing decisions, IP consults the routing table, which is stored in memory on a host computer or router. Because all IP hosts perform some form of IP routing, routing tables are not exclusive to IP routers.

How the router uses the routing table

The routing table stores information about IP networks and how they can be reached, either directly or indirectly. There are a series of default entries based on the configuration of the host and additional entries that can be entered either manually, by using TCP/IP utilities, or dynamically, through interaction with routers. When an IP packet is to be forwarded, the router uses the routing table to determine:

- *The next-hop IP address.* For a direct delivery, the forwarding IP address is the destination IP address in the IP packet. For an indirect delivery, the forwarding IP address is the IP address of a router.
- *The interface to be used for the forwarding.* The interface identifies the physical or logical interface, such as a network adapter that is used to forward the packet to either its destination or the next router.

Types of entries in the IP routing table

The following table lists the fields of a route entry and describes the information that they contain.

Route field	Information
Network ID	The network ID or destination corresponding to the route. The ID can be class-based, a subnet, a supernet, or an IP address for a host route. In Windows Server 2003, this is the Network Destination column.
Network mask	The mask used to match a destination IP address to the network ID. In the routing table, this is the Netmask column.
Next hop	The IP address of the next hop. In the routing table in Windows Server 2003, this is the Gateway column.

(continued)

Route field	Information
Interface	An indication of which network interface is used to forward the IP packet.
Metric	A number used to indicate the cost of the route so that the best route can be selected. Commonly used to indicate the number of hops to the network ID.

Types of routes

The following table describes the types of routes.

Type of route	Description
Directly attached network ID	A route for network IDs that are directly attached. The Next Hop field can be blank or can contain the IP address of the interface on that network.
Remote network ID	A route for network IDs that are not directly attached but are available across other routers. The Next Hop field is the IP address of a local router.
Host route	A route to a specific IP address. Host routes allow routing to occur on a per-IP-address basis. The network ID is the IP address of the specified host, and the network mask is 255.255.255.255.
Default route	A route that is used when a more specific network ID or host route is not found. The network ID is 0.0.0.0 with a network mask of 0.0.0.0.
Persistent routes	A route added by using the –p switch. When used with the Add command, this switch adds the route to the routing table and to the Windows Server 2003 registry. The route is automatically added to the routing table each time TCP/IP is initialized.

The default routing table for a client running Windows Server 2003

The following table shows the default routing table for a client running Windows Server 2003 with a single network adapter, IP address 192.168.0.53, subnet mask 255.255.255.0, and default gateway 192.168.0.1.

Network destination	Net mask	Gateway	Interface	Metric	Purpose
0.0.0.0	0.0.0.0	192.168.0.1	192.168.0.53	20	Default route
127.0.0.0	255.0.0.0	127.0.0.1	127.0.0.1	1	Loopback or testing network
192.168.0.0	255.255.255.0	192.168.0.53	192.168.0.53	20	Directly attached network
192.168.0.53	255.255.255.255	127.0.0.1	127.0.0.1	20	Local host
192.168.0.255	255.255.255.255	192.168.0.53	192.168.0.53	20	Network broadcast
224.0.0.0	240.0.0.0	192.168.0.53	192.168.0.53	20	Multicast
255.255.255.255	255.255.255.255	192.168.0.53	192.168.0.53	1	Limited broadcast

Guidelines for Troubleshooting IP Routing by Using the Routing Table

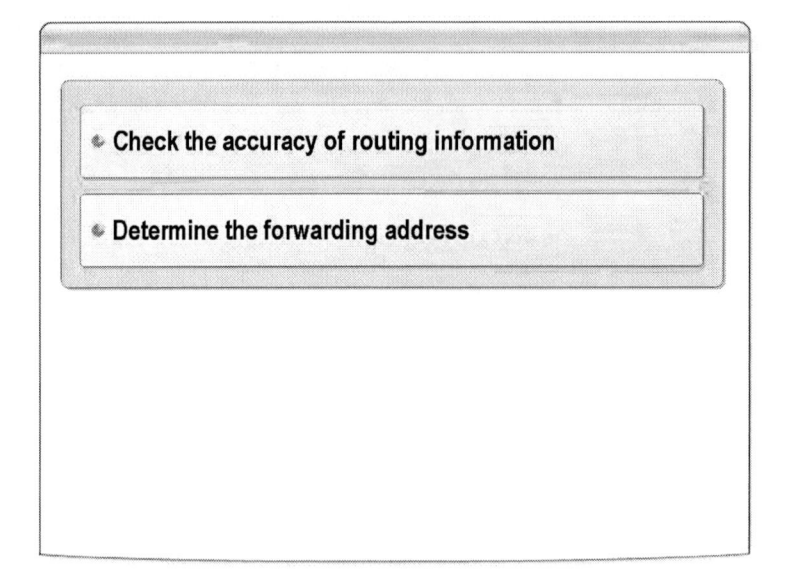

- Check the accuracy of routing information
- Determine the forwarding address

Introduction

You can use the routing tables in Windows to assist you in isolating connectivity issues. Examining the tables will help you to determine whether an incorrect entry is contributing to a problem.

How to use the table to identify route errors

If the route for a packet sent out by a host is incorrect, the packet will not arrive at its destination, and an error message will be sent to the host. You can examine the routing table to determine the route that was attempted.

To determine the forwarding, or next-hop, IP address from a route in the routing table:

- If the gateway address is the same as the interface address, the forwarding IP address is set to the destination IP address of the IP packet.
- If the gateway address is not the same as the interface address, the forwarding IP address is set to the gateway address.

Examples of matching routes

When traffic is sent to 192.168.0.55, the most specific matching route is the route for the directly attached network (192.168.0.0, 255.255.255.0). The forwarding IP address is set to the destination IP address (157.60.16.48), and the interface is the network adapter that has been assigned the IP address 157.60.27.90.

When sending traffic to 131.107.1.100, the most specific matching route is the default route (0.0.0.0, 0.0.0.0). The forwarding IP address is set to the gateway address (192.168.0.1), and the interface is the network adapter that has been assigned the IP address 192.168.0.53.

How to view the IP routing table

To view the IP routing table on a computer running Windows Server 2003, type **route print** at a command prompt. You can also use the **netstat –r** command.

Practice: Using IP Routing

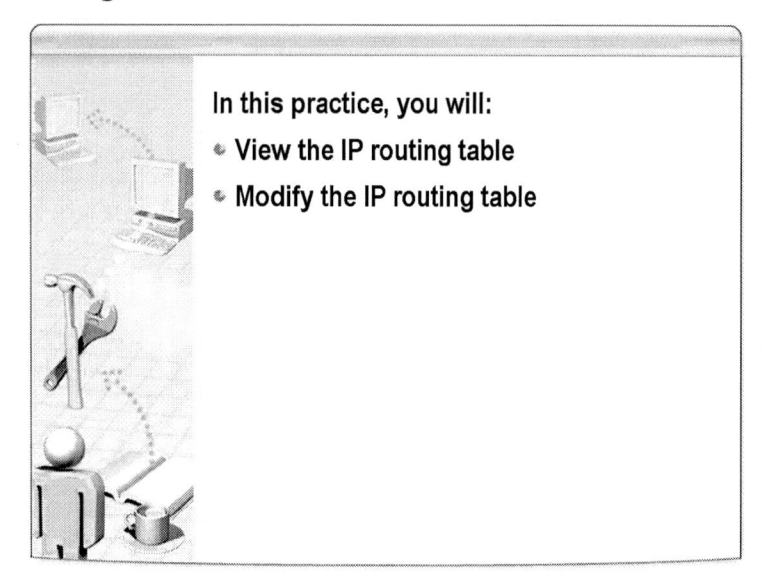

> In this practice, you will:
> - View the IP routing table
> - Modify the IP routing table

Objectives

In this practice, you will:

- View the IP routing table.
- Modify the IP routing table.

Instructions

Ensure that the DEN-DC1 and DEN-CL1 virtual machines are running.

Practice

▶ **View the IP routing table**

1. On DEN-CL1, log on to the **CONTOSO** domain as **Administrator**, with a password of **Pa$$w0rd**.
2. Click **Start**, click **Run**, type **cmd**, and then click **OK**.
3. Type **route print** and then press ENTER.

    Are there any persistent routes listed?

    _____

    The network destination for the default gateway is listed as 0.0.0.0. What is the IP address of the default gateway?

    _____

4. Type **ipconfig /all**, and then press ENTER.

    What is the IP address of the default gateway?

    _____

▶ Modify the IP routing table

1. Type **route delete 0.0.0.0** and then press ENTER.
2. Type **ipconfig /all** and then press ENTER.

   What is the IP address of the default gateway?

   _____

3. At a command prompt, type **route add 0.0.0.0 mask 0.0.0.0 10.10.0.254** and then press ENTER.
4. At the command prompt, type **ipconfig /all** and then press ENTER.

   What is the IP address of the default gateway?

   _____

Important Shut down DEN-DC1 and DEN-CL1 without saving your changes.

Lesson: Overcoming the Limitations of the IP Addressing Scheme

- Multimedia: How IP Addresses Are Wasted
- What Are Private and Public IP Addresses?
- What Is VLSM?
- What Is CIDR?
- How CIDR Is Used for Supernetting
- What Is IPv6?
- Practice: Overcoming the Limitations of the IP Addressing Scheme

Introduction

There are limitations of the IP addressing scheme that can prevent you from using the best scheme for your network and that result in a large number of addresses that remain unused. In this lesson, you will learn how you can overcome some of these limitations and increase the effectiveness of your IP addressing scheme.

Lesson objectives

After completing this lesson, you will be able to:

- Describe how IP addresses are wasted.
- Describe private and public IP addresses.
- Describe what variable-length subnet masks (VLSMs) are and how to use them.
- Describe classless interdomain routing (CIDR).
- Describe how CIDR is used for supernetting.
- Explain IP version 6 (IPv6).
- Overcome the limitations of the IP addressing scheme.

Multimedia: How IP Addresses Are Wasted

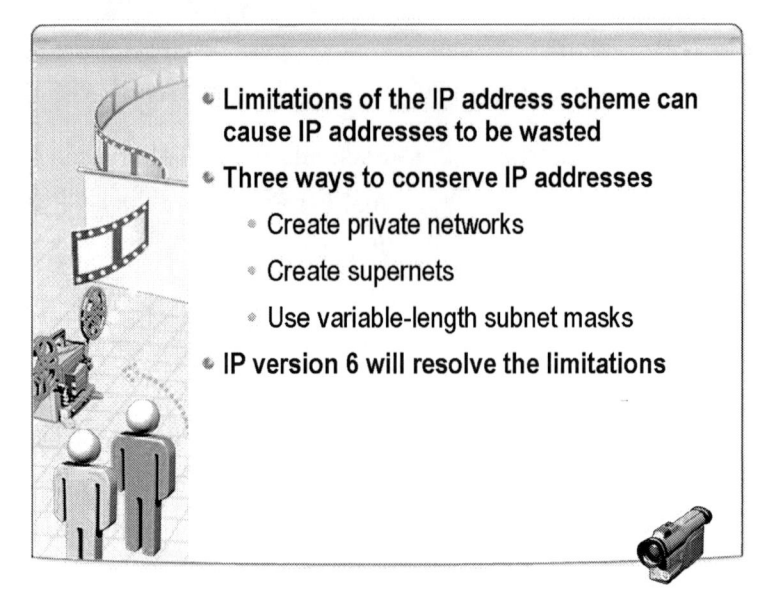

- Limitations of the IP address scheme can cause IP addresses to be wasted
- Three ways to conserve IP addresses
  - Create private networks
  - Create supernets
  - Use variable-length subnet masks
- IP version 6 will resolve the limitations

File location

To view the multimedia presentation *How IP Addresses Are Wasted*, open the Web page on the Student Materials compact disc, click **Multimedia**, and then click the title of the presentation.

Objectives

After this presentation, you will be able to describe:

- How the limitations of the IP address scheme can cause IP addresses to be wasted.
- Three ways to conserve IP addresses.

What Are Private and Public IP Addresses?

> **Private addresses:**
> - Do not have to be registered
> - Can be assigned by the network administrator
> - Are used on computers that are not accessed by the Internet
>
> **Public addresses:**
> - Are assigned by an ISP
> - Consist of unique class-based blocks
> - Are kept to a limited number

Introduction

All the computers on your network that are accessible from the Internet require a registered IP address; however, not every computer that can access the Internet requires a registered IP address. You can use private or public IP addresses, depending on network requirements.

Private IP addresses

Private IP addresses are special network addresses that are intended for use on private networks and are not registered to anyone. You can assign these addresses without obtaining them from an ISP. You can use private addresses for computers that are not required to be accessible from the Internet.

Note Networks use a firewall or some other security technology to protect their systems from intrusion by outside computers. These firewalls provide computers with access to Internet resources without making them accessible to other systems on the Internet.

A private IP address is never assigned as a public address and never duplicates public addresses.

IP addresses reserved for private networks

The following IP addresses are reserved for private networks:

- 10.0.0.0 through 10.255.255.255
- 172.16.0.0 through 172.31.255.255
- 192.168.0.0 through 192.168.255.255

Note For more information about private IP addresses, see RFC 1918 under **Additional Reading** on the Student Materials compact disc.

How a host with a private IP address sends requests to the Internet	A host that has a private address must send its Internet traffic requests to an application layer gateway (such as a proxy server) that has a valid public address. Or the host must have network address translation (NAT) to translate the private address into a valid public address and then send its requests to the Internet.
Public addresses	When public addresses are assigned, routes are programmed into the routers of the Internet so that traffic sent to the assigned public addresses can reach those locations. Traffic sent to destination public addresses is transmitted across the Internet.

What Is VLSM?

> **Using VLSM, you can:**
> - **Create different-size subnets to match the number of hosts in each subnet**
> - **Significantly reduce the number of unused IP addresses**

Definition

VLSM is a method of creating different-size subnet masks to conserve IP addresses. When you use fixed-length subnet masks on an internetwork that has subnets with different requirements for the maximum number of hosts, a large proportion of the addresses might be wasted. By using VLSM, you can allocate the appropriate number of IP addresses to each subnet rather than using fixed-length subnet masks.

How equal-size subnets waste IP addresses

Subnetting was originally used to subdivide a class-based network ID into a series of equal-size subnets. For example, a 4-bit subnetting of a Class B network ID produced 16 equal-size subnets. However, the number of hosts per subnet is rarely if ever of equal size. This inequality results in many wasted IP addresses.

How VLSM conserves IP addresses

Subnetting does not require equal-size subnets, so you can conserve IP addresses by using VLSM to create different-size subnets that best match the number of hosts in each subnet. For example, on a network segmented into three departments, you could subnet a Class C network as follows:

Description	Hosts	Network ID	Subnet mask
Head Office	126	192.168.10.0	255.255.255.128
Department 1	62	192.168.10.128	255.255.255.192
Department 2	62	192.168.10.192	255.255.255.192

What Is CIDR?

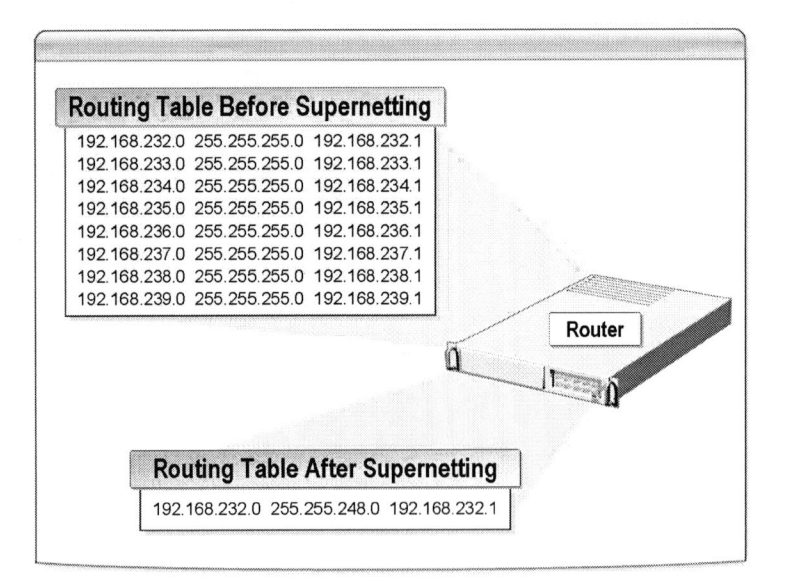

```
Routing Table Before Supernetting
192.168.232.0  255.255.255.0  192.168.232.1
192.168.233.0  255.255.255.0  192.168.233.1
192.168.234.0  255.255.255.0  192.168.234.1
192.168.235.0  255.255.255.0  192.168.235.1
192.168.236.0  255.255.255.0  192.168.236.1
192.168.237.0  255.255.255.0  192.168.237.1
192.168.238.0  255.255.255.0  192.168.238.1
192.168.239.0  255.255.255.0  192.168.239.1

Router

Routing Table After Supernetting
192.168.232.0  255.255.248.0  192.168.232.1
```

Definition

CIDR reduces the size of routing tables by allowing the aggregation of multiple class-based networks into a single routing table entry. This is called *supernetting*.

Why CIDR is required

When class-based routing is used, routers have a routing table entry for each class-based network. This is not a problem on most WANs and LANs, but it is a problem for very large networks such as the Internet. An Internet router could conceivably be forced to track over two million networks.

Supernetting is often used to conserve Class B addresses by combining contiguous groups of Class C addresses. The Class C addresses must have the same high-order bits, and the subnet mask is shortened by borrowing bits from the network ID and assigning them to the host ID portion to create a custom subnet mask.

Example of using CIDR for 2000 hosts

When a company has 2000 hosts on its TCP/IP network that must be accessed from the Internet, the company can attempt to obtain the following from an ISP:

- A single Class B network ID. This approach would waste 63,000 addresses.
- Eight different Class C addresses that can support 8 x 254 = 2032 hosts. This means poorer routing performance, because each router requires eight entries in its routing table for each of the eight networks to which packets can be forwarded.
- A single block of addresses that allows 2000 hosts. Using supernetting, an ISP allocates a block of eight contiguous Class C network IDs in such a way that they can be expressed as a single routing table entry.

How CIDR Is Used for Supernetting

Class C Example

	Network ID	Network ID (binary)
Starting	192.168.44.0/24	**11000000.10101000.00101100**.00000000
Ending	192.168.47.0/24	**11000000.10101000.00101111**.00000000

CIDR Entry

Network ID	Subnet mask (binary)
192.168.44.0/22	**11000000.10101000.001011**00.00000000

Introduction

When you use CIDR to implement supernetting, you are combining multiple addresses into a single network ID, thereby increasing the efficiency of IP address allocation and reducing the number of unused IP addresses.

How CIDR creates the entry for the routing table

To supernet several Class C networks, bits must be taken from the network ID and allocated to the host ID. This is done by modifying the subnet mask.

In the following table, four Class C network IDs are allocated, starting with network ID 192.168.44.0. The bolded bits are the network IDs.

Description	Binary	Decimal
Original network 1	**11000000.10101000.00101100**.00000000	192.168.44.0
Original network 2	**11000000.10101000.00101101**.00000000	192.168.45.0
Original network 3	**11000000.10101000.00101110**.00000000	192.168.46.0
Original network 4	**11000000.10101000.00101111**.00000000	192.168.47.0
Original subnet mask	**11111111.11111111.11111111**.00000000	255.255.255.0
Supernetted network	**11000000.10101000.001011**00.00000000	192.168.44.0
New subnet mask	**11111111.11111111.111111**00.00000000	255.255.252.0
First host	**11000000.10101000.001011**00.00000001	192.168.44.1
Last host	**11000000.10101000.001011**11.11111110	192.168.47.254
Broadcast	**11000000.10101000.001011**11.11111111	192.168.47.255

The first 22 bits of the original Class C network IDs are the same. The last two bits of the third octet vary from 00 to 11. The supernetted network uses only the first 22 bits as part of the network ID.

Note Because subnet masks are used to define supernetting, class-based network IDs must be allocated in groups corresponding to multiples of 2.

CIDR notation

Subnet masks are a fairly cumbersome way of expressing how many bits are in the network ID of an IP address. CIDR notation is a faster way to express the same information. To indicate that 22 bits are part of the network ID, add **/22** after the IP address—for example, **192.168.44.0/22**.

Address-space perspective

The use of CIDR to allocate addresses promotes a new perspective on IP network IDs. The CIDR block 192.168.40.0, 255.255.252.0 can be thought of in two ways:

- As a block of eight Class C network IDs
- As an address space in which 22 bits are fixed and 10 bits are assignable

In the latter perspective, IP network IDs lose their class-based heritage and become separate IP address spaces, subsets of the original IP address space defined by the 32-bit IP address. This is the current and correct perspective, as the original Internet address classes have been made obsolete by CIDR.

Each IP network ID (class-based, subnetted, or CIDR block) is an address space in which certain bits are fixed (the network ID bits) and certain bits are variable (the host bits). The host bits are assignable as host IDs or, by using subnetting techniques, can be used in whatever manner best suits the needs of the organization.

Requirements for using CIDR

For routers to support CIDR, they must be able to exchange routing information in the form of network ID–network mask pairs. RIP for IP version 2, OSPF, and Border Gateway Protocol version 4 (BGPv4) are routing protocols that support CIDR. RIP for IP version 1 does not support CIDR.

What Is IPv6?

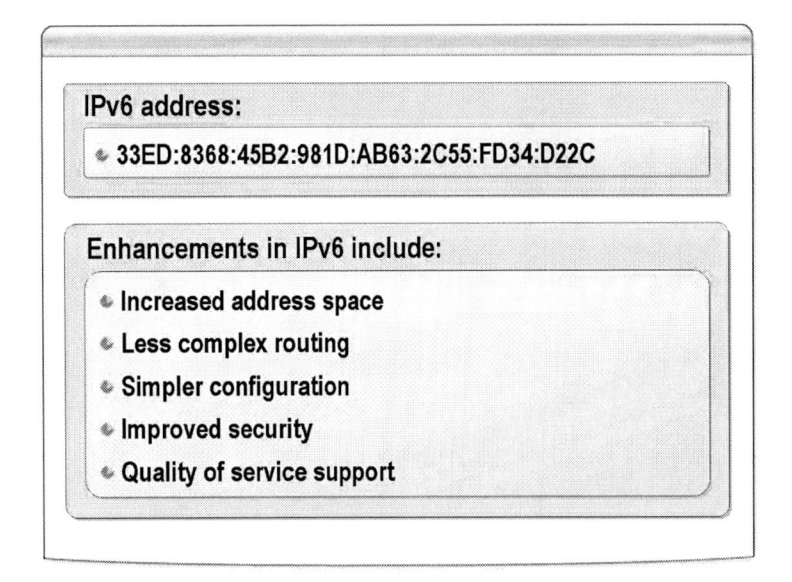

> **IPv6 address:**
> - 33ED:8368:45B2:981D:AB63:2C55:FD34:D22C
>
> **Enhancements in IPv6 include:**
> - Increased address space
> - Less complex routing
> - Simpler configuration
> - Improved security
> - Quality of service support

Definition

IP version 6 (IPv6) is an enhanced network-layer protocol that replaces IPv4, which is currently used in most TCP/IP networks. The most obvious change in IPv6 is the size of the address. IPv6 uses 128-bit addresses that are expressed in hexadecimal. An example of an IPv6 address is 33ED:8368:45B2:981D:AB63:2C55:FD34:D22C.

IPv6 improvements

IPv6 offers a number of improvements over IPv4, including the following:

- *IPv6 has increased address space.* By using a 128-bit address instead of the 32-bit addresses of IPv4, the number of available addresses is increased millions of times. This will eliminate IP shortages on the Internet and allow every computer, and other devices, to have a unique Internet addressable IP address. NAT will no longer be required to work around IP shortages.

- *IPv6 routing is less complex.* The Internet currently uses a mix of class-based and classless routing, which increases routing complexity. IPv6 does not have address classes and will reduce routing complexity on the Internet.

- *IPv6 configuration is simpler.* IPv6 addresses can be assigned to hosts automatically without implementing DHCP. Automatic address assignment is built in to the protocol.

- *IPv6 is more secure.* IPv6 is designed to allow secure communication by using Internet Protocol Security (IPSec). Current implementations of IPSec on IPv4 are options and sometimes interoperate poorly.

- *IPv6 supports quality of service.* Quality of service (QOS) for IPv4 is optional and has limited functionality. In IPv6, QOS is built into the protocol.

IPv6 implementation

Implementation of IPv6 on the Internet and on corporate networks has been slow. This is for several reasons:

- Wide use of NAT for corporate environments has reduced the need for additional IP addresses.
- The return of unused IP addresses from organizations has resulted in more efficient use of IPv4 addresses.

Practice: Overcoming the Limitations of the IP Addressing Scheme

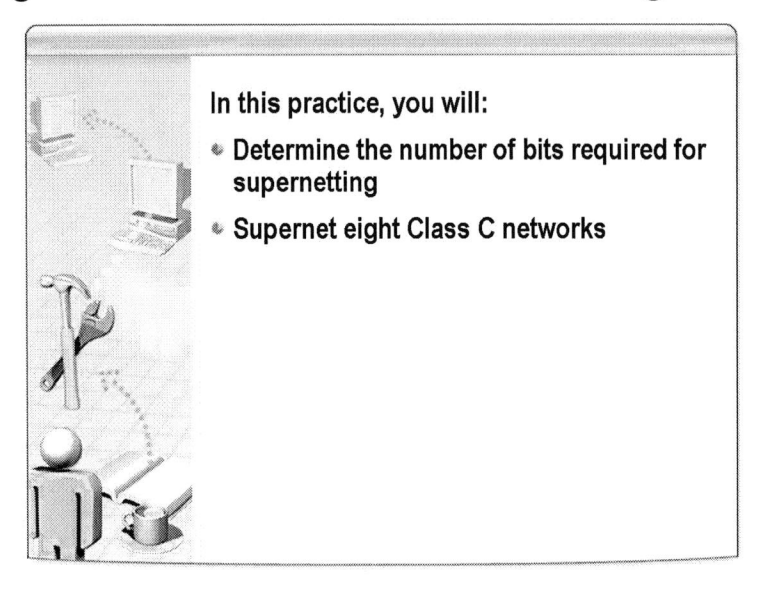

In this practice, you will:
- Determine the number of bits required for supernetting
- Supernet eight Class C networks

Objectives

In this practice, you will:

- Determine the number of bits required for supernetting.
- Supernet eight Class C networks.

Instructions

No virtual machines are required for this practice.

Practice

▶ **Determine the number of bits required for supernetting**

- Using the formula 2^n, fill in the following table.

Number of bits	Number of subnets
1	
2	
3	
5	

▶ Supernet eight Class C networks

- Fill in the following table and calculate the new network, first host, last host, and broadcast addresses.

Description	Binary	Decimal
Original network 1	11000000.10101000.11101000.00000000	192.168.232.0
Original network 2	11000000.10101000.11101001.00000000	192.168.233.0
Original network 3	11000000.10101000.11101010.00000000	192.168.234.0
Original network 4	11000000.10101000.11101011.00000000	192.168.235.0
Original network 5	11000000.10101000.11101100.00000000	192.168.236.0
Original network 6	11000000.10101000.11101101.00000000	192.168.237.0
Original network 7	11000000.10101000.11101110.00000000	192.168.238.0
Original network 8	11000000.10101000.11101111.00000000	192.168.239.0
Original subnet mask	11111111.11111111.11111111.00000000	255.255.255.0
New subnet mask	11111111.11111111.11111000.00000000	255.255.248.0
New network	11000000.10101000.11101000.00000000	
First host	11000000.10101000.11101.00000001	
Last host	11000000.10101000.11101.11111110	
Broadcast	11000000.10101000.11101.11111111	

Lab: Assigning IP Addresses in a Multiple-Subnet Network

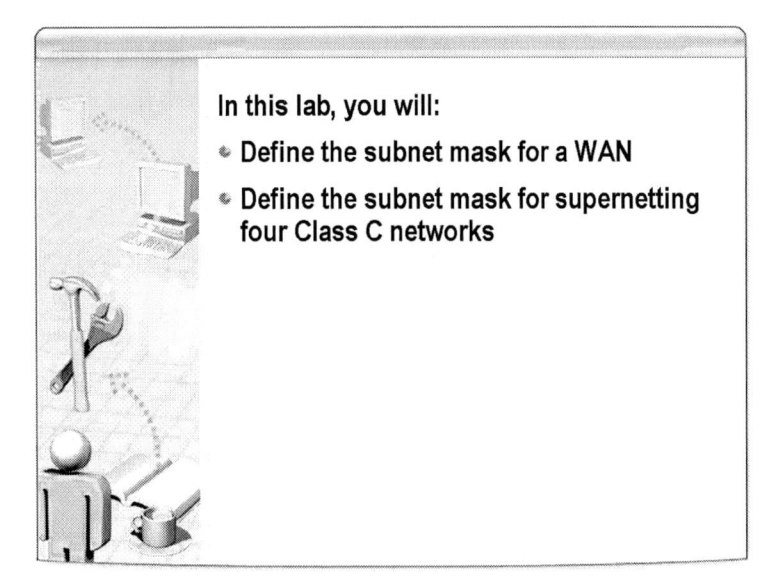

In this lab, you will:
- Define the subnet mask for a WAN
- Define the subnet mask for supernetting four Class C networks

Objectives

After completing this lab, you will be able to:

- Define the subnet mask for a WAN.
- Define the subnet mask for supernetting four Class C networks.

Estimated time to complete this lab: 15 minutes

Exercise 1
Defining the Subnet Mask for a WAN

Your company is designing an integrated WAN for eight locations using a Class B network (172.23.0.0). The IP structure for the WAN should include room for future growth of at least four additional locations and maximize the number of hosts on each subnet. Each location must have its own subnet. Use the following table to define the subnets.

Description	Binary	Decimal
Original network	**10101100.00010111**.00000000.00000000	172.23.0.0
Original subnet mask	**11111111.11111111**.00000000.00000000	255.255.0.0
New subnet mask		
Subnet 1		
Subnet 2		
Subnet 3		
Subnet 4		

Exercise 2
Defining the Subnet Mask for Supernetting Four Class C Networks

Your company has been assigned four Class C networks for a single location. To reduce complexity on your network, you have decided to combine all four networks into a single supernetted network. Use the following table to define the subnet mask, network ID, first host, last host, and broadcast addresses for the supernetted network.

Description	Binary	Decimal
Original network 1	**11000000.10101000.11001100**.00000000	192.168.204.0
Original network 2	**11000000.10101000.11001100**.00000000	192.168.205.0
Original network 3	**11000000.10101000.11001100**.00000000	192.168.206..0
Original network 4	**11000000.10101000.11001100**.00000000	192.168.207.0
Original subnet mask	**11111111.11111111.11111111**.00000000	255.255.255.0
Supernetted network		
New subnet mask		
First host		
Last host		
Broadcast		

Module 3: Configuring a Client IP Address

Contents

Overview	1
Lesson: Configuring a Client to Use a Static IP Address	2
Lesson: Configuring a Client to Obtain an IP Address Automatically	10
Lesson: Using Alternate Configuration	20
Lab: Configuring Hosts to Connect to a Network Running the TCP/IP Protocol Suite	26
Course Evaluation	35

Information in this document, including URL and other Internet Web site references, is subject to change without notice. Unless otherwise noted, the example companies, organizations, products, domain names, e-mail addresses, logos, people, places, and events depicted herein are fictitious, and no association with any real company, organization, product, domain name, e-mail address, logo, person, place or event is intended or should be inferred. Complying with all applicable copyright laws is the responsibility of the user. Without limiting the rights under copyright, no part of this document may be reproduced, stored in or introduced into a retrieval system, or transmitted in any form or by any means (electronic, mechanical, photocopying, recording, or otherwise), or for any purpose, without the express written permission of Microsoft Corporation.

The names of manufacturers, products, or URLs are provided for informational purposes only and Microsoft makes no representations and warranties, either expressed, implied, or statutory, regarding these manufacturers or the use of the products with any Microsoft technologies. The inclusion of a manufacturer or product does not imply endorsement of Microsoft of the manufacturer or product. Links are provided to third party sites. Such sites are not under the control of Microsoft and Microsoft is not responsible for the contents of any linked site or any link contained in a linked site, or any changes or updates to such sites. Microsoft is not responsible for webcasting or any other form of transmission received from any linked site. Microsoft is providing these links to you only as a convenience, and the inclusion of any link does not imply endorsement of Microsoft of the site or the products contained therein.

Microsoft may have patents, patent applications, trademarks, copyrights, or other intellectual property rights covering subject matter in this document. Except as expressly provided in any written license agreement from Microsoft, the furnishing of this document does not give you any license to these patents, trademarks, copyrights, or other intellectual property.

© 2005 Microsoft Corporation. All rights reserved.

Microsoft, Active Directory, Excel, MS-DOS, PowerPoint, Windows, Windows Media, Windows NT, and Windows Server are either registered trademarks or trademarks of Microsoft Corporation in the United States and/or other countries.

All other trademarks are property of their respective owners.

Overview

- Configuring a Client to Use a Static IP Address
- Configuring a Client to Obtain an IP Address Automatically
- Using Alternate Configuration

Introduction

This module describes how to configure an Internet Protocol (IP) address for a client computer running Microsoft® Windows®. An IP address is required for each computer and device on a network that is running the Transmission Control Protocol/Internet Protocol (TCP/IP) suite. The IP address identifies a computer's location on the network. When you assign an IP address to a client, you ensure that the client can be accurately identified on the network when it sends and receives data.

Note In this module, the term *client* refers to a computer running a Windows operating system on a network running TCP/IP. The term *host* includes clients and refers to any device on the network that has an IP address.

Objectives

After completing this module, you will be able to:

- Configure a client to use a static IP address.
- Configure a client to use a dynamic IP address.
- Configure a client with an alternate IP configuration.

Lesson: Configuring a Client to Use a Static IP Address

- Static and Dynamic IP Addresses
- Static TCP/IP Configuration
- How to Use Ipconfig for Viewing the TCP/IP Configuration
- Practice: Configuring a Client to Use a Static IP Address

Introduction

Assigning an IP address is a fundamental procedure for you to establish client network connectivity. By default, clients running Microsoft Windows are configured to obtain an IP address automatically by using DHCP. However, there will be instances in which it is necessary for you to assign manually and confirm the assignment of an IP address. An IP address that is manually assigned is called a *static address*.

Lesson objectives

After completing this lesson, you will be able to:

- Describe static and dynamic IP addressing.
- View the static TCP/IP configuration.
- View the configuration of TCP/IP by using the Ipconfig command-line utility.
- Configure a client to use a static IP address.

Static and Dynamic IP Addresses

> **IP addresses can be:**
> - **Static**
>   - Addresses that are manually assigned and do not change over time
> - **Dynamic**
>   - Addresses that are automatically assigned for a specific length of time and might change

Introduction

You can assign either static or dynamic IP addresses for client computers, depending on your network configuration and on the computer's function. In most cases, clients have dynamic IP addresses.

What is a static IP address?

A static IP address is an address that always remains the same and must be manually configured. When you assign static IP addresses, you must manually configure the address for each computer on your network.

When to use a static IP address

You use a static IP address when:

- A client is using an application that requires an IP address that does not change.
- You do not have a Dynamic Host Configuration Protocol (DHCP) server on your network.
- You are isolating network connectivity issues for a client computer and want to determine whether a DHCP server is incorrectly configured.

Managing static IP addresses

Every host on your TCP/IP network must be configured with a unique IP address. If the same IP address is assigned to a second host, one of the hosts will lose network connectivity.

On a small network, configuring the individual TCP/IP hosts and keeping track of their IP addresses is relatively straightforward. However, on a large network, managing IP addresses can be challenging, and in this case, you can use DHCP to simplify the task by assigning dynamic IP addresses.

What is a dynamic IP address?

A *dynamic address* is an address that is automatically assigned for a specific length of time and can change. You use DHCP to assign dynamic addresses. When you assign IP addresses automatically, you can configure the addresses for an entire network from a single location and then dynamically assign them to each computer.

Static TCP/IP Configuration

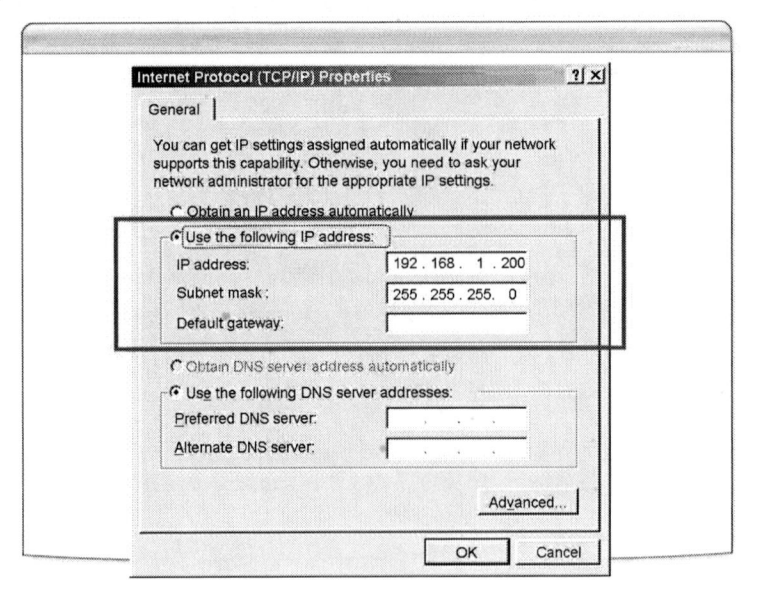

![Internet Protocol (TCP/IP) Properties dialog box showing "Use the following IP address" selected with IP address 192.168.1.200 and Subnet mask 255.255.255.0]

Introduction

In some situations, you might need to view the IP address information for a specific client. For example, a client on your network might not be able to communicate with other computers on the network. In this situation, you must know the IP addresses of the other computers to identify the problem.

How to view a static IP address

You can use the **Internet Protocol (TCP/IP) Properties** dialog box to view static TCP/IP information.

By using the **Internet Protocol (TCP/IP) Properties** dialog box, you can determine whether the IP address configuration has been performed dynamically or statically. If the IP address is static, you can then view the IP address, subnet mask, and default gateway in this dialog box. However, if the IP address has been configured dynamically by using DHCP or Automatic Private IP Addressing (APIPA), you cannot determine the values of the TCP/IP configuration options by using this dialog box.

Preferred DNS server

Incorrect configuration of the preferred DNS server in static configurations is the most common cause of network logon problems. In a domain-based environment, the preferred DNS server should be an internal DNS server with domain information, not an Internet DNS server.

Advanced TCP/IP settings

The Advanced TCP/IP Settings dialog box allows you to configure additional TCP/IP settings not available in the **Internet Protocol (TCP/IP) Properties** dialog box. Some of the settings that you can configure are:

- *Additional IP Addresses*. A client can be configured with multiple IP addresses.
- *Additional Default Gateways*. Additional default gateways can be configured for fault tolerance.
- *Additional DNS Servers*. Additional DNS servers can be configured for enhanced fault tolerance.
- *DNS Suffix search*. You can configure which DNS suffixes are used when searching for host names.
- *DNS Suffix registration*. You can configure which DNS suffixes are used when registering this host by using dynamic DNS.
- *WINS configuration*. You can configure multiple Windows Internet Naming Service (WINS) servers for fault tolerance and enable or disable network basic input/output system (NetBIOS).
- *TCP/IP filtering*. TCP/IP filtering can be enabled as an alternative to Windows Firewall.

Note Additional information about DNS and WINS configuration can be found in Module 4, "Configuring a Client for Name Resolution."

How to Use Ipconfig for Viewing the TCP/IP Configuration

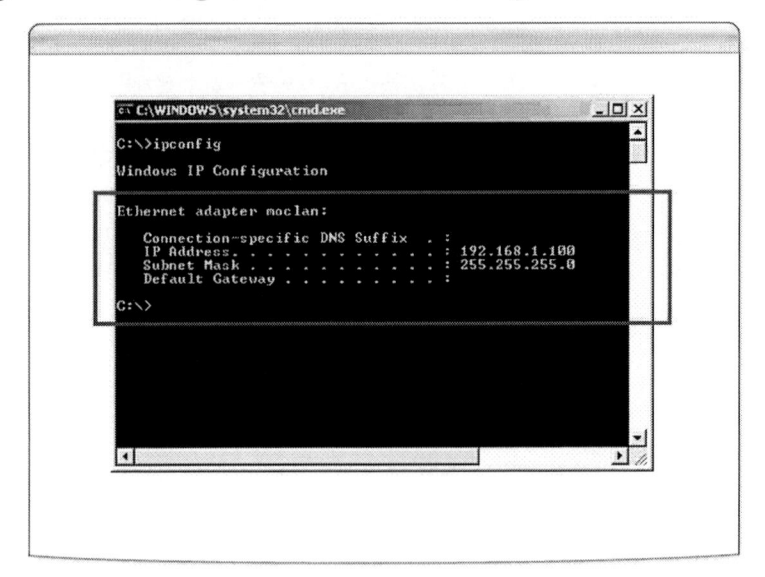

Introduction

When you want to obtain information about static or dynamic IP addresses, you can use Ipconfig. You can also use Ipconfig to view information about static IP addresses not provided when you use the Internet Protocol (TCP/IP) Properties dialog box.

What is Ipconfig?

Ipconfig is a command-line utility that you can use to view, but not set, the TCP/IP configuration options on a client, including the IP address, subnet mask, and default gateway. Ipconfig provides additional information that is not available in the **Internet Protocol (TCP/IP) Properties** dialog box, such as the media state (connected or disconnected).

Ipconfig syntax

The basic command syntax for this utility is **ipconfig**. To start the Ipconfig utility, at a command prompt, type **ipconfig**. The values of the three primary configuration parameters are displayed. The following table contains options that can be used with Ipconfig.

Option	Description
/?	Displays the help message.
/all	Displays all of the current TCP/IP configuration values, including the IP address, subnet mask, default gateway, and WINS and DNS configurations.
/release	Releases the dynamic IP address of the specified adapter.
/renew	Renews the dynamic IP address of the specified adapter.
/flushdns	Purges the DNS resolver cache.
/registerdns	Refreshes all DHCP leases and reregisters DNS names.
/displaydns	Displays the contents of the DNS resolver cache.
/showclassid	Displays all the DHCP ClassIDs allowed for the specified adapter.
/setclassid	Modifies the DHCP ClassID.

Ipconfig DNS options

A DNS host record is used to resolve a DNS name to an IP address. DNS host records are used extensively by the Active Directory® directory service and management tools. If the IP address of a host changes, some functionality might be lost. You can force the host record to be updated on the DNS server by using the **ipconfig** command with the **/registerdns** option.

After a client has resolved a DNS name to an IP address, the result is stored in the DNS resolver cache. If the IP address of a remote computer changes and the host record is updated, the client will still resolve the name of the remote computer to the original IP address because it is stored in the DNS resolver cache. You can clear the contents of the DNS resolver cache by using **ipconfig** with the **/flushdns** option.

Connection status

The **Support** tab in the **Local Area Connection Status** dialog box also allows you to view static or dynamic TCP/IP configuration information. The information displayed on this tab is similar to running **ipconfig** without options. Clicking the **Details** button displays information similar to what you would receive by running **ipconfig /all**.

Note More information about DNS name resolution can be found in Module 4, "Configuring a Client for Name Resolution."

Practice: Configuring a Client to Use a Static IP Address

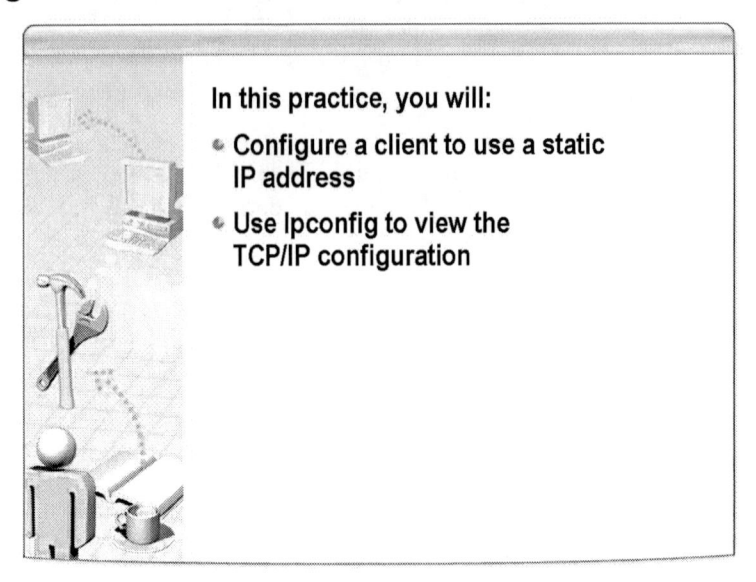

Objectives

In this practice, you will:

- Configure a client to use a static IP address.
- Use Ipconfig to view the TCP/IP configuration.

Instructions

Ensure that the DEN-DC1 and DEN-CL1 virtual machines are running.

Practice

▶ **Configure a client to use a static IP address**

1. On DEN-CL1, log on to the **CONTOSO** domain as **Paul**, with a password of **Pa$$w0rd**.
2. Click **Start**, and then click **Control Panel**.
3. Click **Network Connections**.
4. Double-click **Local Area Connection**.
5. Click **Properties**.
6. Click **Internet Protocol (TCP/IP)**, and then click **Properties**.
7. Click **Use the following IP address**.
8. In the **IP address** box, change the IP address to **10.10.0.21**.
9. In the **Subnet mask** box, verify that the subnet mask is **255.255.0.0**.
10. In the **Preferred DNS server** box, verify that the DNS server address is **10.10.0.2**.
11. To close the **Internet Protocol (TCP/IP) Properties** dialog box, click **OK**.
12. To close the **Local Area Connection Properties** dialog box, click **Close**.
13. Click the **Support** tab. Notice that the **Address Type** setting is manually configured.
14. To close the **Local Area Connection Status** dialog box, click **Close**.
15. Close the Network Connections window.

▶ Use Ipconfig to view the TCP/IP configuration

1. Click **Start**, click **Run**, type **cmd**, and then click **OK**.
2. Type **ipconfig**, and then press ENTER.
3. Verify that the **IP Address** setting is **10.10.0.21**.
4. Verify that the **Subnet Mask** attribute is **255.255.0.0**.
5. Close the command prompt window.

Important Do not shut down the virtual machines.

Lesson: Configuring a Client to Obtain an IP Address Automatically

- **What Is DHCP?**
- **Multimedia: The Role of DHCP in the Network Infrastructure**
- **DHCP Address Renewal**
- **DHCP Server Configuration**
- **Practice: Configuring a Client to Obtain an IP Address Automatically**

Introduction

Windows Server 2003 includes DHCP, a TCP/IP standard that you can use to automatically assign dynamic IP addresses and other TCP/IP configuration parameters to client computers on your network. When you use DHCP, you centralize the management of IP addresses and other TCP/IP configuration settings, thereby simplifying your administrative tasks.

Lesson objectives

After completing this lesson, you will be able to:

- Describe DHCP.
- Describe the role of DHCP in the network.
- Describe renewing an IP address.
- Describe configuring a DHCP server.
- Configure a client to obtain an IP address automatically.

What Is DHCP?

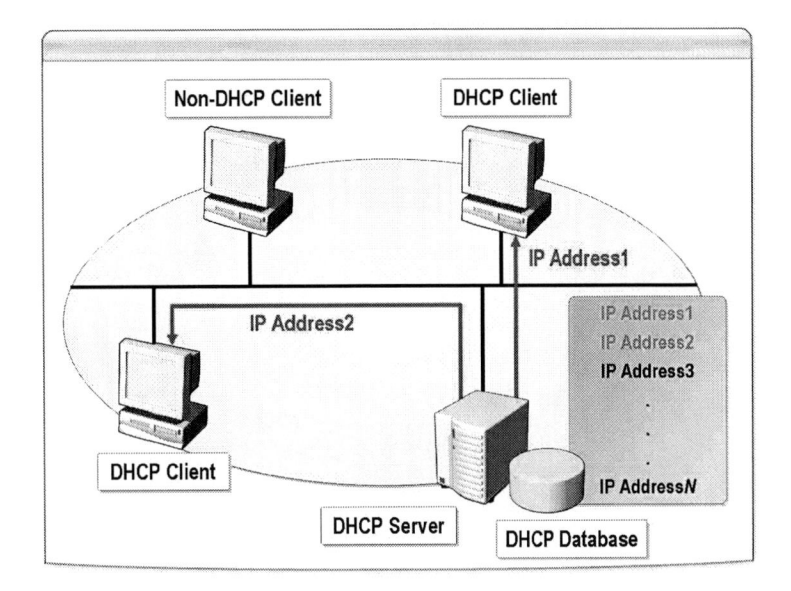

Definition

DHCP is a service and a protocol that work together to automatically assign IP addresses and other configuration settings to the computers on a network. DHCP dynamically assigns IP addresses to clients from a pool of addresses.

Benefits of using DHCP

When you use DHCP, you:

- Do not have to manually configure each client with an IP address.
- No longer have to maintain a record of each individual IP address that you assign.
- Can automatically assign a new IP address when you move a client from one subnet to another.
- Can release the IP address of a computer that is offline for a specific amount of time, and then reassign the address to another computer.
- Reduce the possibility of address duplication, because DHCP automatically tracks IP address assignments.
- Can rely on the DHCP server to detect unauthorized DHCP servers on the network.

How DHCP works

When a DHCP server receives a request from a DHCP client, it selects an IP address from a pool of addresses (called a *scope*) defined in its database and offers the address to the DHCP client. If the client accepts the offer, the IP addressing information is leased to the client for a specified period. As the lease interval progresses, the client renews the address assignment each time it logs on to the network. If the lease expires without a renewal, the IP address is returned to the pool for reassignment. Certain addresses in the scope might be excluded from distribution because they are already assigned as static addresses.

The DHCP server provides the client with the following basic information:

- IP address
- Subnet mask

Other information can be distributed by using DHCP as well, such as a default gateway address, DNS server addresses, and WINS server addresses.

How to enable DHCP

You must enable clients in the network to use DHCP by selecting **Obtain an IP address automatically** in the **Internet Protocol (TCP/IP) Properties** dialog box; this option is selected by default in Windows XP.

Note For more information about DHCP, see RFC 2131 under **Additional Reading** on the Student Materials compact disc and Course 2277, *Implementing, Managing, and Maintaining a Microsoft Windows Server™ 2003 Network Infrastructure: Network Services.*

Module 3: Configuring a Client IP Address 13

Multimedia: The Role of DHCP in the Network Infrastructure

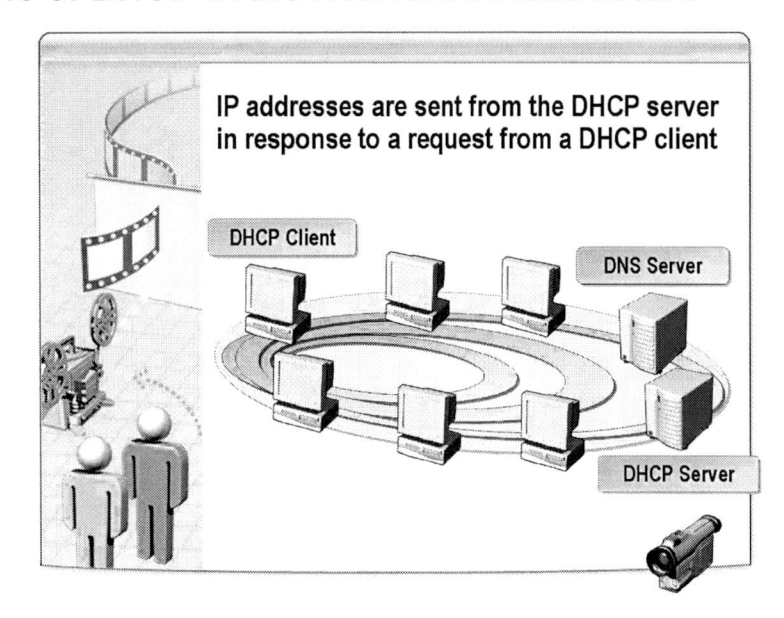

IP addresses are sent from the DHCP server in response to a request from a DHCP client

DHCP Client
DNS Server
DHCP Server

File location

To view the multimedia presentation *The Role of DHCP in the Network Infrastructure*, open the Web page on the Student Materials compact disc, click **Multimedia**, and then click the title of the presentation.

Objectives

At the end of this presentation, you will be able to describe how DHCP:

- Assigns TCP/IP configuration data to clients.
- Manages IP address allocation.
- Ensures that IP address conflicts do not occur.
- Provides configuration data for a specific period.

DHCP Address Renewal

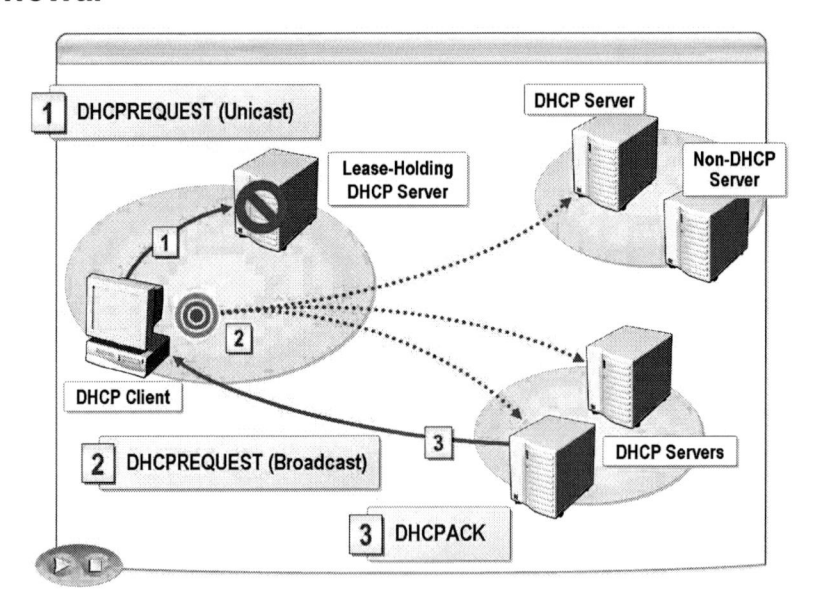

Introduction

When you identify a connectivity problem with a client on your network, an effective first step is to release and renew the IP address manually. This action frequently resolves the issue. For example, when you move a client from one subnet to another, the IP address might not be automatically updated for the new subnet. In this case, releasing and renewing the IP address might be all you need to do to solve the problem.

Automatic renewal of IP addresses

In most cases, the client retains the settings assigned to it by the DHCP server until someone explicitly changes them or forces a reassignment. However, when the server dynamically allocates settings, the client leases its IP address for a certain period of time (configured at the server) and must renew the lease to continue using it.

The length of an IP address lease is typically measured in days and is generally based on whether computers are frequently moved around the network or whether IP addresses are in short supply. Shorter leases generate more network traffic, but they enable DHCP servers to reclaim unused addresses faster. For a relatively stable network, longer leases reduce the amount of traffic that DHCP generates.

The lease renewal process

The lease renewal process begins when a *bound client* (a DHCP client with a leased address) reaches what is known as the *renewal time value*, or *T1 value*, of its lease. By default, the renewal time value is 50 percent of the lease period. When a client reaches this point, it enters the *renewing state* and begins generating DHCPREQUEST messages as follows:

1. The client transmits a unicast DHCPREQUEST message to the server that holds the lease.

   If the server is available to receive the message, it responds with either a DHCPACK message, which renews the lease and restarts the lease time clock, or a DHCPNACK message, which terminates the lease and forces the client to begin the address assignment process again from the beginning.

   A DHCPREQUEST to the server that holds the lease is also sent by the client when the client is restarted. If the IP address is available, the lease will be treated like a renewal. If the address is not available, the client receives a DHCPNAK message and restarts the lease process.

2. If the server does not respond to the DHCPREQUEST unicast message, the client continues to send messages until it reaches the *rebinding time value*, or *T2 value*, which defaults to 87.5 percent of the lease period. At this point, the client enters the *rebinding state* and begins transmitting broadcast DHCPREQUEST messages, soliciting an address assignment from any DHCP server on the network.

3. A server can respond with either a DHCPACK or a DHCPNACK message.

   If the lease time expires with no response from any DHCP server, the client's IP address is released, and all of its TCP/IP communication ceases, except for the transmission of broadcast DHCPDISCOVER messages. The DHCPDISCOVER broadcasts are used to request configuration parameters from a DHCP server.

DHCP Server Configuration

> DHCP server configuration tasks include:
> - Authorizing the DHCP server
> - Creating scopes
> - Creating reservations

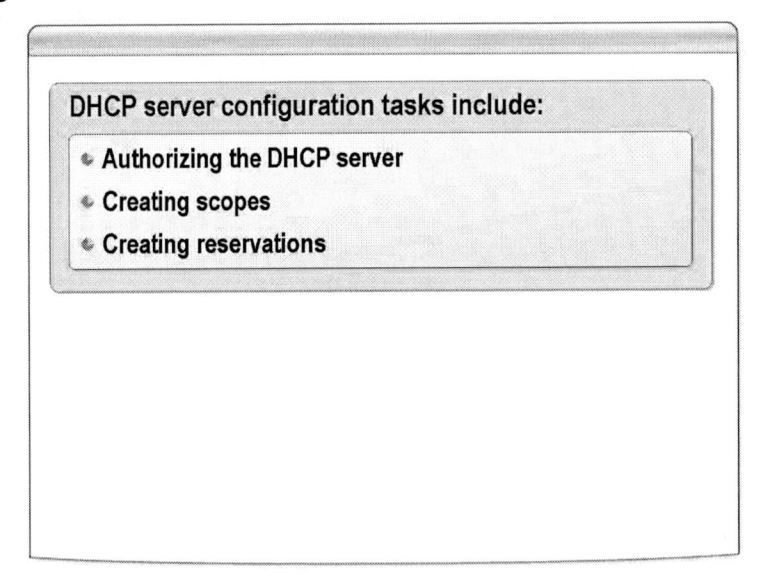

Introduction

A DHCP server is required to hand out DHCP addresses to clients. On many networks, this role is performed by a server running Windows; however, it can also be done by most routers.

Authorizing a DHCP server

After the DHCP service is installed, DHCP servers running Windows 2000 Server or Windows Server 2003 must be authorized in Active Directory to assign IP addresses to clients. The ability to authorize DHCP servers can be controlled and delegated. Restricting DHCP server authorization allows senior networking staff to control who can install and configure DHCP servers to prevent errors. "Rogue" DHCP servers (a DHCP server that has not been or cannot be authorized in Active Directory) can cause serious connectivity problems on corporate networks.

Creating scopes

A *scope* is a range of valid IP addresses that are available for lease or assignment to client computers on a particular subnet. You configure a scope on the DHCP server to determine the pool of IP addresses that the server can assign to DHCP clients. A scope must be activated before a DHCP server uses it.

A scope has many possible configuration properties. Some of the configuration properties are required; others are optional. The following table lists some of the available properties.

Scope property	Description
Scope Name (required)	The name of the scope in Active Directory
Start IP Address (required)	The first IP address that can be leased to clients
End IP Address (required)	The last IP address that can be leased to clients
Subnet Mask (required)	The subnet mask that is delivered to clients with the IP addresses

(*continued*)

Scope property	Description
Lease Duration (required)	The period that the DHCP server holds an issued IP address for a client before removing the lease
Router	A DHCP option that allows DHCP clients to access remote networks
Exclusion Range	The range of IP addresses in the scope that are excluded from being leased

Creating DHCP reservations

A *reservation* is a specific IP address, within a scope, that is permanently reserved for a specific DHCP client. Reservations allow devices to have a static IP address without having to visit the device to configure it statically. Additionally, if IP address changes are needed in the future, the IP address of the device can be easily changed by editing the existing reservation or creating a new reservation.

To use a reservation, you must know the media access control (MAC) address of the device being configured. The DHCP server correlates DHCP clients to reservations by using the MAC address of the client.

Practice: Configuring a Client to Obtain an IP Address Automatically

In this practice, you will:
- Configure a client for DHCP
- Release and renew an IP address

Objectives

In this practice, you will:

- Configure a client for DHCP.
- Release and renew an IP address.

Instructions

Ensure that the DEN-DC1 and DEN-CL1 virtual machines are running.

Practice

▶ **Configure a client for DHCP**

1. On DEN-CL1, click **Start**, and then click **Control Panel**.
2. Click **Network Connections**.
3. Double-click **Local Area Connection**.
4. Click **Properties**.
5. Click **Internet Protocol (TCP/IP)**, and then click **Properties**.
6. Click **Obtain an IP address automatically**, click **Obtain DNS server address automatically**, and then click **OK**.
7. To close the **Internet Protocol (TCP/IP) Properties** dialog box, click **OK**.
8. To close the **Local Area Connection Properties** dialog box, click **Close**.
9. Click the **Support** tab. Notice that the **Address Type** property is assigned by DHCP. This may take a few seconds to complete.
10. To close the **Local Area Connection Status** dialog box, click **Close**.
11. Close the Network Connections window.

▶ Release and renew an IP address

1. Click **Start**, click **Run**, type **cmd**, and then click **OK**.
2. At the command prompt, type **ipconfig /all**, and then press ENTER.
3. Verify that the **DHCP enabled** attribute is **Yes** and that you have an IP address.
4. At the command prompt, type **ipconfig /release**, and then press ENTER.

   The IP address and subnet mask of your adapter should read **0.0.0.0**. You may receive an error message stating that the local area connection has limited or no connectivity.
5. At the command prompt, type **ipconfig /renew**, and then press ENTER.

   You should now have a valid IP address and subnet mask.
6. At the command prompt, type **ipconfig /all**, and then press ENTER.
7. Note the time of the **Lease Obtained** attribute. What date and time does it show?

   _____

   _____

8. Close the command prompt window.

Important Do not shut down the virtual machines.

Lesson: Using Alternate Configuration

- What Is Alternate Configuration?
- What Is Automatic Private IP Addressing?
- Practice: Using Alternate Configuration

Introduction

Alternate Configuration is a feature of Windows Server 2003 that you can use to streamline multiple-network connectivity. Alternate Configuration is useful when you are using a computer on more than one network and at least one of the networks does not have a DHCP server. Mobile computer users can use Alternate Configuration to assign IP addresses automatically on both office and home networks without having to reconfigure TCP/IP settings manually.

Lesson objectives

After completing this lesson, you will be able to:

- Describe Alternate Configuration.
- Describe automatic private IP addressing.
- Configure and use Alternate Configuration for TCP/IP.

What Is Alternate Configuration?

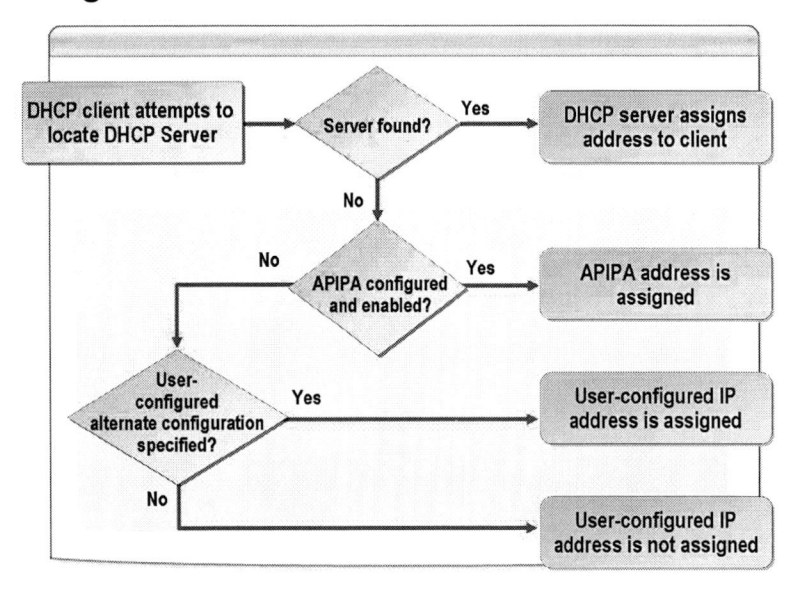

Definition

Alternate Configuration is another way to assign IP addresses. There are two Alternate Configuration methods: User-Configured Alternate Configuration (also known as a static address) and Automatic Private IP Addressing (APIPA). Alternate Configuration is used only if DHCP fails to obtain an IP address.

How to determine which Alternate Configuration method to use

User-Configured Alternate Configuration provides more detailed parameters than APIPA. In situations for which you require a specific IP address and subnet mask for a client, or if you require a default gateway, DNS server, or WINS server, you should use Alternate Configuration.

APIPA is most useful in situations where a reserved IP address in the range 169.254.0.1 through 169.254.255.254 is acceptable and you do not need access to a default gateway, DNS server, or WINS server. APIPA functions without any user configuration.

How Alternate Configuration works

By default, a client computer first tries to contact a DHCP server on the network to dynamically obtain a configuration for each installed network connection. When the client contacts the server:

- If a DHCP server is reached and the leased configuration is successful, TCP/IP configuration is completed.

- If a DHCP server is not reached, by default the computer instead uses either APIPA or a user-configured alternate configuration to configure TCP/IP.

When specifying a user-configured alternate configuration, you can also specify a default gateway, WINS servers, and DNS servers.

The **Alternate Configuration** tab is visible only if **Obtain an IP address automatically** is selected on the **General** tab in the **Internet Protocol (TCP/IP) Properties** dialog box.

What Is Automatic Private IP Addressing?

APIPA:
- Used if a DHCP server cannot be contacted
- Assigns IP addresses on the 169.254.0.0/16 network
- Cannot be used with:
  - Active Directory
  - Internet connectivity
  - Multiple subnets
  - DNS or WINS servers

Definition

APIPA is one of two methods that you can use to specify an alternate configuration. When you use APIPA, you can create a functioning, single-subnet TCP/IP network without having to manually configure the TCP/IP protocol or set up a DHCP server. APIPA eliminates errors associated with missing IP addresses that often occur in single-network small-office or home-office networks.

How APIPA works

If a DHCP server cannot be reached to assign an IP address automatically and APIPA has been selected as the mode of alternate configuration, Windows selects an address in the reserved IP addressing class ranging from 169.254.0.1 through 169.254.255.254 and assigns the subnet mask of 255.255.0.0.

In addition to receiving an address on the 169.254.0.0 network, Microsoft Windows XP clients using APIPA also display a warning icon in the system tray. This icon is often overlooked by users, and might be missed when they are describing the problem to the help desk.

APIPA limitations

The limitations of APIPA make it unsuitable for even most small networks. APIPA does not assign DNS servers, WINS servers, or a default gateway. Using APIPA is not appropriate for networks that have any of the following characteristics:

- Active Directory
- Internet connectivity
- Multiple subnets
- DNS servers
- WINS servers

Disabling APIPA

Some network administrators prefer to disable APIPA on client computers. However, in Windows XP the warning icon displayed to users is exactly the same as when APIPA is used. If APIPA is disabled, clients that would normally be configured with an APIPA address will display an IP address of 0.0.0.0 when Ipconfig is run.

To disable APIPA, you must edit the registry. In the key HKEY_LOCAL_MACHINE\SYSTEM\CurrentControlSet\Services\Tcpip\Parameters, add a DWORD value named **IPAutoconfigurationEnabled** with a value of **0**.

Note For more information about APIPA, see article 220874, "How to Use Automatic TCP/IP Addressing Without a DHCP Server," in the Microsoft Knowledge Base.

Practice: Using Alternate Configuration

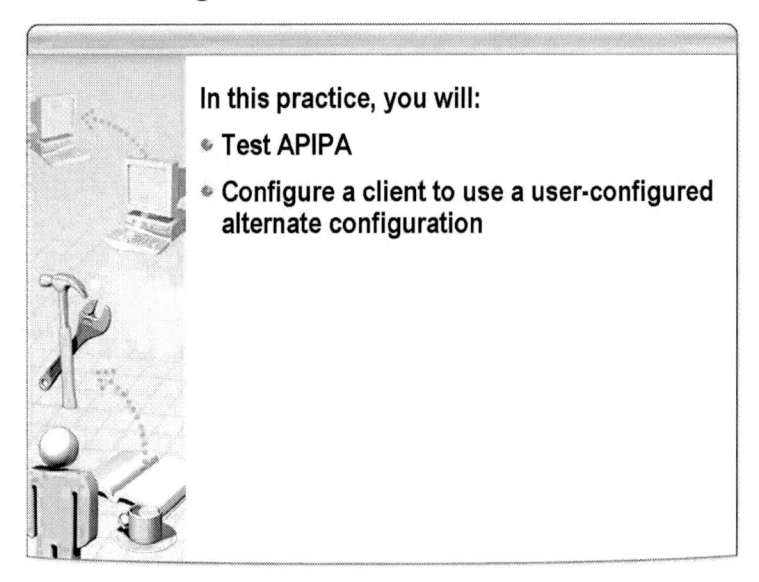

In this practice, you will:
- Test APIPA
- Configure a client to use a user-configured alternate configuration

Objectives

In this practice, you will:
- Test APIPA.
- Configure a client to use a user-configured alternate configuration.

Instructions

Ensure that the DEN-DC1 and DEN-CL1 virtual machines are running.

Practice

▶ **Test APIPA**

1. Log on to DEN-DC1 as **Administrator** with the password of **Pa$$w0rd**.
2. On DEN-DC1, click **Start**, point to **Administrative Tools**, and then click **DHCP**.
3. Click **DEN-DC1.contoso.msft**.
4. Right-click **DEN-DC1.contoso.msft**, point to **All Tasks**, and then click **Stop**.
5. On DEN-CL1, click **Start**, click **Run**, type **cmd**, and then click **OK**.
6. Type **ipconfig /release**, and then press ENTER.
7. Type **ipconfig /renew**, and then press ENTER. After a couple of minutes, an error message will be displayed, indicating that a DHCP server could not be contacted.
8. Type **ipconfig**, and then press ENTER. An address on the 169.254.0.0 network will be displayed.
9. Close the command prompt window.

▶ Configure a client to use a user-configured alternate configuration

1. On DEN-CL1, click **Start**, and then click **Control Panel**.
2. Click **Network Connections**.
3. Double-click **Local Area Connection**.
4. Click **Properties**.
5. Click **Internet Protocol (TCP/IP)**, and then click **Properties**.
6. On the **Alternate Configuration** tab, click **User configured**.
7. In the **IP address** box, type **10.10.0.20**.
8. In the **Subnet mask** box, type **255.255.0.0**.
9. In the **Default gateway** box, type **10.10.0.1**.
10. In the **Preferred DNS server** box, type **10.10.0.2**.
11. In the **Preferred WINS server** box, type **10.10.0.2**.
12. To close the **Internet Protocol (TCP/IP) Properties** dialog box, click **OK**.
13. To close the **Local Area Connection Properties** dialog box, click **Close**.
14. Click the **Support** tab.

    Notice that the **Address Type** setting is **Alternate Manually Configured**.
15. To close the **Local Area Connection Status** dialog box, click **Close**.
16. Close the Network Connections window.
17. Click **Start**, click **Run**, type **cmd**, and then click **OK**.
18. Type **ipconfig**, and then press ENTER.

    The IP address 10.10.0.20 will be displayed.
19. Close the command prompt window.
20. On DEN-DC1, right-click **DEN-DC1.contoso.msft**, point to **All Tasks**, and then click **Start**.
21. Close the DHCP window.

Important Do not shut down the virtual machines.

Lab: Configuring Hosts to Connect to a Network Running the TCP/IP Protocol Suite

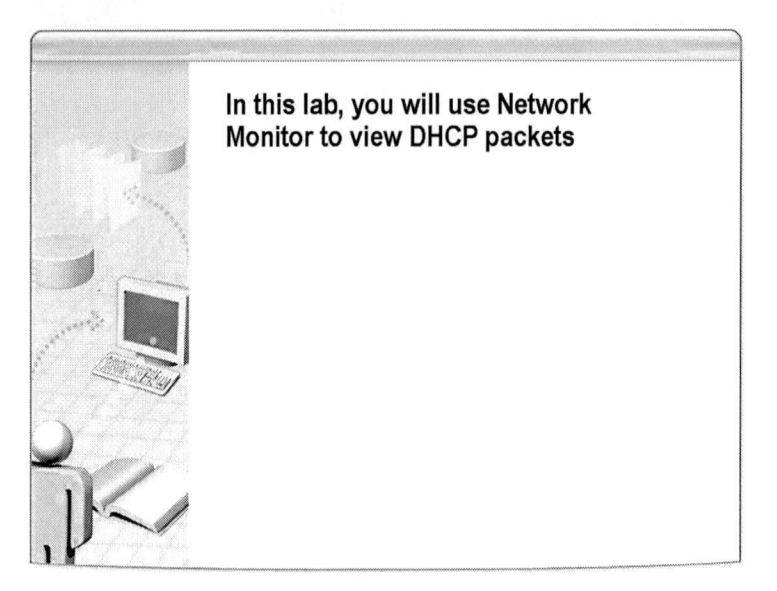

In this lab, you will use Network Monitor to view DHCP packets

Objective In this lab, you will use Network Monitor to view DHCP packets.

Instructions Ensure that the DEN-DC1 and DEN-CL1 virtual machines are running.

Estimated time to complete this lab: 10 minutes

Exercise 1
Viewing DHCP Packets

In this exercise, you will view the DHCP packets sent between a DHCP client and a DHCP server. Viewing the DHCP packets reinforces the DHCP communication process and can be used to confirm that proper communication is occurring.

Scenario

A client computer on your network has been intermittently obtaining unusual IP configuration information from DHCP. You will view the DHCP packets passed between the client and the DHCP server to verify that the proper communication process is occurring. To do this, you use Network Monitor.

Tasks	Detailed steps
1. Ensure that DEN-CL1 has a dynamic IP address.	a. If necessary, on DEN-CL1, log on to the **CONTOSO** domain as **Paul** with the password of **Pa$$w0rd**. b. Open a command prompt window. c. Renew the IP address by using **ipconfig**.
2. Start capturing packets on DEN-DC1.	a. If necessary, log on to DEN-DC1 as **Administrator** with the password of **Pa$$w0rd**. b. Open Network Monitor. c. If necessary, select **Local Area Connection** for the network. d. Start a capture.
3. Renew the IP address on DEN-CL1.	▪ Renew the IP address by using ipconfig.
4. View the DHCP packets in Network Monitor.	a. Stop and view the capture. b. Filter the capture to show only DHCP packets. c. View the details of each DHCP packet.
5. Complete the lab exercise.	a. Close all programs and shut down all computers. Do not save changes. b. To prepare for the next module, start the DEN-DC1 and DEN-CL1 virtual computers.

Course Evaluation

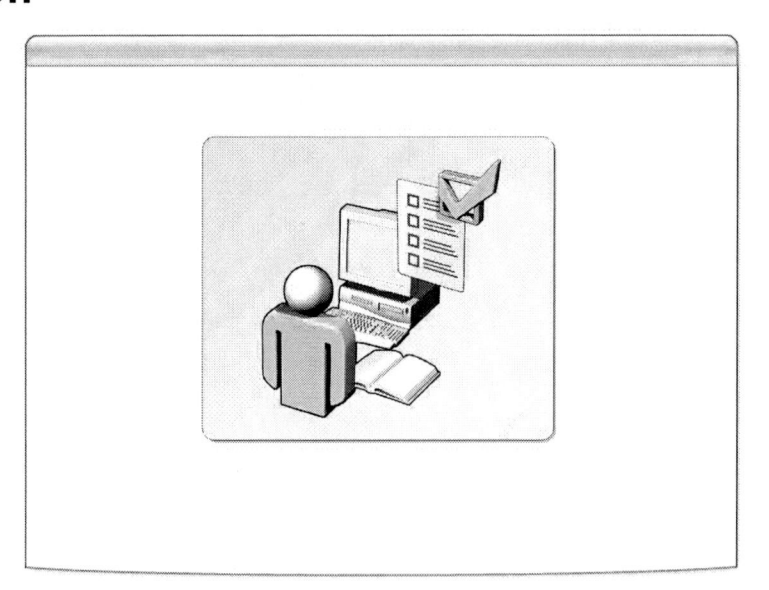

Your evaluation of this course will help Microsoft understand the quality of your learning experience.

At a convenient time before the end of the course, please complete a course evaluation, which is available on the Metrics That Matter page of the Knowledge Advisors Web site at http://www.metricsthatmatter.com/MTMStudent/ClassListPage.aspx?&orig=6&VendorAlias=survey.

Microsoft will keep your evaluation strictly confidential and will use your responses to improve your future learning experience.

Module 4: Configuring a Client for Name Resolution

Contents

Overview	1
Lesson: Overview of Name Resolution	2
Lesson: Resolving Host Names	7
Lesson: Resolving NetBIOS Names	18
Lab: Configuring a Client for Name Resolution	31

Information in this document, including URL and other Internet Web site references, is subject to change without notice. Unless otherwise noted, the example companies, organizations, products, domain names, e-mail addresses, logos, people, places, and events depicted herein are fictitious, and no association with any real company, organization, product, domain name, e-mail address, logo, person, place or event is intended or should be inferred. Complying with all applicable copyright laws is the responsibility of the user. Without limiting the rights under copyright, no part of this document may be reproduced, stored in or introduced into a retrieval system, or transmitted in any form or by any means (electronic, mechanical, photocopying, recording, or otherwise), or for any purpose, without the express written permission of Microsoft Corporation.

The names of manufacturers, products, or URLs are provided for informational purposes only and Microsoft makes no representations and warranties, either expressed, implied, or statutory, regarding these manufacturers or the use of the products with any Microsoft technologies. The inclusion of a manufacturer or product does not imply endorsement of Microsoft of the manufacturer or product. Links are provided to third party sites. Such sites are not under the control of Microsoft and Microsoft is not responsible for the contents of any linked site or any link contained in a linked site, or any changes or updates to such sites. Microsoft is not responsible for webcasting or any other form of transmission received from any linked site. Microsoft is providing these links to you only as a convenience, and the inclusion of any link does not imply endorsement of Microsoft of the site or the products contained therein.

Microsoft may have patents, patent applications, trademarks, copyrights, or other intellectual property rights covering subject matter in this document. Except as expressly provided in any written license agreement from Microsoft, the furnishing of this document does not give you any license to these patents, trademarks, copyrights, or other intellectual property.

© 2005 Microsoft Corporation. All rights reserved.

Microsoft, Active Directory, Excel, MS-DOS, PowerPoint, Windows, Windows Media, Windows NT, and Windows Server are either registered trademarks or trademarks of Microsoft Corporation in the United States and/or other countries.

All other trademarks are property of their respective owners.

Overview

- Overview of Name Resolution
- Resolving Host Names
- Resolving NetBIOS Names

Introduction

As part of the Microsoft® Windows Server™ 2003 installation process, you specify a name by which the computer is known to the network. The Microsoft Windows® Setup program refers to this as a computer name, and it is used to generate other names, such as a network basic input/output system (NetBIOS) name and Domain Name System (DNS) host name. To use NetBIOS names on a Transmission Control Protocol/Internet Protocol (TCP/IP) network, there must be mechanisms that resolve the names into Internet Protocol (IP) addresses and then into media access control (MAC) addresses, which are needed for TCP/IP communication. This module describes the various types of name resolution mechanisms provided by the Windows operating systems and how to use them for clients on your network.

Note In this module, the term *client* refers to a computer running a Windows operating system on a network running TCP/IP. The term *host* includes clients and refers to any device on the network that has an IP address.

Objectives

After completing this module, you will be able to:

- Describe how name resolution occurs.
- Describe how host names are used and resolved.
- Describe how NetBIOS names are used and resolved.

Lesson: Overview of Name Resolution

- **Multimedia: The Name Resolution Process**
- **Types of Names That Computers Use**

Introduction

You must configure the client computers on your network so that their computer names can be resolved into IP addresses. When you configure clients for name resolution, you are ensuring that they can communicate with other computers using computer names. For two hosts to communicate on a network, the MAC address of each host must be identified. An IP address is associated with a MAC address, and a computer name is associated with an IP address. Name resolution is the process of obtaining the IP address associated with the computer name. Knowing the various methods for resolving computer names assists you in performing these administrative tasks successfully.

Lesson objectives

After completing this lesson, you will be able to:

- Describe the name resolution process used by Windows clients.
- Describe why computers use names and the two types of names that they use.

Multimedia: The Name Resolution Process

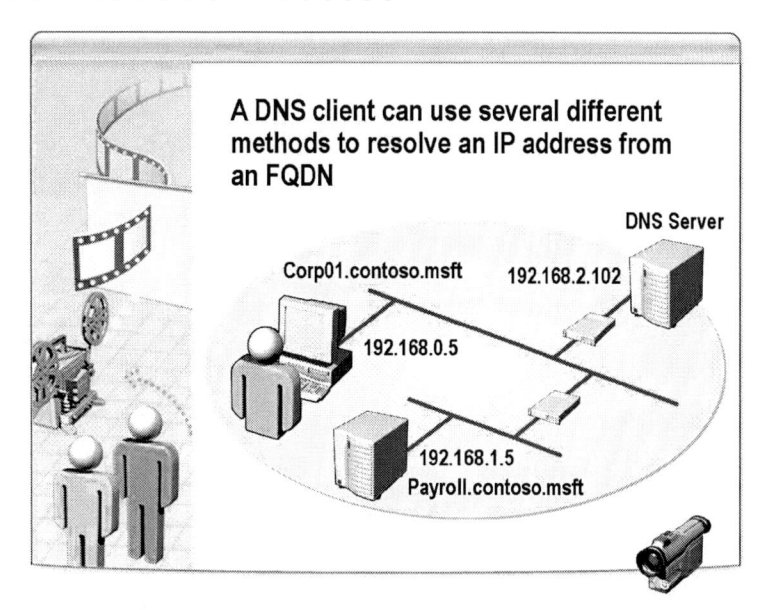

> A DNS client can use several different methods to resolve an IP address from an FQDN
>
> DNS Server
> Corp01.contoso.msft   192.168.2.102
> 192.168.0.5
> 192.168.1.5
> Payroll.contoso.msft

File location To view the multimedia presentation *The Name Resolution Process*, open the Web page on the Student Materials compact disc, click **Multimedia**, and then click the title of the presentation.

Objective Upon completion of this presentation, you will be able to describe the methods that a DNS client can use to resolve an IP address from a fully qualified domain name (FQDN).

Types of Names That Computers Use

Name	Description
Host names	• Up to 255 characters in length • Can contain alphabetic and numeric characters, periods, and hyphens • Part of FQDN
NetBIOS names	• Represent a single computer or group of computers • 15 characters used for the name • 16th character identifies service • Flat namespace

Introduction

TCP/IP identifies source and destination computers by their IP addresses. However, computer users are much better at remembering and using names than numbers, so common, or user-friendly, names are assigned to the computer's IP address. These names are either NetBIOS names or host names.

Note Earlier versions of Windows require NetBIOS to support networking capabilities. Windows 2000, Windows XP, and Windows Server 2003 support NetBIOS for backward compatibility with earlier versions of Windows, but they do not require NetBIOS.

Choosing a name type

The name type used by an application is determined by the application developer. Windows operating systems allow applications to request network services through either Windows Sockets or NetBIOS. If an application requests network services through Windows Sockets, host names are used. If an application requests services through NetBIOS, a NetBIOS name is used.

Most current applications, including Internet applications, use Windows Sockets to access network services. NetBIOS is used by many earlier Windows applications. Windows 98 and earlier versions of Windows use only NetBIOS for file sharing. Windows 2000, Windows XP, and Windows Server 2003 use both Windows Sockets and NetBIOS for file sharing.

Note Windows Sockets applications allow users to specify the destination host by IP address or host name. NetBIOS applications require the use of a NetBIOS name.

Host name

A host name is a user-friendly name that is associated with a computer's IP address to identify it as a TCP/IP host. The host name can be up to 255 characters in length and can contain alphabetic and numeric characters, periods, and hyphens.

Note Although a host name can be up to 255 characters long, Windows Server 2003 and Windows XP support host names only up to 63 characters in length. The maximum number of characters between periods in a host name is 63.

Host names can be used in various forms. The two most common forms are an alias and an FQDN. An alias is a single name associated with an IP address, such as *payroll*. An alias can be combined with a domain name to create an FQDN. An FQDN is structured for use on the Internet and includes periods as separators. An example of an FQDN is *payroll.contoso.com*.

NetBIOS name

A NetBIOS name is a 16-character name that is used to identify a NetBIOS resource on the network. A NetBIOS name can represent a single computer or a group of computers. The first 15 characters are used for the name. The final character is used to identify the resource or service that is being referred to on the computer.

The NetBIOS namespace is flat, meaning that names can be used only once within a network. NetBIOS names cannot be organized into a hierarchical structure, as can be done with FQDNs.

How NetBIOS names are constructed

The 15-character name can include the computer name, the domain name, and the name of the user who is logged on. The sixteenth character is a 1-byte hexadecimal identifier.

For example, the sixteenth character identifying the Windows Server 2003 Messenger service has the 1-byte hexadecimal identifier 03h. On a computer running Windows Server 2003 named SERVER12, the Messenger service would be uniquely identified on the network with the NetBIOS name SERVER12   [03h]. (Note: the extra spaces make the name 15 characters long.) A NetBIOS name is also distinguished by whether it is:

- A unique name, which applies to a single IP address.
- A group name, which applies to multiple IP addresses.
- A multihomed name, which apples to a group of IP addresses assigned to a single host.

Common suffixes for NetBIOS names

The following table shows some of the more common suffixes that constitute the hidden sixteenth character of a NetBIOS name and the networking service with which they are associated.

Suffix (hex)	First 15 characters	Networking service
00	Computer name	Workstation service
00	Domain name	Domain name
03	Computer name	Messenger service
03	User name	Messenger service
20	Computer name	File Server service
1B	Domain name	Domain master browser
1C	Domain name	Domain controllers
1D	Domain name	Master browser
1E	Domain name	Browser service election

Tip To view the NetBIOS names registered for your computer, use the **nbtstat –n** command.

Lesson: Resolving Host Names

- Purpose of a Hosts File
- What Is DNS?
- How Windows Clients Use the DNS Suffix
- DNS Resolver Cache
- The Host Name Resolution Process
- Practice: Resolving Host Names

Introduction

Host names are used for basic network services in Windows 2000, Windows XP, and Windows Server 2003. Proper resolution of host names to IP addresses is essential to the proper functioning of a Windows-based network. Network administrators must understand host name resolution in Windows to troubleshoot problems with host name resolution.

Lesson objectives

After completing this lesson, you will be able to:

- Describe the purpose of a Hosts file.
- Describe what DNS is and how DNS is used to provide name resolution.
- Describe how Windows clients use the DNS suffix.
- Describe the DNS resolver cache.
- Describe the host name resolution process.
- Configure host name resolution.

Purpose of a Hosts File

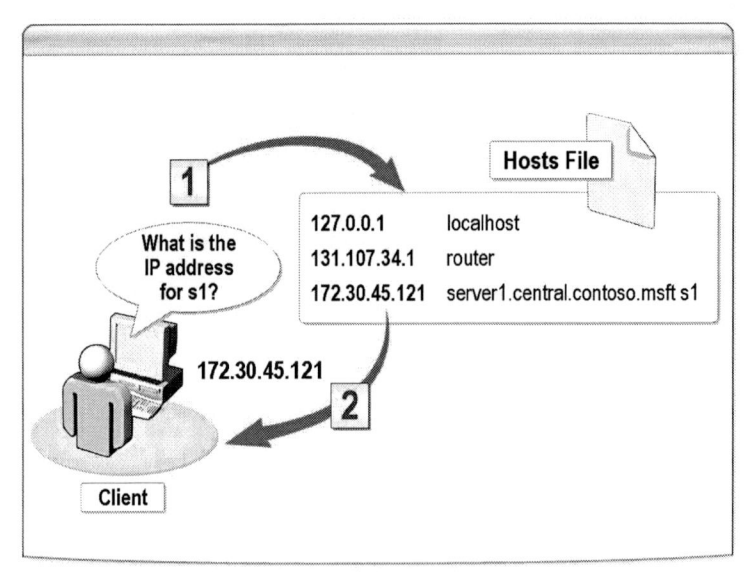

Introduction

A Hosts file is a text file that provides a local method for resolution of host names into their respective IP addresses on a TCP/IP network. Most networks do not use a Hosts file because maintaining the file on each individual computer and server is difficult. However, a Hosts file is often used during troubleshooting because adding an entry to a Hosts file is faster than reconfiguring a DNS server.

Hosts file entries

The following example shows three Hosts file entries:

```
127.0.0.1           localhost
131.107.34.1        router
172.30.45.121       server1.central.contoso.msft s1
```

The server with the IP address 172.30.45.121 can be referred to by its FQDN, *server1.central.contoso.msft*, or alias, *s1*. Using an alias allows a user to refer to the server without typing the entire FQDN.

Guidelines for using the Hosts file

Use the following guidelines to create and edit entries in the Hosts file:

- You can assign multiple host names to the same IP address.
- Entries in the Hosts file for Windows Server 2003 and Windows 2000 are not case sensitive.
- To create an entry, use the IP address of the computer followed by the FQDN. You can complete the entry with a comment. You use the pound sign (#) as a prefix for this optional comment.
- To locate the Hosts file, use the appropriate path as follows:
  - Microsoft Windows NT®, Windows 2000, and Windows XP:
    %SystemRoot%\system32\drivers\etc\Hosts
  - Windows 95 or Windows 98:
    \%WinDir%\Hosts

Common causes of Hosts file problems

Connectivity issues associated with the Hosts file are commonly caused by one or more of the following:

- The Hosts file does not contain the particular host name.
- The host name in the Hosts file or in the command is misspelled.
- The IP address for the host name in the Hosts file is invalid or incorrect.

What Is DNS?

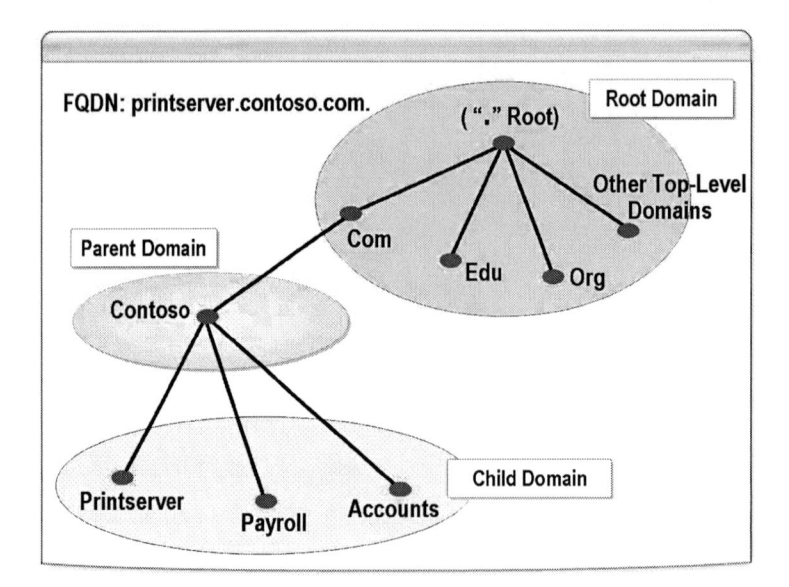

Diagram: FQDN: printserver.contoso.com. Root Domain ("." Root) with Com, Edu, Org, and Other Top-Level Domains. Parent Domain Contoso under Com. Child Domain containing Printserver, Payroll, and Accounts under Contoso.

Definition

DNS is a service that uses a distributed database to resolve FQDNs and other host names to IP addresses. All server versions of Windows 2003 include a DNS service. When you use DNS, you are enabling users on your network to apply user-friendly names, instead of IP addresses, to network resources.

How DNS resolves names to IP addresses

DNS uses a database of names and IP addresses to provide this service. DNS client software performs queries on and updates to the DNS database. A user trying to locate a print server can use the DNS name *printserver.contoso.com*, for example, and have that name resolved to an IP address such as 172.16.23.55.

Note For more information about DNS, see RFCs 1034 and 1035 under **Additional Reading** on the Student Materials compact disc.

The DNS namespace

DNS groups information about network resources into a hierarchical structure of *domains*. The hierarchical structure of domains is an inverted tree structure beginning with a *root domain* at its apex and descending into separate branches with common levels of *parent domains* and downward further into singular *child domains*. The representation of the entire hierarchical domain structure is known as a DNS *namespace*.

The Internet uses a single DNS namespace with multiple root servers. To participate in the Internet DNS namespace, a domain name must be registered with a DNS registrar. This ensures that no two organizations attempt to use the same domain name.

If hosts located on the Internet do not need to resolve names in your domain, you can host a domain internally, without registering it. However, you must still ensure that the domain name is unique from Internet domain names, or connectivity to Internet resources might be affected. A common way to ensure uniqueness is to create an internal domain in the .local domain. The .local domain is reserved for internal use in much the same way that private IP addresses are reserved for internal use.

A DNS namespace can be created in any TCP/IP network by hosting the DNS root domain on a DNS server, but each DNS namespace must be separate from all other DNS namespaces, as they are separate hierarchies. The DNS namespace on the Internet is the most common DNS namespace, but you can create a separate DNS namespace within your network with its own root domain that is entirely unrelated to the Internet DNS namespace.

DNS nodes

Each name in the DNS namespace is typically called a *node*. A DNS node, such as *ftp.contoso.com*, could represent a DNS domain, a host name, or a network service.

DNS and Active Directory

DNS is essential to the proper functioning of the Active Directory® directory service. Active Directory stores service location information in DNS. Clients require access to the service information in DNS to locate domain controllers and global catalog servers. Active Directory domains use the same naming structure as DNS domains.

Note For more information about DNS and the domain namespace, see Module 4, "Resolving Host Names by Using Domain Name System," in Course 2277, *Implementing, Managing, and Maintaining a Microsoft Windows Server 2003 Network Infrastructure: Network Services*.

How Windows Clients Use the DNS Suffix

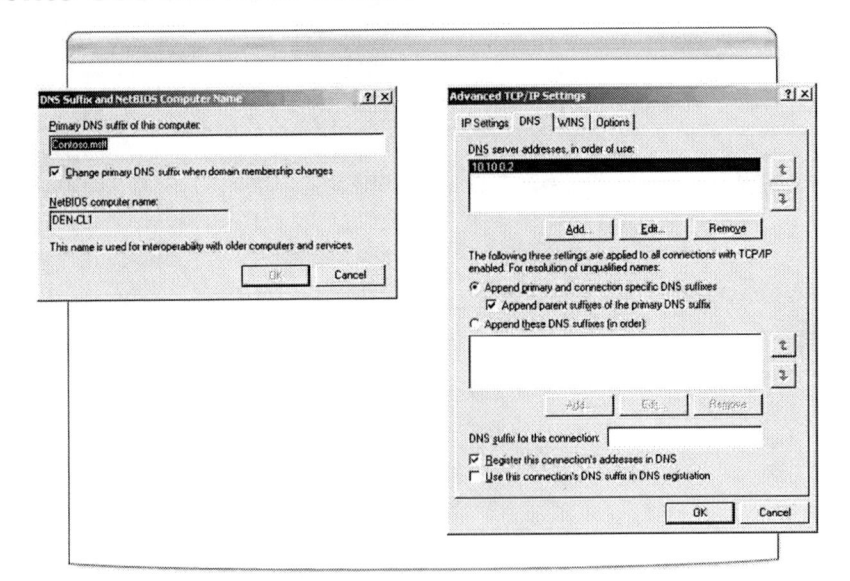

Introduction

A DNS suffix is used by a client for both resolving and registering DNS names. During host name resolution, the client attempts to resolve the host name by appending all configured DNS suffixes to the host name. During DNS name registration, the client registers its host name in DNS domains matching each configured DNS suffix.

In most cases, only a single DNS suffix, the *primary* DNS suffix, is configured. However, the ability to add additional DNS suffixes allows users to resolve resource host names in multiple domains without using FQDNs.

Primary DNS suffix

For clients that are members of an Active Directory domain, the primary DNS suffix is the same as the Active Directory domain. Client computers register their host names in DNS by using the primary DNS suffix. Client computers also resolve host names by using the primary DNS suffix.

If the "Append parent suffixes of the primary DNS suffix" option is selected, all parent domains of the primary DNS suffix will be used to resolve host names. For example, if a client is configured with the primary DNS suffix *contoso.msft*, that client will attempt to resolve host names by appending *contoso.msft* and *msft*.

The primary DNS suffix is configured in the **DNS Suffix and Netbios Computer Name** dialog box, which can be opened from the **Computer Name** tab in the **System Properties** dialog box. Other DNS suffix settings are configured on the **DNS** tab in the **Advanced TCP/IP Settings** dialog box.

Connection-specific DNS suffix	On a multihomed computer, you can apply a DNS suffix to a single adapter with a connection-specific DNS suffix. The connection-specific DNS suffix will be used in addition to the primary DNS suffix when host names are resolved.

When a multihomed computer registers its host name in DNS, only the IP address of the specified connection is registered in the domain specified in the connection-specific DNS suffix. In the domain specified in the primary DNS suffix, all IP addresses on the multihomed computer are registered. The "Use this connection's DNS suffix in DNS registration" option must be selected.

A connection-specific DNS suffix is typically used when a service is bound to only a single IP address on a multihomed computer. For example, a developer might have configured a test Web server to use only the IP address on the second network adapter in his client. |
| **Additional DNS suffixes** | In complex environments with many DNS domains, you can configure DNS suffixes in addition to the primary DNS suffix and any connection-specific DNS suffixes. Many large companies have several DNS domains for backward compatibility with earlier systems. These companies would configure additional DNS suffixes to enable host name resolution in several domains. |
| **Full computer name** | The full computer name of a Windows client is the concatenation of the single-label host name, such as *corp01*, and a multilabel primary DNS suffix name, such as *sales.contoso.com*. Using the host and primary DNS suffix examples, the full computer name is *corp01.sales.contoso.com*. The host name is the same as the computer name specified during the installation of Windows Server 2003. |

DNS Resolver Cache

> The DNS resolver cache:
> - Speeds DNS queries
> - Reduces network traffic
> - Caches DNS lookup attempts
> - Is displayed by using ipconfig /displaydns
> - Is cleared by using ipconfig /flushdns

Introduction

The DNS resolver cache is used to speed up DNS queries and reduce network traffic. Clients always check the DNS resolver cache before sending a query to a DNS server. If a name is in the cache, the cached information is used rather than querying the DNS server.

DNS resolver cache contents

Each time a client attempts to resolve a host name through DNS, the result is added to the DNS resolver cache. If the query result is positive, the name stays in the cache for the period of time specified by the DNS server that hosts the record. In most cases, this is about 24 hours. If the result is negative, the failed attempt is cached for 300 seconds (5 minutes).

The DNS resolver cache also contains all host names specified in the Hosts file. If the Hosts file is modified, the contents are reloaded. Caching the Hosts file is more efficient than reading it each time a host name is resolved. Cache entries loaded from the Hosts file do not expire.

Controlling the DNS resolver cache

You can use Ipconfig to view and clear the DNS resolver cache. The command **ipconfig /displaydns** displays the contents of the DNS resolver cache. The command **ipconfig /flushdns** clears the contents of the DNS resolver cache. Clearing the DNS resolver cache is useful when an incorrect DNS record has been fixed but the incorrect result is still cached on the client.

The Host Name Resolution Process

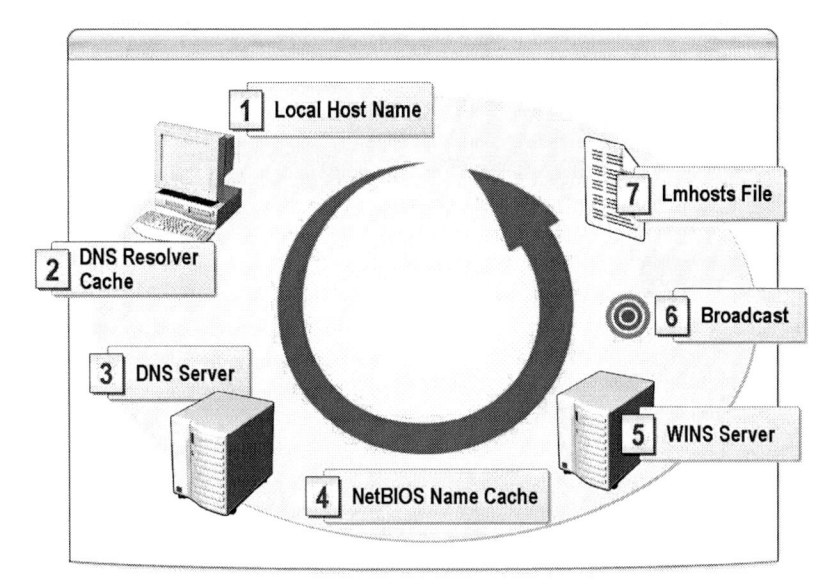

Introduction

When an application uses Windows Sockets and a host name is specified, TCP/IP will use the DNS resolver cache and DNS when attempting to resolve the host name. If NetBIOS over TCP/IP is enabled, TCP/IP will also use NetBIOS name resolution methods when resolving host names. NetBIOS over TCP/IP is enabled by default.

The host name resolution process

When NetBIOS over TCP/IP is enabled, the host name resolution process is as follows:

1. Windows checks whether the host name is the same as the local host name.
2. Windows searches the DNS resolver cache.
3. Windows sends a DNS request to its configured DNS servers.
4. Windows converts the host name to a NetBIOS name and checks the local NetBIOS name cache.
5. Windows contacts its configured Microsoft Windows Internet Naming Service (WINS) servers.
6. Windows broadcasts as many as three NetBIOS Name Query Request messages on the directly attached subnet.
7. Windows searches the Lmhosts file.

The name resolution process stops when the first IP address is found for the name.

Note For more information about host name resolution, see Chapter 7, "Host Name Resolution," in *TCP/IP Fundamentals for Microsoft Windows* on the Microsoft Web site.

Practice: Resolving Host Names

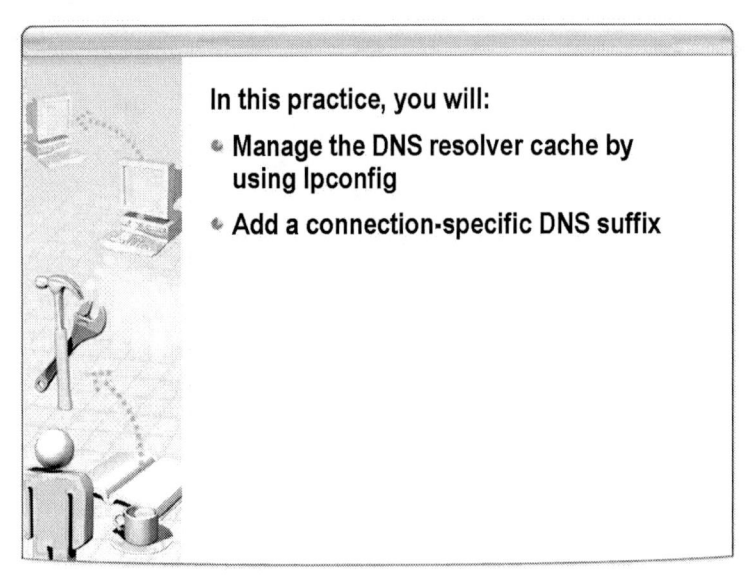

In this practice, you will:
- Manage the DNS resolver cache by using Ipconfig
- Add a connection-specific DNS suffix

Objectives

In this practice, you will:

- Manage the DNS resolver cache by using Ipconfig.
- Add a connection-specific DNS suffix.

Instructions

Be sure that the DEN-DC1 and DEN-CL1 virtual machines are started.

Practice

▶ **Manage the DNS resolver cache by using Ipconfig**

1. On DEN-CL1, log on as **Paul**, with a password of **Pa$$w0rd**.
2. Click **Start**, click **Run**, type **cmd**, and then click **OK**.
3. At the command prompt, type **ipconfig /displaydns** and then press ENTER. Observe the DNS entries displayed. You might need to scroll up in the command prompt window. Notice that DEN-DC1 is in the list.
4. Type **ipconfig /flushdns** and then press ENTER.
5. Type **ipconfig /displaydns** and then press ENTER. Notice that DEN-DC1 is no longer in the list.
6. Click **Start**, point to **All Programs**, point to **Accessories**, and then click **Notepad**.
7. Click **File**, and then click **Open**. In the **Files of type** box, select **All Files**, browse to **C:\Windows\system32\drivers\etc\hosts**, and then click **Open**.
8. Scroll to the bottom of the Hosts file, and then type **127.0.0.5 testhost**.
9. Click **File**, click **Save**, and then close Notepad.
10. At the command prompt, type **ipconfig /displaydns**, and then press ENTER. Notice that **testhost** is now listed.
11. Close the command prompt window.

▶ Add a connection-specific DNS suffix

1. Click **Start**, click **Run**, type **cmd**, and then click **OK**.
2. Type **ipconfig /all** and then press ENTER. Notice that the primary DNS suffix is **contoso.msft**.
3. Type **ping DEN-DC1.contoso.msft** and then press ENTER. This test is successful because a DNS record has been created for DEN-DC1 in contoso.msft.
4. Type **ping DEN-CL1.testdom.msft** and then press ENTER. This test is unsuccessful because a DNS record has not been created for DEN-CL1 in testdom.msft.
5. Click **Start**, click **Control Panel**, double-click **Network Connections**, right-click **Local Area Connection**, and then click **Properties**.
6. Click **Internet Protocol (TCP/IP)**, click **Properties**, click **Advanced**, and then click the **DNS** tab.
7. In the **Suffix for this connection** box, type **testdom.msft**.
8. Select the **Use this connection's DNS suffix in DNS registration** check box.
9. Click **OK** twice, click **Close**, and then close Network Connections.
10. At the command prompt, type **ipconfig /registerdns** and then press ENTER. This command forces your client to reregister its host name with the DNS server.
11. Type **ping DEN-CL1.testdom.msft** and then press ENTER. This time, the ping is successful because a DNS record has been created for DEN-CL1 in testdom.msft.
12. Close the command prompt window.

Important Do not shut down the virtual machines.

Lesson: Resolving NetBIOS Names

* What Is NetBIOS?
* What Is NetBT?
* Types of NetBT Nodes
* What Is Nbtstat?
* What Is Lmhosts?
* What Is WINS?
* The NetBIOS Name Resolution Process
* Practice: Resolving NetBIOS Names

Introduction

NetBIOS acts to connect applications in the session and transport layers of TCP/IP, providing messaging and resource allocation. NetBIOS establishes logical names on the network, establishes sessions between two logical names on the network, and supports reliable data transfer between computers that have established a session. Understanding how NetBIOS functions in a network will assist you in understanding network communications.

Lesson objectives

After completing this lesson, you will be able to:

- Describe NetBIOS.
- Describe NetBT and why it is necessary.
- List the types of NetBT nodes.
- Describe Nbtstat.
- Describe an Lmhosts file and when to use it.
- Describe WINS.
- Describe the NetBIOS name resolution process.
- Configure a client to use Lmhosts and WINS.

What Is NetBIOS?

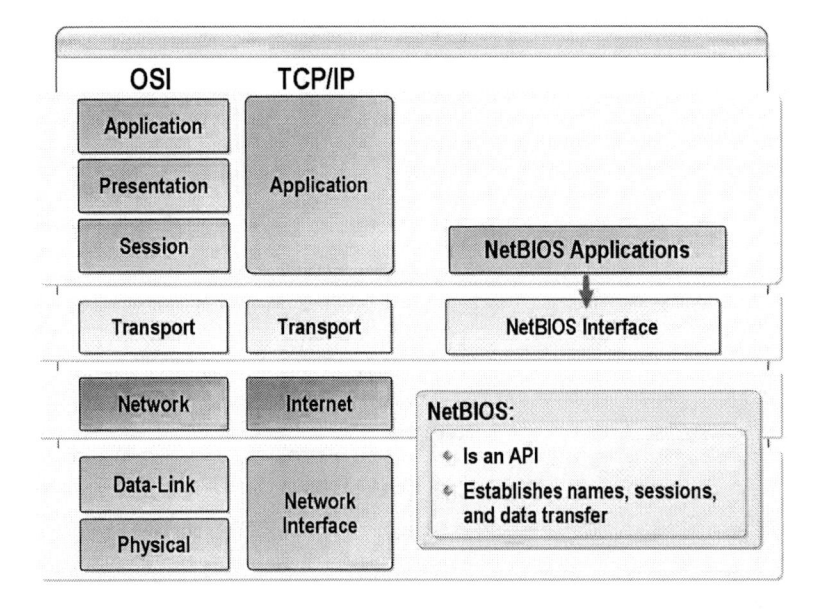

Introduction

NetBIOS is a specification created by IBM and Microsoft that allows distributed applications to access each other's network services independent of the transport protocol being used. It integrates with TCP/IP, running at the session and transport levels.

NetBIOS establishes names on the network, establishes sessions between two named services on the network, and supports reliable data transfer between computers that have established a session.

Definition of NetBIOS

NetBIOS provides network input/output services to support client/server applications on a network. From an architectural viewpoint, the NetBIOS specification defines:

- An interprocess communication (IPC) mechanism and application programming interface (API) that allow applications that are NetBIOS-enabled to communicate remotely over a network and request services from lower levels of the TCP/IP protocol stack. This is the primary and original definition of NetBIOS.

- A protocol operating at the session and transport layers of the Open Systems Interconnection (OSI) reference model that enables functions such as session establishment and termination as well as name registration, name renewal, and name resolution.

Note For more information about the TCP/IP and OSI models, see Module 1, "Reviewing the Suite of TCP/IP Protocols." in this course.

What Is NetBT?

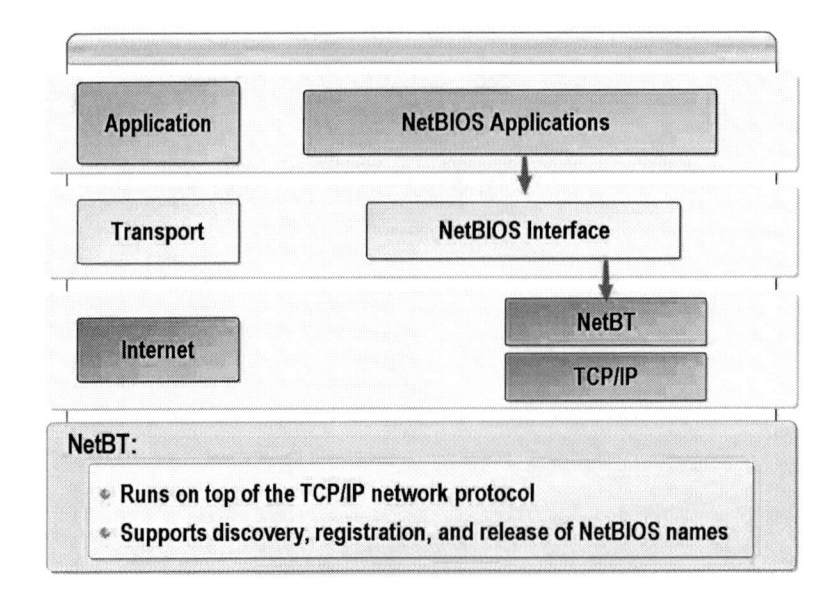

NetBT:
- Runs on top of the TCP/IP network protocol
- Supports discovery, registration, and release of NetBIOS names

Introduction

By default, NetBIOS names do not function over a TCP/IP network. Windows Server 2003 enables NetBIOS clients to communicate over TCP/IP by providing the NetBIOS over TCP/IP (NetBT) protocol. By using this protocol, you are ensuring that NetBIOS-based applications can use TCP/IP to provide NetBIOS network services to NetBIOS applications. To effectively provide network communication between NetBIOS applications and hosts, you must understand NetBIOS naming functions.

What NetBT does

NetBT is composed of the NetBIOS session-layer protocol and the APIs running on top of TCP/IP. NetBT supports NetBIOS sessions, NetBIOS datagrams, and naming functions such as the discovery, resolution, and release of NetBIOS names on a TCP/IP network.

How NetBT determines the method for naming functions

There are several ways that NetBT can perform naming functions. For example, NetBT can use a broadcast, a NetBIOS Name Server (NBNS) such as a WINS server, or both. The node type of the network device determines how NetBIOS naming functions are performed. *Node* refers to any uniquely addressable device on a network. The node type also determines the order in which the functions are performed.

The following list describes the NetBIOS naming functions:

- *NetBIOS name resolution*. NetBT hosts that want to communicate with similar hosts must issue a NetBIOS Name Query Request to resolve the NetBIOS name to its IP address.

- *NetBIOS name registration.* NetBT hosts must register their unique NetBIOS names when they are initialized on a network to ensure that there are no duplicate names on the network. NetBIOS name registration can be done either by broadcasts or by unicast messages sent to a WINS server. Either or both methods can be used, and in either order, depending on the NetBT node type of the host.

- *NetBIOS name release.* NetBT hosts must release their NetBIOS names when they are shut down or when a particular NetBIOS-enabled service is stopped on the server. This enables the released name to be used by another host. NetBIOS name release can be done by broadcasts or by unicast messages sent to a WINS server. Either or both methods can be used in either order, depending on the NetBT node type of the host.

Types of NetBT Nodes

NetBt Node Types	
B-node (broadcast)	Uses NetBIOS broadcast name queries
P-node (peer-to-peer)	Uses NBNS
M-node (mixed)	A combination of B-node and P-node; uses broadcast by default
H-node (hybrid)	A combination of B-node and P-node; uses NBNS by default
Microsoft enhanced B-node	Uses the Lmhosts file

Introduction

The method that NetBT applies to perform naming functions depends on the node type of the client.

NetBT node types

The NetBT node types are listed in the following table.

Node type	Method (in the order applied)	Description
B-node (broadcast)	Broadcast only	Uses broadcast NetBIOS name queries for name registration and name resolution. Typically not forwarded by routers, so limited to the local subnet. Can create excessive broadcast traffic for large subnets.
P-node (peer-to-peer)	NBNS only	Uses NBNS only. WINS is the Microsoft implementation of an NBNS.
M-node (mixed)	Broadcast, NBNS	A combination of B-node and P-node. Uses broadcast by default. If unable to resolve a name, uses NBNS.
H-node (hybrid)	NBNS, broadcast	A combination of P-node and B-node. Uses NBNS by default. Default node type for Microsoft clients if an NBNS is configured on the network.
Microsoft enhanced B-node	NetBIOS name cache, broadcast, Lmhosts file	An enhanced broadcast that uses the Lmhosts file. Default node type for Microsoft clients if no NBNS is configured on the network.

> **Tip** You can configure the NetBIOS node type on a client running Windows Server 2003 by using the registry, but the preferred way is to configure the Dynamic Host Configuration Protocol (DHCP) to specify the node type to the client.

Handwritten notes:

Net Bios

Can we Buy Larger Hard Drive?

Cache, wins, Broadcast, Lm Host, Host, DNS

Bnodes (C, B, L, H, D)
Pnodes (C, W, L, H, D)
Mnodes (C, B, W, L, H, D)
HBnodes - (Regular)

What Is Nbtstat?

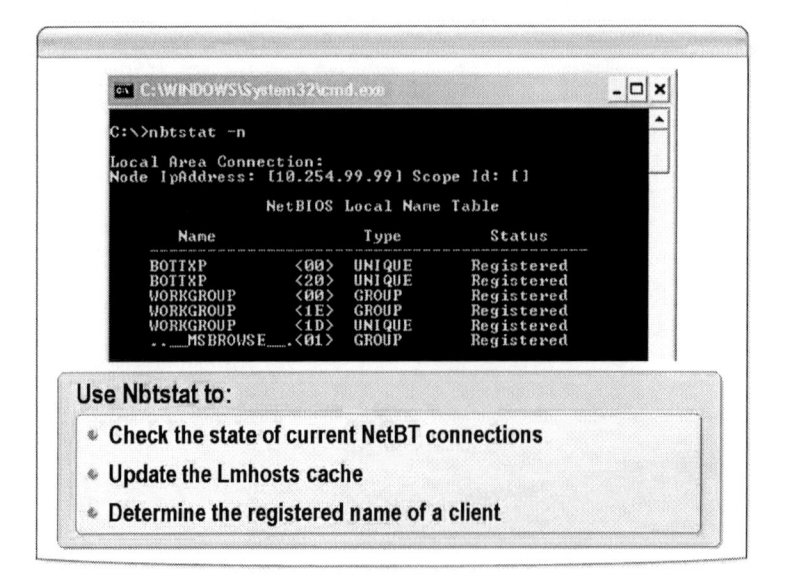

```
C:\>nbtstat -n
Local Area Connection:
Node IpAddress: [10.254.99.99] Scope Id: []

            NetBIOS Local Name Table

       Name              Type         Status
    ---------------------------------------------
    BOTTXP        <00>  UNIQUE     Registered
    BOTTXP        <20>  UNIQUE     Registered
    WORKGROUP     <00>  GROUP      Registered
    WORKGROUP     <1E>  GROUP      Registered
    WORKGROUP     <1D>  UNIQUE     Registered
    ..__MSBROWSE__.<01> GROUP      Registered
```

Use Nbtstat to:
- Check the state of current NetBT connections
- Update the Lmhosts cache
- Determine the registered name of a client

Introduction

Nbtstat is a TCP/IP utility that displays information about the NetBT connections that Windows uses when communicating with other computers on the TCP/IP network. Nbtstat is installed by default on computers running Windows Server 2003.

What Nbtstat displays

Nbtstat displays NetBT protocol statistics, NetBIOS name tables for both the local computer and remote computers, and the NetBIOS name cache. The NetBIOS name table is the list of NetBIOS names that correspond to NetBIOS applications running on that computer. You can use Nbtstat to refresh the NetBIOS name cache and the names registered with WINS.

How to use Nbtstat

You can use Nbtstat to:

- View NetBT statistics on the computer.
- Determine the status of the computer's current network connections.
- Preload entries in an Lmhosts file into the NetBIOS name cache.
- View the NetBIOS name of a computer.
- Isolate NetBIOS name resolution issues.

To use Nbtstat, run **nbtstat** from a command prompt window.

Examples of Nbtstat displays

nbtstat -n displays the NetBIOS names of the host that have been registered on the system.

nbtstat -c displays the current contents of the NetBIOS name cache, which contains the NetBIOS name to IP address mappings for other hosts on the network.

Tip You can run **nbtstat -a** *ComputerName* to obtain the local NetBIOS name table on *ComputerName* as well as its MAC address.

What Is Lmhosts?

> **An Lmhosts file:**
> - Is a text file that maps NetBIOS names to IP addresses
> - Overcomes broadcast limitations
> - Can be used for troubleshooting
> - Should not have entries for DHCP clients
> - Is stored in *systemroot*\system32\drivers\etc

Definition

Lmhosts is a text file that allows you to map NetBIOS names to IP addresses. Lmhosts is not used in most networks because it is difficult to maintain on many computers. The Lmhosts file has no file extension.

Why use Lmhosts?

Early networks that required NetBIOS name resolution used broadcasts to resolve NetBIOS names to IP addresses. However, as networks became larger and incorporated multiple subnets, NetBIOS name resolution did not work because broadcasts are not propagated across routers. Lmhosts eliminates the issue by allowing the client to resolve the name locally rather than requiring broadcasts.

Another reason to use Lmhosts is for troubleshooting. Adding a NetBIOS name to Lmhosts is a quick and easy way to ensure that a client can properly resolve a NetBIOS name.

Guidelines for editing Lmhosts

Use the following guidelines when editing Lmhosts:

- Use the default location of the *systemroot*\system32\drivers\etc folder.
- View the Lmhosts example file Lmhosts.sam for configuration information.
- To create an entry, use the IP address of the computer, followed by at least one space or tab and the NetBIOS name of the computer.

> **Caution** You should not add an Lmhosts entry for a computer that is a DHCP client because the IP addresses of DHCP clients change dynamically. To avoid problems, make sure that the computers for which names are entered in the Lmhosts files are configured with static IP addresses.

- You must place each entry on a separate line. Add a carriage return after the final entry in the file.

- You can use uppercase and lowercase characters and special characters in NetBIOS names. For example, *AccountingDC* is a mixed-case name, and *HumanRscSr\0x03* specifies a name with a special character. If a name is enclosed in double quotation marks, it is used exactly as entered.

- Entries in the Lmhosts file can represent computers that are running Windows Server 2003 and earlier, as well as Microsoft LAN Manager and Microsoft Windows for Workgroups version 3.11 with Microsoft TCP/IP. There is no need to distinguish between different platforms in the Lmhosts file.

- Use the pound sign (#) to mark the start of a comment. You can also use # to designate special keywords. For example, the keyword #PRE will cause the entry to be preloaded into the NetBIOS name cache.

Note For information about the keywords that you can use in the Lmhosts file, see "Creating Entries in the LMHOSTS File" in the *Microsoft Windows 2000 Resource Kit* on the Microsoft Web site.

What Is WINS?

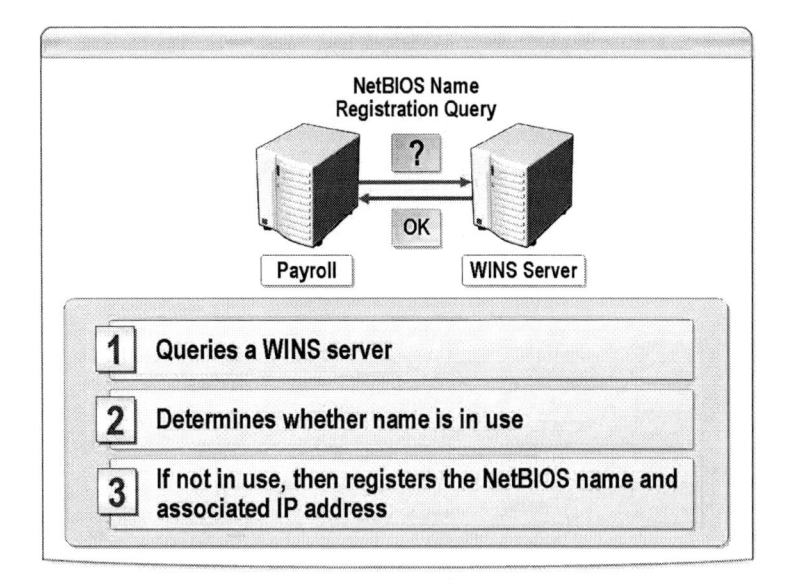

NetBIOS Name Registration Query

Payroll ↔ ? / OK ↔ WINS Server

1. Queries a WINS server
2. Determines whether name is in use
3. If not in use, then registers the NetBIOS name and associated IP address

Introduction

WINS is an NBNS that you can use to resolve NetBIOS names to IP addresses when computers on your network are running Windows Server 2003, Windows 2000, Windows NT 4.0, Windows 98, or Windows 95.

Benefits of using WINS

WINS provides a centralized database for registering dynamic mappings of NetBIOS names used on a network. WINS is built on a protocol that registers, resolves, and releases NetBIOS names by using unicast transmissions, rather than repeated transmissions of broadcast messages. This protocol allows the system to work across routers and eliminates the need for an Lmhosts file, restoring the dynamic nature of NetBIOS name resolution and allowing the system to work seamlessly with DHCP. For example, when dynamic addressing through DHCP creates new IP addresses for computers that move between subnets, the WINS database tracks the changes automatically.

Note WINS supports the NetBT mode of operation defined in RFCs 1001 and 1002 as *p-node*.

WINS client requirements

WINS is the Microsoft implementation of a NetBIOS name server. For WINS to function properly on a network, each client must:

- Register its NetBIOS name in the WINS database. When a client starts up, it will register its name with its configured WINS server.
- Renew its name registration at intervals. Client registrations are temporary, and from time to time a WINS client must renew its name or its lease will expire.
- Release names from the database when shutting down. When a WINS client no longer requires a name—for example, when it is shut down—the client sends a message instructing the WINS server to release its name.

The NetBIOS Name Resolution Process

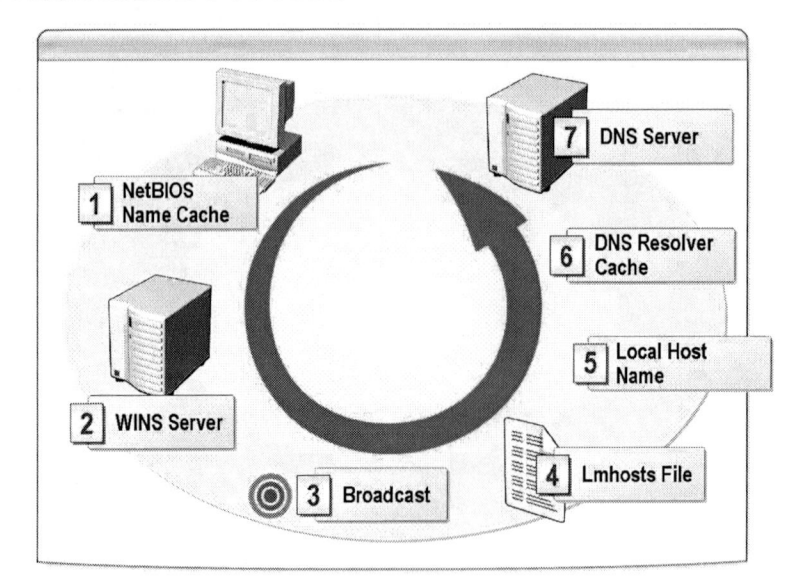

Introduction

The NetBIOS name resolution process varies, depending on the NetBT node type that is specified. However, in most cases, the default NetBT node type is not altered. If all NetBIOS name resolution methods fail, clients will attempt to use host name resolution methods to resolve NetBIOS names.

The host name resolution process

When a WINS server is configured on the client, the NetBIOS name resolution process is as follows:

1. Windows checks the local NetBIOS name cache.
2. Windows contacts its configured WINS servers.
3. Windows broadcasts as many as three NetBIOS Name Query Request messages on the directly attached subnet.
4. Windows searches the Lmhosts file.
5. Windows checks whether the NetBIOS name is the same as the local host name.
6. Windows searches the DNS resolver cache.
7. Windows sends a DNS request to its configured DNS servers.

The name resolution process stops when the first IP address is found for the name.

Practice: Resolving NetBIOS Names

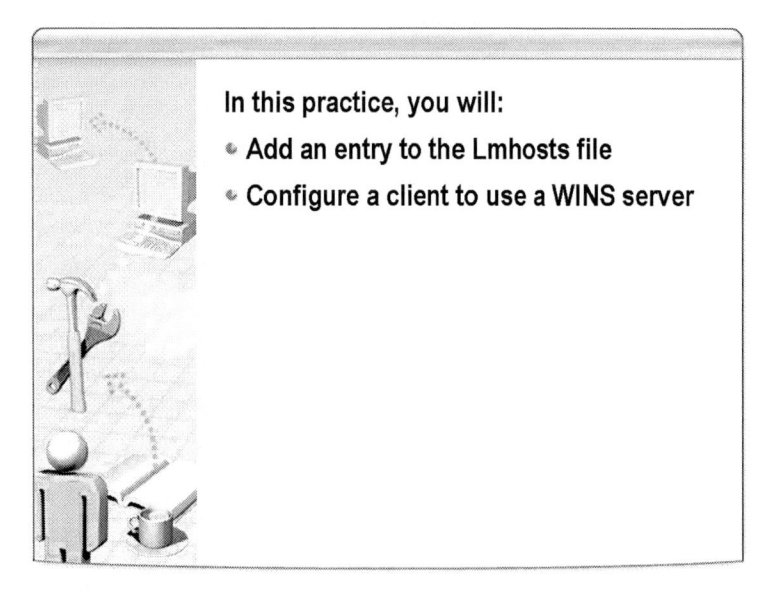

In this practice, you will:
- Add an entry to the Lmhosts file
- Configure a client to use a WINS server

Objectives

In this practice, you will:
- Add an entry to the Lmhosts file.
- Configure a client to use a WINS server.

Instructions

Ensure that the DEN-DC1 and DEN-CL1 virtual machines are running.

Practice

▶ **Add an entry to the Lmhosts file**

1. On DEN-CL1, log on as **Paul**, with a password of **Pa$$w0rd**.
2. Click **Start**, click **Run**, type **cmd**, and then click **OK**.
3. Type **nbtstat –c** and then press ENTER. Notice that **testserver** is not listed.
4. Click **Start**, click **Control Panel**, and then click **Folder Options**.
5. Click the **View** tab, clear the **Hide extensions for known file types** check box, and then click **OK**.
6. At a command prompt, type **copy C:\Windows\system32\drivers\etc\lmhosts.sam C:\Windows\system32\drivers\etc\lmhosts** and then press ENTER.
7. Click **Start**, point to **All Programs**, point to **Accessories**, and then click **Notepad**.
8. Click **File**, and then click **Open**.
9. In the **Files of type** box, select **All Files**.
10. Browse to **C:\Windows\system32\drivers\etc**, click **lmhosts**, and then click **Open**.
11. Scroll to the bottom of Lmhosts, type **10.10.0.58 testserver #PRE**, and then press ENTER.
12. Click **File**, click **Save**, and then close Notepad.

13. At the command prompt, type **nbtstat –R** and then press ENTER. This reloads the NetBIOS name cache, including entries in Lmhosts marked with **#PRE**.
14. Type **nbtstat –c** and then press ENTER. Notice that **testserver** is now listed.
15. Close the command prompt window.

▶ **Configure a client to use a WINS server**

1. Click **Start**, click **Control Panel**, click **Network Connections**, right-click **Local Area Connection**, and then click **Properties**.
2. Click **Internet Protocol (TCP/IP)**, and then click **Properties**.
3. Click **Advanced**, and then click the **WINS** tab.
4. Click the **Add** button, type **10.10.0.2** and then click **Add**.
5. Click **OK** twice, and then click **Close**.
6. Click **Start**, click **Run**, type **cmd**, and then click **OK**.
7. Right-click **Local Area Connection**, and then click **Status**.
8. Click the **Support** tab, and then click **Details**. Notice that the WINS server is now configured.
9. Click **Close** twice, and then close Network Connections.

Important Do not shut down the virtual machines.

Lab: Configuring a Client for Name Resolution

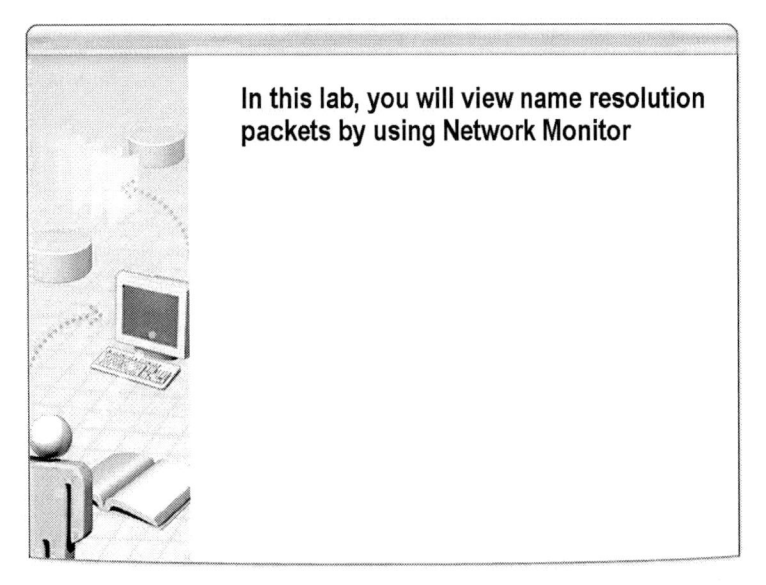

In this lab, you will view name resolution packets by using Network Monitor

Objective

After completing this lab, you will be able to view name resolution packets by using Network Monitor.

Instructions

Ensure that the DEN-DC1 and DEN-CL1 virtual machines are running.

Estimated time to complete this lab: 15 minutes

Exercise 1
Viewing DNS Packets

In this exercise, you will view the DNS packets sent between a client and a DNS server. This is useful for troubleshooting host name resolution problems.

Scenario

A client computer on your network has been intermittently having problems resolving host names. You will view the DNS packets between the client and the DNS server to verify that the proper communication process is occurring. To do this, you use Network Monitor.

Tasks	Detailed steps
1. Start capturing packets on DEN-DC1.	a. Open Network Monitor. b. If necessary, select **Local Area Connection** for the network. c. Start a capture.
2. Clear the DNS cache on DEN-CL1.	a. Open a command prompt window. b. Clear the DNS cache by using Ipconfig.
3. On DEN-CL1, ping DEN-DC1.	▪ Ping DEN-DC1.
4. View the DNS packets in Network Monitor.	a. Stop and view the capture. b. Filter the capture to show only DNS packets. c. View the details of each DNS packet.
5. Start capturing packets on DEN-DC1.	▪ Start a capture.
6. On DEN-CL1, ping DEN-DC2.	a. Ping DEN-DC2. b. Close the command prompt window.
7. View the DNS packets in Network Monitor.	a. Stop and view the capture. b. Filter the capture to show only DNS packets. c. View the details of each DNS packet. d. Close Network Monitor.
8. Complete the lab exercise.	a. Close all programs and shut down all computers. Do not save changes. b. To prepare for the next module, start the DEN-DC1 and DEN-CL1 virtual computers.

Module 5: Isolating Common Connectivity Issues

Contents

Overview	1
Lesson: Analyzing Client Startup Communication	2
Lesson: Determining the Causes of Connectivity Issues	10
Lesson: Using Network Utilities and Tools to Isolate Connectivity Issues	20
Lab: Isolating Common Connectivity Issues	39
Course Evaluation	45

Information in this document, including URL and other Internet Web site references, is subject to change without notice. Unless otherwise noted, the example companies, organizations, products, domain names, e-mail addresses, logos, people, places, and events depicted herein are fictitious, and no association with any real company, organization, product, domain name, e-mail address, logo, person, place or event is intended or should be inferred. Complying with all applicable copyright laws is the responsibility of the user. Without limiting the rights under copyright, no part of this document may be reproduced, stored in or introduced into a retrieval system, or transmitted in any form or by any means (electronic, mechanical, photocopying, recording, or otherwise), or for any purpose, without the express written permission of Microsoft Corporation.

The names of manufacturers, products, or URLs are provided for informational purposes only and Microsoft makes no representations and warranties, either expressed, implied, or statutory, regarding these manufacturers or the use of the products with any Microsoft technologies. The inclusion of a manufacturer or product does not imply endorsement of Microsoft of the manufacturer or product. Links are provided to third party sites. Such sites are not under the control of Microsoft and Microsoft is not responsible for the contents of any linked site or any link contained in a linked site, or any changes or updates to such sites. Microsoft is not responsible for webcasting or any other form of transmission received from any linked site. Microsoft is providing these links to you only as a convenience, and the inclusion of any link does not imply endorsement of Microsoft of the site or the products contained therein.

Microsoft may have patents, patent applications, trademarks, copyrights, or other intellectual property rights covering subject matter in this document. Except as expressly provided in any written license agreement from Microsoft, the furnishing of this document does not give you any license to these patents, trademarks, copyrights, or other intellectual property.

© 2005 Microsoft Corporation. All rights reserved.

Microsoft, Active Directory, Excel, MS-DOS, PowerPoint, Windows, Windows Media, Windows NT, and Windows Server are either registered trademarks or trademarks of Microsoft Corporation in the United States and/or other countries.

All other trademarks are property of their respective owners.

Overview

- Analyzing Client Startup Communication
- Determining the Causes of Connectivity Issues
- Using Network Utilities and Tools to Isolate Connectivity Issues

Introduction

The information in this module introduces you to a process for isolating common connectivity issues and also describes how you can use network utilities and tools as part of this process. To maintain network connectivity, you must be able to isolate issues that interrupt it. When you isolate connectivity issues, you are assisting systems engineers in resolving these issues as rapidly as possible.

Objectives

After completing this module, you will be able to:

- Describe client startup communication.
- Determine the causes of connectivity issues.
- Describe the utilities and tools used to resolve connectivity issues.

Lesson: Analyzing Client Startup Communication

- Client Startup Communication Process
- Client Startup Communication Issues
- Practice: Analyzing Client Startup Communication

Introduction

One of the most common times when users experience problems is during logon. Understanding the client startup communication process will help you understand how to fix logon problems.

Lesson objectives

After completing this lesson, you will be able to:

- Describe the client startup communication process.
- Identify client startup communication issues.
- Analyze client startup communication.

Client Startup Communication Process

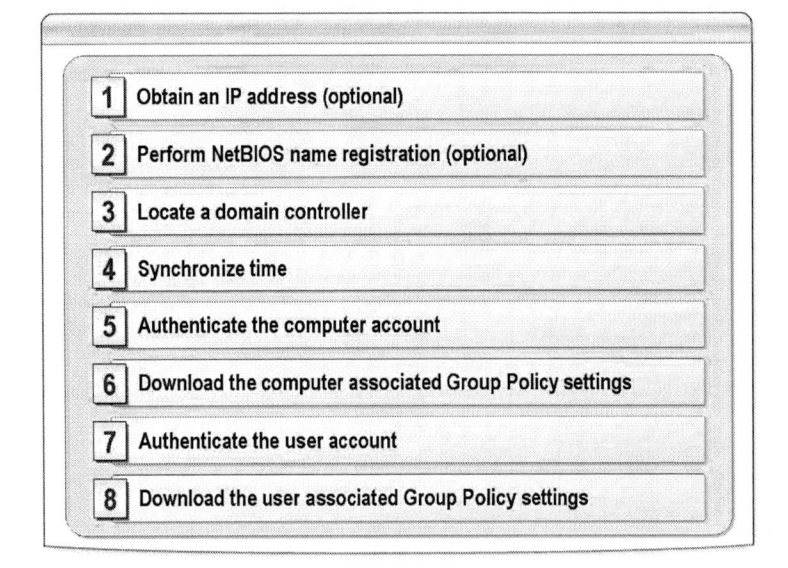

> 1. Obtain an IP address (optional)
> 2. Perform NetBIOS name registration (optional)
> 3. Locate a domain controller
> 4. Synchronize time
> 5. Authenticate the computer account
> 6. Download the computer associated Group Policy settings
> 7. Authenticate the user account
> 8. Download the user associated Group Policy settings

Introduction

Each time a client is started, a consistent communication process is performed. All the steps in the communication process must be properly completed for a client to access all network resources. If any step is unsuccessful, the client might not be able to log on.

Steps in client startup communication

The client startup communication steps are as follows:

1. Obtain an Internet Protocol (IP) address (optional).

   If a client is configured to obtain an IP address automatically, it will obtain an IP address from a Dynamic Host Configuration Protocol (DHCP) server or by using automatic configuration. This step is not performed for clients with a static IP address.

2. Perform network basic input/output system (NetBIOS) name registration (optional).

   If NetBIOS over Transmission Control Protocol/Internet Protocol (TCP/IP) is enabled on a client, it will register its computer name as a NetBIOS name and will register itself as a member of the domain. This step is not performed for clients with NetBIOS over TCP/IP disabled.

3. Locate a domain controller.

   Clients locate a domain controller by using Domain Name System (DNS). They query for the Lightweight Directory Access Protocol (LDAP) service records in the local site. The query returns the host name of a domain controller and the TCP port number.

4. Synchronize the time.

   Time synchronization is essential for authentication using the Kerberos version 5 authentication protocol. To ensure that the time is synchronized, clients will synchronize their clocks with the domain controller in their domain by using the Network Time Protocol (NTP).

5. Authenticate the computer account.

   The computer account is authenticated using the Kerberos protocol. This is necessary before a user can log on to the network.

6. Download the computer-associated Group Policy settings.

   After the computer account is authenticated, it is able to download the computer-associated Group Policy settings. These settings are downloaded only if they have been modified; otherwise, a cached version is used. However, version verification is done each time.

7. Authenticate the user account.

   All the preceding steps are completed before the logon window is displayed to the user. The user can then log on. Kerberos is used to perform the authentication.

8. Download the user-associated Group Policy settings.

   Similar to computer-associated Group Policy settings, user-associated Group Policy settings are downloaded after user authentication. These settings are downloaded only if they have been modified; otherwise, a cached version is used. However, version verification is performed each time.

Client Startup Communication Issues

> **Common issues encountered with client startup communication:**
> - Unable to obtain an IP address
> - Duplicate NetBIOS names
> - Incorrect DNS server configuration
> - Time not synchronized with the network
> - Computer account cannot authenticate
> - User account cannot authenticate

Introduction

When any step in the client startup communication process fails, there will be issues. Most of these issues result in reduced performance or some resources being unavailable.

Issues and symptoms

To fix client startup communication problems, you must understand their symptoms. The following table lists client startup communication problems and the symptoms that indicate that they are occurring.

Issue	Symptoms
Unable to obtain an IP address.	Clients without an IP address still allow domain users to log on using cached credentials. However, the clients will not be able to access any network resources.
Duplicate NetBIOS names.	Duplicate NetBIOS names prevent clients from registering a NetBIOS name. If there is a duplicate NetBIOS name, all NetBIOS services will be unavailable. In Microsoft® Windows® 2000, Windows XP, and Windows Server™ 2003, this has a minimal impact, because file sharing and printer sharing do not require NetBIOS. A warning message will appear, indicating that there is a name conflict.
Incorrect DNS server configuration.	The most common symptom of the DNS server being incorrectly configured on a client is a slow network logon—typically, two minutes or more. This is because the client attempts to find a domain controller by using DNS before failing over to locating a domain controller by using NetBIOS. If NetBIOS name resolution also cannot locate a domain controller, the client will not be authenticated to the network and will not have access to network resources.

(*continued*)

Issue	Symptoms
Time not synchronized with the network.	If there is more than a five-minute time difference between clients and the domain controller to which they are logging on, they will receive an error message indicating that they cannot be logged on due to a time difference between the client and server. Network resources will be inaccessible. This should occur only when a client has been reconfigured to obtain time from a source other than a local domain controller, or a local domain controller has the incorrect time.
Computer account cannot authenticate.	If a computer account cannot authenticate, its trust with the domain is broken, and it cannot log on domain users, except with cached credentials. Additionally, new Group Policy settings will not be downloaded. This can occur when a client is reimaged by using an image older than 30 days. Computer accounts change their passwords every 30 days, and an image older than 30 days will not have the current password. Events in the system log will indicate that the computer account could not be authenticated. To fix this, reset the computer account.
User account cannot authenticate.	When a user account cannot authenticate, the following message will appear: "The system could not log you on." This is typically due to an incorrect password or user name. However, this also happens when the **Log On To** box is not configured with the correct name.

Practice: Analyzing Client Startup Communication

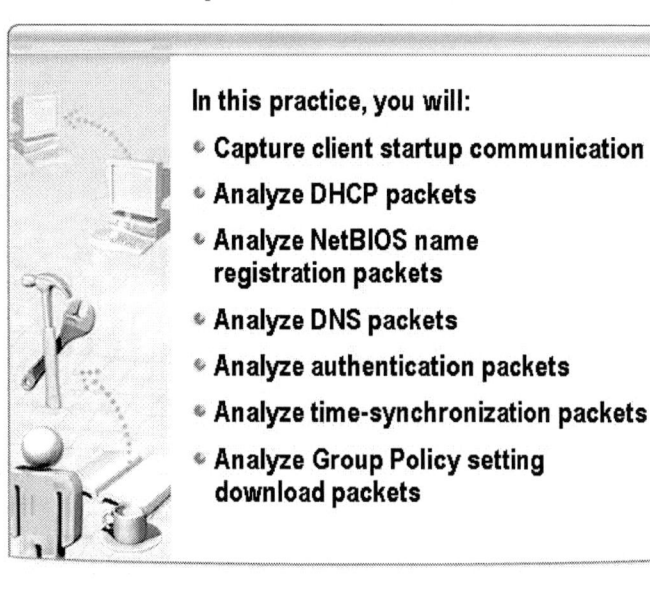

Objectives

In this practice, you will:

- Capture client startup communication.
- Analyze DHCP packets.
- Analyze NetBIOS name registration packets.
- Analyze DNS packets.
- Analyze authentication packets.
- Analyze time-synchronization packets.
- Analyze Group Policy settings download packets.

Instructions

Ensure that the DEN-DC1 virtual machine is running. The DEN-CL1 virtual machine should not be running.

Practice

▶ **Capture client startup communication**

1. On DEN-DC1, log on as **Administrator**, with a password or **Pa$$w0rd**.
2. Click **Start**, point to **Administrative Tools**, and then click **Network Monitor**.
3. Click **OK** to begin selecting the network on which you want to capture data.
4. Expand **Local Computer**, click **Local Area Connection**, and then click **OK**.
5. On the **Capture** menu, click **Start**.
6. Start the DEN-CL1 virtual machine.
7. On DEN-DC1, watch the number of frames being captured in Network Monitor. When the number of frames has stabilized (approximately 175 to 250 frames), take note of the Time Elapsed. This is the time for prelogon communication. Notice that most of the communication will take place after the **Welcome To Windows** dialog box appears.

8. On DEN-CL1, log on as **Paul**, with a password of **Pa$$word**.
9. On DEN-DC1, watch the number of frames being captured in Network Monitor. When the number of frames has stabilized (approximately 650 frames), on the **Capture** menu, click **Stop and View**.

▶ **Analyze NetBIOS name registration packets**

1. On the **Display** menu, click **Filter**.
2. Double-click **Protocol==Any**.
3. Click **Disable All**.
4. Under **Disabled Protocols**, double-click **NBT**, and then click **OK** twice. Read the first 10 NBT packets. The first few are broadcasts registering the NetBIOS name DEN-CL1 for the client. The next few register the client in the CONTOSO domain.

▶ **Analyze DNS packets**

1. On the **Display** menu, click **Filter**.
2. Double-click **Protocol==NBT**.
3. Click **Disable All**.
4. Under **Disabled Protocols**, double-click **DNS**, and then click **OK**.
5. Click **OK**. Notice that only 16 frames are now visible. These are the DNS packets.
6. Double-click the first DNS packet. In the middle pane, notice the name that the query is for. This is the client locating a logon server.
7. Click the second DNS packet, and in the middle pane, select **DNS**. Read the ASCII text in the bottom pane. The DNS server has responded with DEN-DC1.contoso.msft as the domain controller.
8. Click the fifth DNS packet. This packet is the client resolving DEN-DC1.contoso.msft to an IP address.

▶ **Analyze authentication packets**

1. On the **Display** menu, click **Filter**.
2. Add a filter for User Datagram Protocol (UDP) Port 88.
    a. Double-click **Protocol==DNS**.
    b. Click the **Property** tab, scroll down, and then expand **UDP**.
    c. Click **Destination Port**, click the **Decimal** button, type **88** in the **Value** box, and then click **OK**.
    d. With **UDP** selected, click the **OR** button, and then click the **Expression** button.
    e. Under **UDP**, click **Source Port**, and then click **OK**.
3. Click **OK**. The visible frames are the Kerberos authentication for both the computer account and the user account.

▶ **Analyze time synchronization packets**

1. On the **Display** menu, click **Filter**.
2. Double-click **UDP:Source Port**, type **123** in the **Value** box, and then click **OK**.
3. Double-click **UDP:Destination Port**, type **123** in the **Value** box, and then click **OK**.
4. Click **OK**. These are the packets for time synchronization.

▶ **Analyze Group Policy settings download packets**

1. On the **Display** menu, click **Filter**.
2. In the **Delete** category, click the **Branch** button.
3. Click **OK** to confirm.
4. In the **Add** category, click the **Expression** button.
5. On the **Property** tab, expand **SMB**, and then click **File name**.
6. Click the **ASCII** button, type **Policies** in the **Value** box, and then click **OK**. Please note that this value is case-sensitive.
7. Click **OK**. The visible packets are the computer-based and user-based Group Policy settings being downloaded to the client.
8. Close **Network Monitor**. Do not save the frame capture.

Lesson: Determining the Causes of Connectivity Issues

- What Are the Common Connectivity Issues?
- Actions to Take Before You Begin Isolating the Issue
- Actions to Take to Isolate the Issue
- Actions to Take to Resolve the Issue
- The Process to Follow After the Issue Is Resolved

Introduction

One of the key elements in isolating a network problem is using a consistent, effective strategy for determining the cause. Many of the trouble calls that you receive will be due to user errors that can be resolved through a little training for the user. When you are faced with a more complex complaint, however, you should follow a set procedure for isolating and resolving the problem.

Lesson objectives

After completing this lesson, you will be able to:

- List common connectivity issues.
- Identify actions to take before isolating the issue.
- Describe how to isolate the issue.
- Describe how to resolve the issue.
- Describe the process to follow after the problem is resolved.

What Are the Common Connectivity Issues?

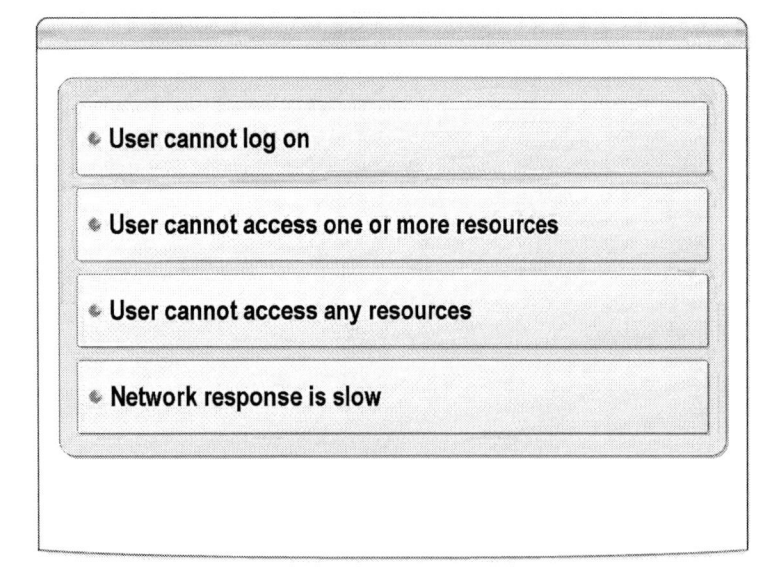

- User cannot log on
- User cannot access one or more resources
- User cannot access any resources
- Network response is slow

Introduction

As a systems administrator, you will not be able to resolve every issue that occurs on your network. However, you should be able to isolate the source of an issue and to determine whether it is one that you can fix or a problem that you need to refer to other experts in your organization.

Common issues

Most issues will be presented to you by users who find that they are unable to perform a specific action on their computers—either something that they were able to do or something that they believe they should be able to do.

There are only a few basic types of complaints:

- User cannot log on.
- User cannot access one or more resources.
- User cannot access *any* resources.
- Network response is slow.

A single basic problem can have a wide variety of causes. For example, a user who cannot log on might simply be entering the wrong password, or all the domain controllers might be offline, or the cause could lie in any of many locations in between. Isolating the problem might be a long and complex process, or it might take only a minute, depending on the cause. The challenge for you is to isolate the single cause from the many possibilities.

Actions to Take Before You Begin Isolating the Issue

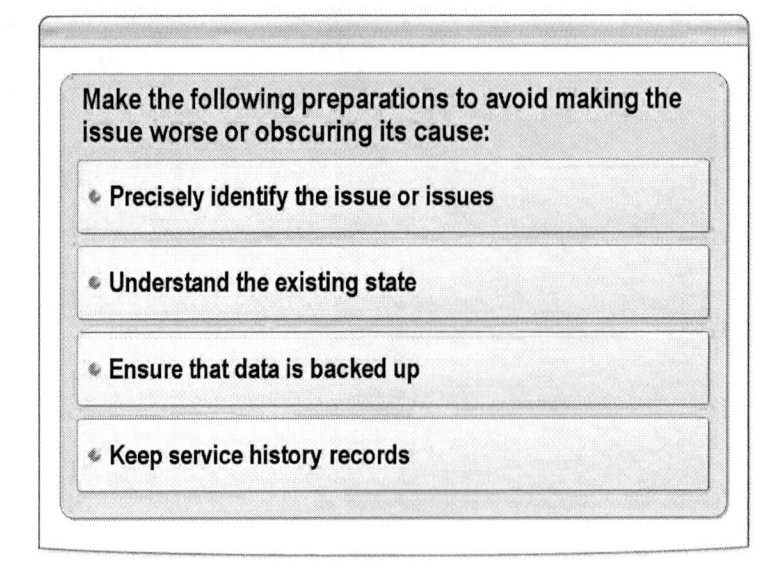

> Make the following preparations to avoid making the issue worse or obscuring its cause:
> - Precisely identify the issue or issues
> - Understand the existing state
> - Ensure that data is backed up
> - Keep service history records

Introduction

If you think that an issue will require a large effort to resolve, you can save yourself time by making preparations that will help you to both proceed as efficiently as possible and avoid making the problem worse.

Precisely identify the issue or issues

It can be difficult to determine the exact nature of an issue from the description given by a user. For this reason, the first action of the isolation is to obtain accurate information about what has occurred.

To understand the nature of an issue, you must know the following:

- What exactly was the user doing when the problem occurred?
- Is this the first time that the problem occurred?
- Which users are affected by the issue? One, a group, or all?
- Which resources are affected by the issue? One, a group, or all?
- Where are the affected resources? A single server or different servers?
- Have there been any recent changes? Network reconfiguration, new software, new hardware?

Understand the existing state

Before changing the configuration of a computer or other device, note its original settings. This can include:

- Noting the client's network configuration, which includes the IP address, the default gateway's IP address, and the subnet mask.
- Noting what services are set to automatic but are not running.
- Reviewing the event log for errors that are occurring before you change the configuration.
- Using the Ping utility to determine the level of connectivity to the gateway and remote computers before you start.

If disabling a feature or changing a setting does not produce the results that you want, use your notes to restore the feature or setting before trying another solution. Not restoring settings can cause new problems and can also make it difficult to determine which of your actions caused a particular effect.

Ensure that data is backed up

Many companies have policies in place dictating that all data must be stored on servers rather than local workstations. However, in most cases, users save some files locally anyway. When troubleshooting a client where there is a risk of data loss, it is important to ensure that any local data is safely backed up. Backups can also be used to restore the system state if problems occur.

Your backup should include the following items:

- The user's personal folder, located in the Documents and Settings folder. This includes the My Documents folder and folders that contain personalization information such as the user's Favorites list and Desktop settings.
- The system state, which includes the registry and other vital system files.

Note A quick way to back up important client data is by using the Backup or Restore Wizard included with Microsoft Windows XP. To start the wizard, in **Control Panel**, in **Performance and Maintenance**, click **Back up your data**.

After you make the backup, consider performing the following steps to check that the data is written correctly to the backup media:

- Use the verification option provided by your backup software.
- Restore a few files from the backup media.

Keep service history records

To detect trends and patterns in your network's performance, you should record each service action that is performed. If you have a small network, you could simply keep the records in a notebook, but larger networks require a more versatile solution.

A useful way to store large numbers of records is to use a database management system to create a service history database with a record for each device on your network. Using a database enables you to search across all your records for similar types of problems or occurrences during a specific time period.

Regardless of the medium on which it is stored, each record should start with baseline performance information gathered when the host was added to the network. Update the baseline information after installing new hardware or software so that you can compare past and current behavior and performance levels.

Your service history records should include:

- Baseline performance data.
- Dates and times of problems and resolutions.
- Changes that you made.
- Reasons for the changes.
- Name of the person who made the changes.
- Positive and negative affects the changes had on the stability and performance of the client and network.
- Information provided by technical support.

Note For more information about creating a configuration management database, see the Information Technology Infrastructure Library (ITIL) and Microsoft Operations Framework (MOF) Web links provided on the Student Materials compact disc.

Actions to Take to Isolate the Issue

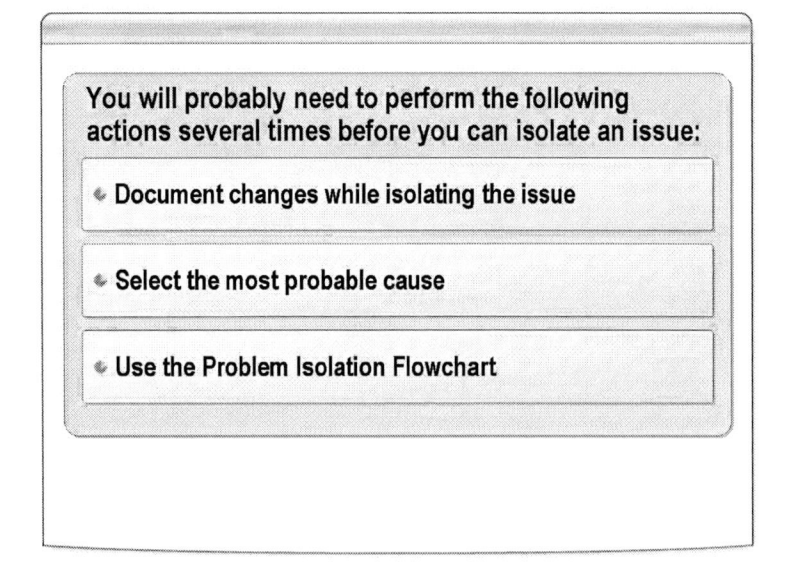

> You will probably need to perform the following actions several times before you can isolate an issue:
>
> * Document changes while isolating the issue
>
> * Select the most probable cause
>
> * Use the Problem Isolation Flowchart

Introduction

Locating the source of a problem might be a long and an arduous process, or it might take only a few minutes. In either case, the Problem Isolation Flowchart (in Appendix B) can help you to identify the shortest path to a solution.

Document changes while isolating the issue

Documenting all changes during troubleshooting is essential to ensure that issues are correctly isolated. Each change made during troubleshooting must be reversed if it does not resolve the problem.

Documenting changes ensures that:

- You do not create additional issues.
- You correctly understand the effects of your changes.

Documenting the steps you take while troubleshooting will also help you review your actions after you resolve the problem. This is useful for complex problems that require lengthy procedures to resolve. Documenting your steps:

- Helps you to verify that you are neither duplicating nor skipping steps.
- Allows others to assist you with the problem.
- Enables you to evaluate the effectiveness of your efforts.
- Makes it possible for you to identify the exact steps to take if the problem should recur.

Note Begin documenting your actions at the start of issue isolation, rather than waiting until you have finished and then attempting to remember all the steps that you took.

Select the most probable cause

When you look for the causes of a problem, begin with the most obvious possibilities. For example, if a client cannot communicate with a file server, do not begin by checking the routers between the two systems. Check the simple, basic details on the client first—such as whether the network cable is connected to the computer.

When isolating network connectivity issues, the fastest way to find the source of the problem is to divide the process into halves. For example, if a client cannot communicate with a server, verify whether the client can communicate with devices halfway between the server and the client. If this is successful, try communicating with a device halfway between the midpoint and the server. Continue this process until the problematic device is found.

Use the Problem Isolation Flowchart

The Problem Isolation Flowchart begins with simple logon problems and progresses in complexity through problems with client configuration, name resolution, routers, firewalls, and other servers. For example, you can use it to isolate an issue such as a single client not obtaining a DHCP address. Following the decision tree, you avoid spending time troubleshooting specific applications or devices such as routers and bridges that apply to more than one computer. Because you know that this issue is applicable to only a single computer, the flowchart directs you away from isolation tasks that involve more than one computer.

The flowchart helps you to take the most effective steps in the most logical order to isolate an issue. Using it will help you to determine whether the problem is a local issue that you can fix by yourself or a broader problem that you will need to refer to other experts in your organization.

Actions to Take to Resolve the Issue

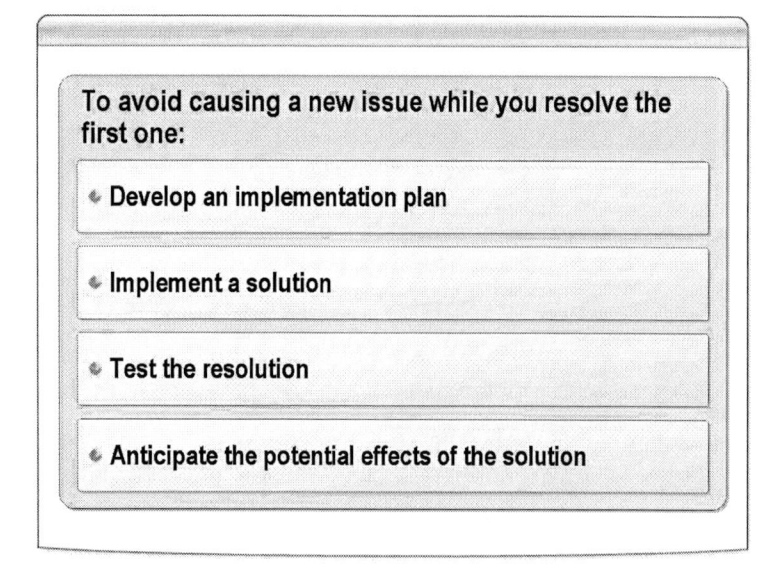

> To avoid causing a new issue while you resolve the first one:
> - Develop an implementation plan
> - Implement a solution
> - Test the resolution
> - Anticipate the potential effects of the solution

Introduction

After you have isolated the source of an issue, you must decide how to resolve it. You can probably fix a simple problem on a client immediately. A larger issue, such as a problem that involves multiple servers that serve hundreds of clients, could require help and cooperation from several groups in your organization.

Develop an implementation plan

After you identify the problem and find a solution that has been tested on one or more computers, you might need an implementation plan if the solution will be deployed across your organization, possibly involving hundreds or thousands of computers. Coordinate your plan with managers and staff members in the affected areas to verify that the schedule does not conflict with important activities.

Your plan can include:

- Estimates of the time and resources that will be needed.
- Provisions for troubleshooting during off-peak work hours.
- A schedule to divide the work into stages.
- Substitute hardware, if the failing equipment performs a vital role, to be used until the equipment can be fixed.

As the number of users grows, the potential loss of productivity due to disruption increases. Your plan must account for dependencies, allow for last-minute changes, and include contingency plans for unforeseen circumstances.

Implement a solution For most problems, you will have a number of potential solutions. When selecting a solution to implement, consider the likelihood that the solution will fix the problem, and how difficult the solution is to implement. It makes sense to try a few quick fixes that are easy to implement before trying an elaborate one, even if the elaborate one is more likely to fix the problem.

After you have isolated the problem to a particular piece of equipment, you can try to determine whether it is being caused by hardware or software. If it is a hardware problem, you might try replacing the unit that is at fault. For example, communication problems might force you to try replacing network cables until you find one that is faulty. If the problem is in a server, you might need to replace components (such as hard drives) until you find the failing piece. If you determine that the problem is caused by software, you can try storing data or running an application on a different computer, or try reinstalling the software on the client that has the problem.

Test the resolution When the issue has been resolved, you should return to the beginning of the process and repeat the task that originally revealed the problem. If the problem no longer occurs, test all the other functions that are related to the changes that you made; this ensures that in fixing one problem, you did not create a new one.

It is at this point that the time you spent documenting the isolation process shows its value. You should repeat exactly the procedures that you used to duplicate the problem, to ensure that the problem the user originally experienced has been eliminated and not just temporarily masked. If the problem was intermittent, it might take time to ascertain whether your solution has been effective. You might need to check with the user several times to make sure that the problem is not recurring.

Anticipate the potential effects of the solution It is important, throughout the troubleshooting process, to keep an eye on the big network picture, and not to let yourself become too involved in the problems experienced by only one user. It is sometimes possible, while implementing a solution to one problem, to create another problem that is more severe or that affects more users.

For example, if users on one subnet are experiencing high traffic levels that reduce their client performance, you might be able to remedy the problem by connecting some of their computers to a different subnet. However, although this solution might help the users with the original problem, you might overload another subnet in the process, causing a new problem that is more severe than the first one. You could consider a more far-reaching solution instead, such as creating a new subnet and then moving some of the affected users to that new subnet.

The Process to Follow After the Issue Is Resolved

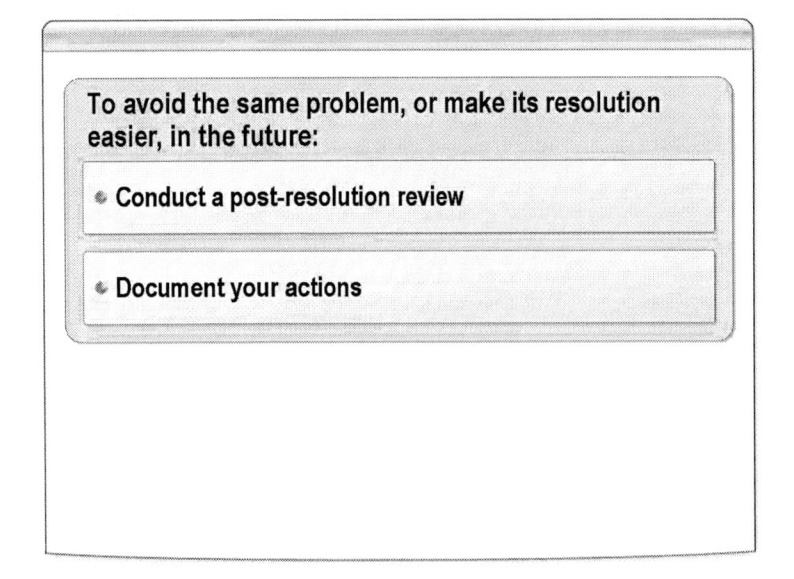

> To avoid the same problem, or make its resolution easier, in the future:
> - Conduct a post-resolution review
> - Document your actions

Introduction

When the network is functioning normally again, review and document just what has happened to avoid (or at least to minimize the impact of) similar problems in the future.

Conduct a post-resolution review

Starting with your compiled documentation, conduct a post-troubleshooting review with the concerned parties, during which they can help you to pinpoint troubleshooting areas that need improvement. Some questions that you might ask during this self-evaluation period include:

- What changes resulted in improvements?
- What changes made the problem worse?
- Was system performance restored to expected levels?
- What work was redundant or unnecessary?
- How effectively were technical support resources used?
- What utility or information was not used that might have helped?
- What unresolved issues require further root-cause analysis?

When it is practical, you should also explain to the user both *what* happened, and *why* it happened. The most important aspect of this conversation is letting the user know whether his or her actions caused the problem, exacerbated it, or made it more difficult to resolve. Such conversations can make the resolution of future issues significantly easier.

Document your actions

The final phase of resolving the issue is to condense your notes and documentation into a concise description of both the problem and its resolution for inclusion in your service history database.

Lesson: Using Network Utilities and Tools to Isolate Connectivity Issues

- Address Resolution Utilities Included with TCP/IP
- Other Utilities Included with TCP/IP
- Actions to Test Connectivity by Using Ping
- Ping Error Messages
- Other Connectivity Testing Tools
- Features of the Network Connections Repair Option
- What Is Network Diagnostics?
- What Is Netsh?
- Practice: Using Network Utilities and Tools to Isolate Connectivity Issues

Introduction

Windows automatically installs most of the utilities that you need for isolating network problems when you install the operating system. There are several additional utilities that you can install from the Windows compact disc when you need them.

Lesson objectives

After completing this lesson, you will be able to:

- Describe how ARP, Nbtstat, and Nslookup are used to isolate connectivity issues.
- Describe how Hostname, Ipconfig, and Netstat are used to isolate connectivity issues.
- Describe how to use the Ping utility to troubleshoot connectivity problems.
- Interpret the error messages created by Ping while troubleshooting connectivity problems.
- Describe how Tracert and Pathping are used to isolate connectivity issues.
- Describe the features of the Network Connections Repair option.
- Describe Network Diagnostics.
- Describe Netsh.
- Isolate connectivity issues by using TCP/IP utilities and tools.

Address Resolution Utilities Included with TCP/IP

> Use IP address resolution command-line utilities included with TCP/IP to:
> - Check IP address to MAC address conversion with ARP
> - Check NetBIOS name to IP address resolution with Nbtstat
> - Check host name to IP address resolution with Nslookup

Introduction

You can use three of the utilities included with TCP/IP to test whether address resolution is being performed properly. The three types of address resolution are:

- IP address to media access control (MAC) address
- NetBIOS name to IP Address
- Host name to IP Address

Use ARP to check IP address to MAC address conversion

ARP converts IP addresses to the MAC addresses that data-link-layer protocols require to transmit frames. To minimize the amount of network traffic that ARP generates, the client stores the resolved hardware addresses in a cache in system memory. The information remains in the cache for a short period (between 2 and 10 minutes) in case the computer has additional packets to send to the same address.

When the network card in a server is changed but retains the same IP address, the client ARP cache will contain outdated information because the new network card will have a different MAC address. Until the cache is updated, clients will be unable to communicate with the server. This problem will resolve itself within 10 minutes. However, it can also be resolved by manually clearing the ARP cache.

Note It is possible to place static entries in the ARP cache. However, this is not recommended, because it is likely to cause network communication problems during network changes and results in minimal network traffic reduction.

Arp.exe uses the following syntax:

```
ARP [-a {ipaddress}] [-n ipaddress] [-s ipaddress hwaddress
{interface}] [-d ipaddress {interface}]
```

- **-a *{ipaddress}*** This parameter displays the contents of the ARP cache. The optional *ipaddress* variable specifies the address of a particular cache entry to be displayed.

- **-n *ipaddress*** This parameter displays the contents of the ARP cache, where *ipaddress* identifies the network interface for which you want to display the cache.

- **-s *ipaddress hwaddress {interface}*** This parameter adds a new entry to the ARP cache, where the *ipaddress* variable contains the IP address of the client, the *hwaddress* variable contains the hardware address of the same client, and the *interface* variable contains the IP address of the network interface in the local system for which you want to modify the cache.

- **-d *ipaddress {interface}*** This parameter deletes the entry in the ARP cache that is associated with the host represented by the *ipaddress* variable. The optional *interface* variable specifies the cache from which the entry should be deleted.

An ARP table as displayed by Arp.exe appears as follows:

```
Interface: 192.168.2.6 on Interface 0x1000003
    Internet Address       Physical Address       Type
    192.168.2.10           00-50-8b-e8-39-7a      dynamic
    192.168.2.99           08-00-4e-a5-70-0f      dynamic
```

Use Nbtstat to check NetBIOS name to IP address resolution

You can use the Nbtstat command-line utility to isolate NetBIOS name resolution problems. For example, use **nbtstat –n** to determine whether a specific NetBIOS name is registered.

When a network is functioning correctly, NetBIOS over TCP/IP (NetBT) resolves NetBIOS names to IP addresses. NetBT uses several options for NetBIOS name resolution, including NetBIOS name cache lookup, Windows Internet Naming Service (WINS) server query, broadcast, LMHOSTS lookup, HOSTS lookup, and DNS server query.

You can use Nbtstat to display a variety of information, including:

- NetBT protocol statistics.

- NetBIOS name tables both for the local client and for remote hosts. The NetBIOS name table is the list of NetBIOS names that corresponds to NetBIOS applications running on the client.

- The contents of the NetBIOS name cache. The NetBIOS name cache is the table that contains NetBIOS name to IP address mappings.

You can also use Nbtstat to refresh both the NetBIOS name cache and the names registered with WINS. The following output is an example of output created by using Nbtstat:

```
C:\Documents and Settings\Administrator>nbtstat -c

Local Area Connection:
Node IpAddress: [10.10.0.50] Scope Id: []

          NetBIOS Remote Cache Name Table

    Name              Type       Host Address    Life [sec]
    ---------------------------------------------------------
    DEN-DC1     <03>  UNIQUE     10.10.0.2         -1
    DEN-DC1     <00>  UNIQUE     10.10.0.2         -1
    DEN-DC1     <20>  UNIQUE     10.10.0.2         -1
```

Use Nslookup to check host name to IP address resolution

Nslookup enables you to generate DNS request messages and also to transmit them to specific DNS servers on the network. Use Nslookup to determine what IP address a particular DNS server has associated with a host name. The basic syntax of Nslookup is as follows:

NSLOOKUP *DNSname DNSserver*

- ***DNSname*** Specifies the DNS name that you want to resolve.
- ***DNSserver*** Specifies the DNS name or IP address of the DNS server that you want to query for the name specified in the *DNSname* variable. If a DNS server is not specified, the primary DNS server in the TCP/IP configuration will be used.

The output generated by the utility looks like the following sample:

```
C:\>nslookup microsoft.com
Server:  den-dc1.contoso.msft
Address:  10.10.0.2

Non-authoritative answer:
Name:    microsoft.com
Address:  207.46.249.222
```

The output sample shows that when queried, the den-dc1.contoso.msft DNS server returns 207.46.249.222 as the IP address associated with microsoft.com. The ability to specify a DNS server makes this utility useful when checking that records on multiple DNS servers are synchronized.

Other Utilities Included with TCP/IP

> Use command-line utilities included with TCP/IP to:
> - Display your client's host name with Hostname
> - Display the IP configuration of your client with Ipconfig
> - Display the network activity on your client with Netstat

Introduction

When Windows is installed, it automatically includes TCP/IP, as well as numerous utilities that you can use to monitor TCP/IP and to check how well TCP/IP is functioning.

Use Hostname to display your client's name

The Hostname utility displays the host name that is assigned to your client. The host name is the computer name of your client.

Use Ipconfig to display the IP configuration of your client

You can use the Ipconfig command-line utility to display the current TCP/IP configuration and to refresh DHCP and DNS settings. Ipconfig will:

- Display current TCP/IP network configuration values.
- Update or release DHCP-allocated leases.
- Display, register, or flush DNS names.

Use Netstat to display the network activity on your client

Netstat displays information about the current network connections of a client running TCP/IP and about the traffic generated by the various TCP/IP protocols. Use Netstat when you want to determine whether a port is available or in use.

A common use of Netstat is to view whether unauthorized services, such as Spyware, are running on a client. All services listening on a TCP or UDP port can be listed by running **netstat –a**. Unknown listings can be tracked down. Be aware that client utilities will also be listed and typically use random course port numbers 1024 and above.

The network connection listing displayed by Netstat on a computer running Windows XP appears as follows:

```
C:\>netstat -a

Active Connections

   Proto  Local Address          Foreign Address         State

   TCP    Den-CL1:epmap          Den-CL1.Contoso.msft:0  LISTENING
   TCP    Den-CL1:microsoft-ds   Den-CL1.Contoso.msft:0  LISTENING
   TCP    Den-CL1:netbios-ssn    Den-CL1.Contoso.msft:0  LISTENING
   TCP    Den-CL1:1043           10.10.0.2:microsoft-ds  TIME_WAIT
   TCP    Den-CL1:1049           10.10.0.2:ldap          TIME_WAIT
   TCP    Den-CL1:1056           10.10.0.2:domain        TIME_WAIT
   TCP    Den-CL1:1028           Den-CL1.Contoso.msft:0  LISTENING
   UDP    Den-CL1:microsoft-ds   *:*
   UDP    Den-CL1:isakmp         *:*
   UDP    Den-CL1:1037           *:*
   UDP    Den-CL1:4500           *:*
   UDP    Den-CL1:ntp            *:*
   UDP    Den-CL1:netbios-ns     *:*
   UDP    Den-CL1:netbios-dgm    *:*
   UDP    Den-CL1:1900           *:*
   UDP    Den-CL1:ntp            *:*
   UDP    Den-CL1:1039           *:*
   UDP    Den-CL1:1900           *:*
```

Actions to Test Connectivity by Using Ping

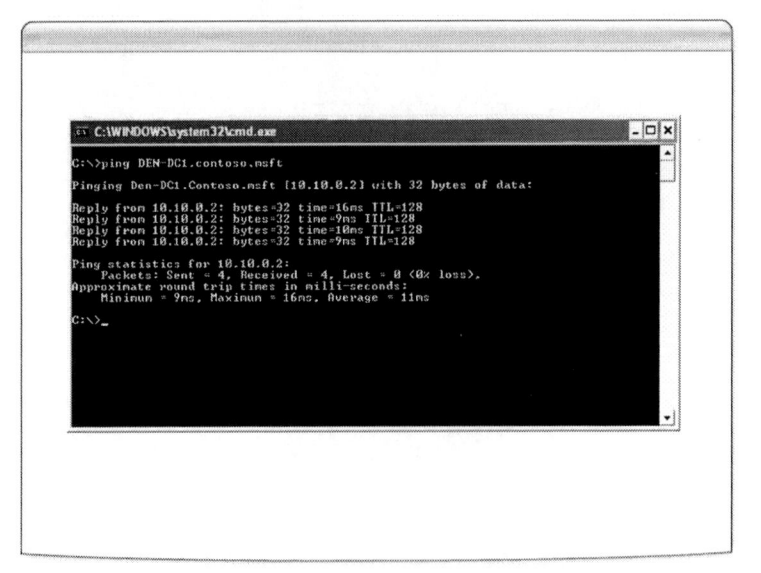

```
C:\>ping DEN-DC1.contoso.msft

Pinging Den-DC1.Contoso.msft [10.10.0.2] with 32 bytes of data:
Reply from 10.10.0.2: bytes=32 time=16ms TTL=128
Reply from 10.10.0.2: bytes=32 time=9ms TTL=128
Reply from 10.10.0.2: bytes=32 time=10ms TTL=128
Reply from 10.10.0.2: bytes=32 time=9ms TTL=128

Ping statistics for 10.10.0.2:
    Packets: Sent = 4, Received = 4, Lost = 0 (0% loss),
Approximate round trip times in milli-seconds:
    Minimum = 9ms, Maximum = 16ms, Average = 11ms

C:\>_
```

Introduction

The Ping utility is one of the most frequently used TCP/IP utilities. When it is used to isolate connectivity issues, Ping tests are done to find the scope of the connectivity issue and the location. When you ping a DNS name, it also tests name resolution.

Testing connectivity to a remote host

The following steps describe how to use the Ping utility to perform tests on your network connectivity. The process starts by testing communication to the remote host and works progressively closer to the local host. An alternative method is to follow these steps in reverse order, starting with step 6.

1. Ping the remote host.

    This confirms whether the connectivity problem still exists. If you can successfully ping a host, you know that the problem is not physical, as packets are able to be transmitted from the client to the remote host. If you can ping a host but cannot access a service on it, the problem is usually with the services.

    In most companies, ping packets are allowed between all subnets. However, some organizations block ping packets to server subnets as a security measure. If this is the case, there will be no response, even if the remote host is operational.

2. Ping another host on the same subnet.

    If this is successful, you know that the problem is limited to accessing the remote host and not a general network problem. After concluding this, you can visit the remote host and begin troubleshooting.

3. Ping a host on another subnet.

    If this is successful, the problem is likely limited to a accessing a single subnet. This might indicate a routing problem. Most routing problems are due to incorrect router configuration or router failure.

4. Ping the default gateway.

   If this is successful, you know that you can communicate on the local network, and the problem is likely a routing problem. Verify that the default gateway is correctly configured.

5. Ping the local client.

   Successfully pinging the IP address of the local client verifies that TCP/IP is correctly configured on the client.

6. Ping the loopback address (127.0.0.1).

   Successfully pinging the loopback address verifies that TCP/IP is both installed and correctly configured on the local client. If the loopback test fails, the IP stack is not responding. Lack of response can occur if the TCP drivers are corrupted, if the network adapter is not working, or if another service is interfering with IP. Open **Event Viewer**, and look for problems reported by Setup or by the TCP/IP service.

   Removing and reinstalling TCP/IP is a common solution to fix problems with pinging the loopback address or the local client. In Windows XP and Windows Server 2003, you cannot remove TCP/IP to reinstall it, but you can reset it by running the command **netsh in tip reset** *logfile*, where *logfile* is a text file that results will be logged to.

   Note For more information about repairing a corrupted TCP/IP stack, see "How to Reset Internet Protocol (TCP/IP) in Windows XP" in the Microsoft Knowledge Base.

7. Temporarily turn off IP Security (IPSec), and then retry all the preceding **ping** commands.

   If none of the preceding **ping** commands are successful, check whether IPSec is enabled. If IPSec is enabled locally, temporarily stop the IPSec Services service in the Services snap-in, and then try pinging again. If network connectivity between hosts works after you stop IPSec, ask the security administrator to troubleshoot the IPSec policy.

Ping Error Messages

> **Common Ping error messages:**
> - TTL expired in transit
> - Destination host unreachable
> - Request timed out
> - Unknown host

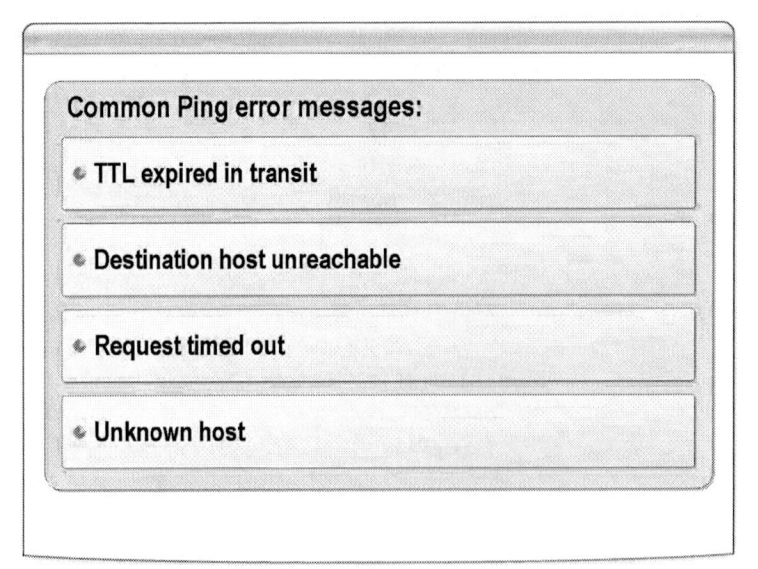

Introduction

Each time you ping a host, the Ping utility will display a message box showing the result—either a successful response or an error message. The type of error is a good clue as to the source of a connectivity problem.

TTL expired in transit

"TTL expired in transit" indicates that the number of hops required to reach the destination exceeds the TTL set by the sending host to forward the packets. The default TTL value for Internet Control Message Protocol (ICMP) Echo Requests sent by Ping is 128. In some rare cases, this is not enough to travel the required number of hops to a destination. You can increase the TTL by using the **-i** switch, to a maximum of 255 hops.

If increasing the TTL value fails to resolve the problem, the packets are being forwarded in a routing loop, a circular path among routers.

Use Tracert to track down the location of the routing loop, which appears as a repeated series of the same IP addresses in the Tracert report. Next, make an appropriate change to the routing tables, or inform the administrator of a remote router of the problem.

Destination host unreachable

"Destination host unreachable" indicates one of two problems: either the local client has no route to the desired destination, or a remote router reports that *it* has no route to the destination. The form of the message can distinguish the two problems. If the message is simply "Destination host unreachable," there is no route from the local client, and the packets to be sent were never put on the network. Use the Route utility to check the local routing table for either a direct route to the destination or a default gateway.

If the message is "Reply from *IP address*: Destination host unreachable," the routing problem occurred at a remote router.

"Request timed out"	In most cases "Request timed out" indicates that the remote host is not responding. This usually indicates a problem on the remote host or a network problem preventing packets from reaching the remote host. However, it is not a router problem, as that would be indicated by the message "Destination host unreachable."
	In most circumstances, the latency to communicate with a remote host is less than 1000 milliseconds, even when accessing hosts around the world on the Internet. Ping allows 4000 milliseconds for a response to be returned before displaying "Request timed out." In rare situations, such as satellite links, "Request timed out" might indicate excessive latency between the client and the host. You can test for excessive latency by increasing the wait time by using the **–w** switch.
Unknown host	This error message appears as "Ping request could not find host *host name*. Please check the name and try again." This indicates that the requested host name cannot be resolved to its IP address; check that the name is entered correctly and that the DNS servers can resolve it.

Other Connectivity Testing Tools

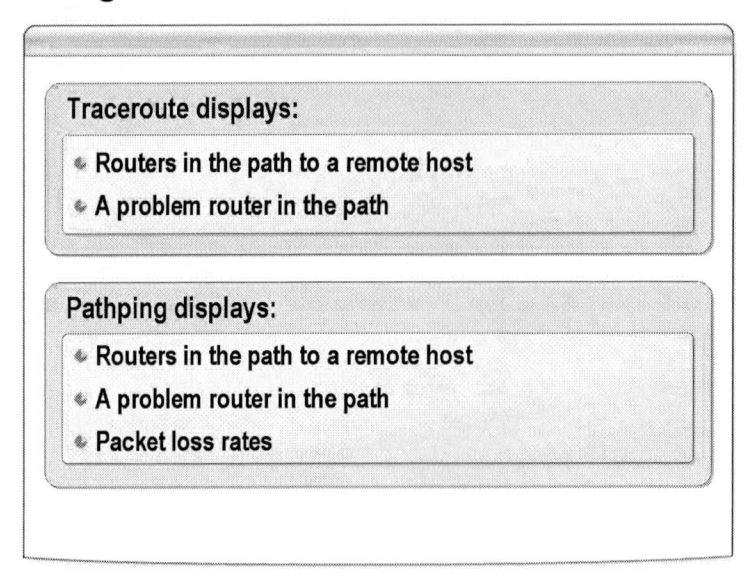

> **Traceroute displays:**
> - Routers in the path to a remote host
> - A problem router in the path
>
> **Pathping displays:**
> - Routers in the path to a remote host
> - A problem router in the path
> - Packet loss rates

Introduction

Traceroute (Tracert) is a variant of the Ping utility that displays the route that packets take to a destination, in addition to the usual Ping messages. Traceroute can show how far your packets are going before they encounter a problem. Pathping combines features of both Ping and Traceroute to obtain additional information about router performance and link reliability that is not available to either of those tools.

Following a packet by using Traceroute

Because of the nature of IP routing, paths through an internetwork can change from minute to minute. Traceroute displays a list of the routers that are currently forwarding packets to a specified destination.

Traceroute uses ICMP Echo and Echo Reply messages, as Ping does, but it changes the value of the TTL field in the IP header. The TTL field is designed to prevent packets from getting caught in router loops that keep them circulating endlessly around the network. The computer generating the packet normally sets a relatively high value for the TTL field; on systems running Windows, the default value is 128. Each router that processes the packet reduces the TTL value by one. If the TTL value reaches zero, the last router discards the packet and transmits an ICMP error message back to the original sender.

When you start Traceroute by using the **tracert** command with the name or IP address of a target computer, the utility generates its first set of Echo Request messages with TTL values of 1. When the messages arrive at the first router on their path, the router decrements their TTL values to 0, discards the packets, and reports the errors to the sender. The error messages contain the router's address, which Traceroute displays as the first hop in the path to the destination. Traceroute's second set of Echo Request messages uses a TTL value of 2, causing the second router on the path to discard the packets and generate error messages. The Echo Request messages in the third set have a TTL value of 3, and so on. Each set of packets travels one hop farther than the previous set before causing a router to return error messages to the source. The list of routers displayed by Traceroute as the path to the destination is the result of these error messages.

Checking packet loss by using Pathping

Like Traceroute, Pathping discovers the path to a destination. However, by default, Pathping sends 100 Echo Request messages to each router between a source and destination over a period of time and then computes results based on the packets returned from each router.

In addition to displaying the path to a destination, Pathping displays the degree of packet loss at any given router. A router with packet loss might indicate congestion or configuration problems.

The path data reported by Pathping includes:

- Information on the intermediate routers visited on the path.
- The round-trip time (RTT) value.
- Link loss information.

Features of the Network Connections Repair Option

> The Network Connections Repair option performs six tasks:
> - Renews DHCP lease
> - Flushes the ARP cache
> - Flushes the NetBIOS name cache
> - Re-registers with a WINS server
> - Flushes the DNS cache
> - Registers a DNS name

Introduction

The Network Connections Repair option combines six of the most commonly used TCP/IP troubleshooting commands in one Windows utility.

Running Network Connections Repair Link

Network Connections Repair Link can be accessed in any of three ways:

- Right-click a network connection icon in the Network Connections folder, and then click **Repair**.
- Right-click the information balloon that appears in the system tray when your IP configuration becomes invalid, and then click **Repair**.
- In the **Status** dialog box, click the **Support** tab, and then click **Repair**.

When selecting a network connection, look in the left-hand column (if shown) for the Repair This Connection link.

The following tasks are performed in the order listed:

Broadcast DHCP lease renewal

This is the equivalent of a DHCP broadcast renewal at 87.5 percent of the lease time. This was chosen because it is safer than actually doing first a DHCP release and then a DHCP renew. If a DHCP server is unavailable to renew the address, the client keeps its current address. If a new DHCP server comes online, the DHCP server cannot acknowledge (NACK) the client and restart the lease process, potentially fixing a client's IP address problem.

Flush the ARP cache

Sometimes an ARP cache entry becomes outdated, and then communication cannot occur again until the bad ARP cache entry expires. It is also possible for a bad static ARP cache entry that never expires to have been placed on the client. The ARP cache is naturally flushed at 2-minute and 10-minute intervals, so this operation is considered safe.

Note If your network relies on static ARP cache entries, make sure that there is a way to reenter the ARP cache addresses after this tool is run.

Flush the NetBIOS name cache	Often the NetBIOS cache can have outdated entries, and then communication cannot occur. Repairing a network connection performs the equivalent of running the **nbtstat –R** command which clears the NetBIOS name cache and then reloads any NetBIOS name entries in the Lmhosts file with the #PRE flag.
Reregister the client's name with a WINS server	Repairing a network connection performs the equivalent of running the **nbtstat –RR** command which reregisters the client's name with a WINS server. This can be very useful in isolating problems with NetBIOS name resolution.
	Note This task simply schedules the name refresh with the operating system; it does not confirm that the refresh was successful.
Flush the DNS cache	Repairing a network connection performs the equivalent of running the **ipconfig /flushdns** command which flushes the DNS resolver cache entries from memory. This can be useful in isolating problems with DNS name resolution.
Register a DNS name	Repairing a network connection reregisters the DNS name of the client with a DNS dynamic update server. This is similar to running the **ipconfig /registerdns** command.

What Is Network Diagnostics?

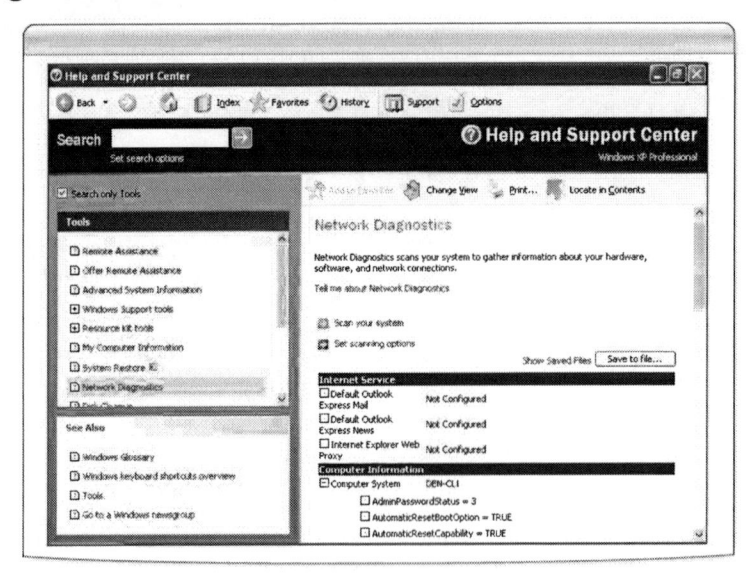

Introduction

The Network Diagnostics utility performs a series of tests to gather important information that can help you isolate the causes of network-related issues. Depending on the options you select, it checks your system for network connectivity and whether your network-related programs and services are running. It also gathers basic information about your computer.

Using Network Diagnostics

Unlike most of the other network utilities, Network Diagnostics is a Windows-based utility rather than a command-line utility. It is accessed by clicking **Help and Support Center** on the **Tools** menu for both Windows XP and Windows Server 2003.

What Is Netsh?

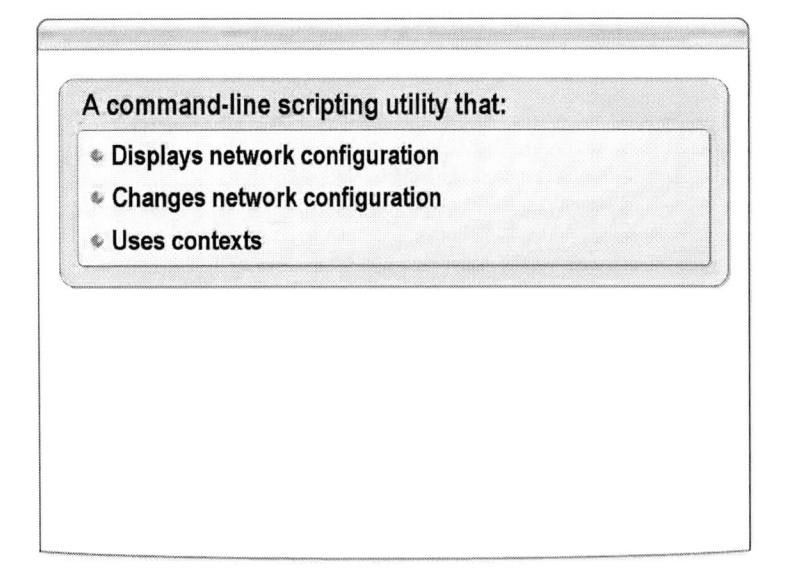

> A command-line scripting utility that:
> - Displays network configuration
> - Changes network configuration
> - Uses contexts

Introduction

Netsh is a command-line scripting utility that allows you to, either locally or remotely, display or modify the network configuration of a computer that is currently running. Netsh also provides a scripting feature that allows you to run a group of commands in batch mode against a specified computer. Netsh can also save a configuration script in a text file for archival purposes or to help you configure other servers.

Netsh contexts

Netsh interacts with other operating system components using dynamic-link library (DLL) files. Each Netsh helper DLL provides an extensive set of features called a context, which is a group of commands specific to a networking component. These contexts extend the functionality of Netsh by providing configuration and monitoring support for one or more services, utilities, or protocols. For example, Dhcpmon.dll provides Netsh the context and set of commands necessary to configure and manage DHCP servers.

You must run the **netsh** command from a command prompt and change to the context that contains the command that you want to use. The contexts that are available to you depend on which networking components you have installed. For example, if you type **dhcp** at the Netsh command prompt, you change to the DHCP context, but if you do not have DHCP installed, the following message appears:

```
The following command was not found: dhcp.
```

The following table lists contexts available in Netsh.

Context	Description
aaaa	Shows and sets the configuration of the authentication, authorization, accounting, and auditing (AAAA) database used by the Internet Authentication Service (IAS) and the Routing and Remote Access Service (RRAS).
bridge	Enables or disables Layer-3 compatibility mode and shows configuration information for the Network Bridge adapters.
dhcp	Administers DHCP servers and provides an equivalent alternative to console-based management.
diag	Administers and troubleshoots operating system and network service parameters.
interface ip	Configures the TCP/IP protocol (including addresses, default gateways, DNS servers, and WINS servers) and displays configuration and statistical information.
interface ipv6	Queries and configures IP version 6 (IPv6) interfaces, addresses, caches, and routes.
interface portproxy	Administers servers that act as proxies between IPv4 and IPv6 networks and applications.
ipsec	Provides an equivalent alternative to the console-based management and diagnostic capabilities provided by the IP Security Policy Management and IP Security Monitor snap-ins available in the Microsoft Management Console (MMC). By using the Netsh commands for IPSec, you can configure and view static or dynamic IPSec main-mode settings, quick-mode settings, rules, and configuration parameters.
ras	Administers remote access servers.
routing	Administers routing servers.
rpc	Changes, resets, or displays selective system-binding settings.
wins	Administers WINS servers.

Practice: Using Network Utilities and Tools to Isolate Connectivity Issues

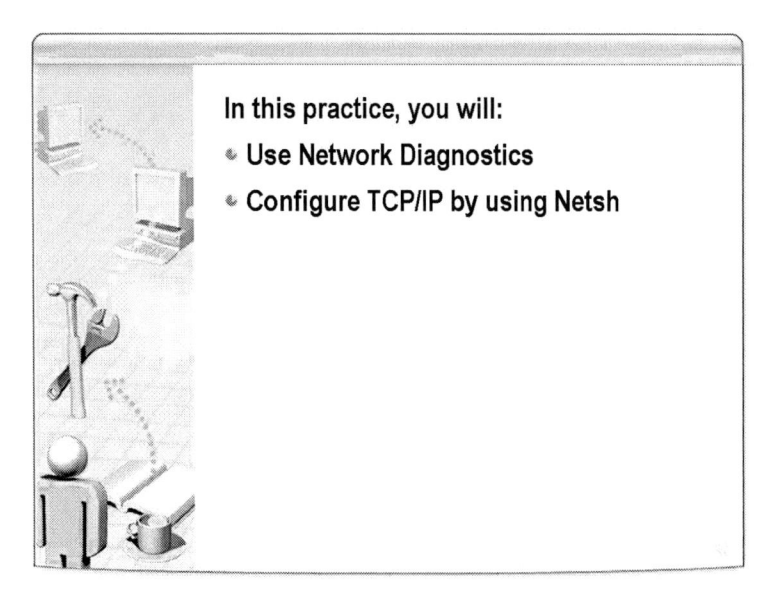

Objectives

In this practice, you will:

- Use Network Diagnostics.
- Configure TCP/IP by using Netsh.

Instructions

Ensure that the DEN-DC1 and DEN-CL1 virtual machines are running.

Practice

▶ **Use Network Diagnostics**

1. On DEN-CL1, log on as **Paul**, with a password of **Pa$$w0rd**.
2. Click **Start**, and then click **Help and Support**.
3. Under **Pick a task**, click **Use Tools to view your computer information and diagnose problems**.
4. In the **Tools** pane, click **Network Diagnostics**.
5. Click **Set scanning options**.
6. Scroll down, and select the **Domain Name System (DNS)** check box and the **Internet Protocol Address** check box. These check boxes are selected in addition to the default selections.
7. Scroll up, and click **Scan your system**.
8. When the report is complete, scroll down, and expand **DNS Servers**. Notice that the status of **DNS Servers** is **Passed**.
9. Expand **DNSServerSearchOrder = 10.10.0.2**. Notice that this displays the communication that Network Diagnostics performed with the DNS server.
10. Expand **Network Adapters**. Notice that a wide variety of network information is listed here.
11. Close **Help and Support Center**.

▶ **Configure TCP/IP by using Netsh**

1. Click **Start**, click **Run**, type **cmd**, and then click **OK**.
2. Type **netsh**, and then press ENTER.
3. Type **interface ip**, and then press ENTER.
4. Type **show**, and then press ENTER.
5. Type **show config**, and then press ENTER. Notice that the address is **10.10.0.20**. We will change the address to **10.10.0.21**.
6. Type **help**, and then press ENTER.
7. Type **set**, and then press ENTER.
8. Type **set address**, and then press ENTER. Read the help message that is displayed.
9. Type **set address name= "Local Area Connection" source=static addr=10.10.0.21 mask=255.255.0.0**, and then press ENTER.
10. Type **show config**, and then press ENTER. Notice that the address is now **10.10.0.21**.
11. Type **reset C:\netshlog.txt**, and then press ENTER.
12. Type **quit**, and then press ENTER.
13. Type **notepad C:\netshlog.txt**, and then press ENTER to view the log file. Read the registry changes that were made.
14. Close Notepad.

▶ **Prepare for the next lab**

- Restart DEN-CL1.

Important Do not shut down the virtual machines.

Lab: Isolating Common Connectivity Issues

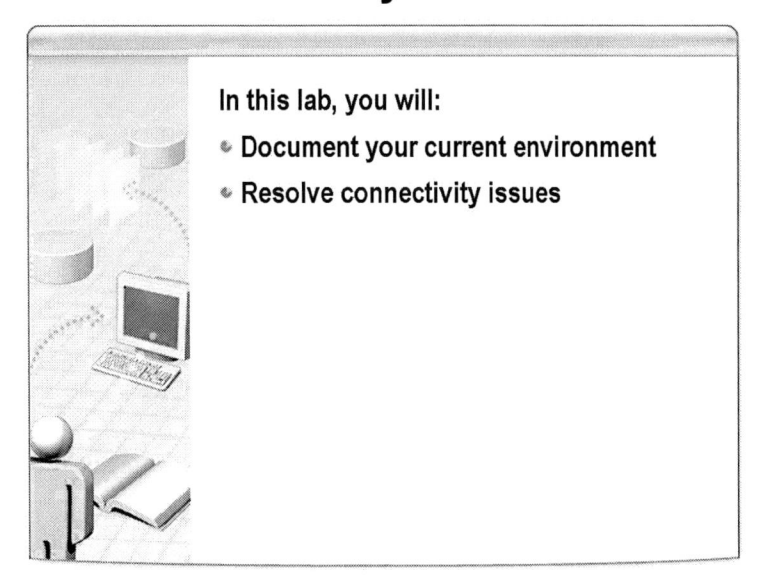

In this lab, you will:
- Document your current environment
- Resolve connectivity issues

Objectives

After completing this lab, you will be able to:

- Document your current environment.
- Resolve connectivity issues.

Prerequisites

Before working on this lab, you must have knowledge of the TCP/IP configuration settings on a client computer running a Windows operating system.

Instructions

Ensure that the DEN-DC1 and DEN-CL1 virtual machines are running.

Scenario

This lab consists of four scenarios. Each scenario outlines a connectivity issue that you will need to resolve. You will use the Network Connectivity Job Aid to isolate client connectivity issues. In each scenario, you will execute a batch file that will introduce an issue into the system. You will then work through a series of steps to isolate and fix the issue.

Note To view the Problem Isolation Flowchart, see Appendix B.

Estimated time to complete this lab: 60 minutes

Exercise 1
Documenting Your Current Environment

As you run the scripts to introduce scenarios, you might be changing the configuration settings of your computer to solve the issue. At the end of each scenario, you will reset your computer. Document your configuration settings by completing the following table, and refer to this table to verify that the settings are correctly configured after you reset your computer.

On DEN-CL1, log on to the CONTOSO domain as **Paul**, with a password of **Pa$$w0rd**.

Item	Configuration
Your computer's IP address	
Your default gateway	
Your primary DNS Server	
Your secondary DNS Server	
Your WINS Server	
Your computer's NetBT node type	

Exercise 2
Resolving Connectivity Issues

This exercise consists of four scenarios. Each scenario outlines a connectivity issue that you will need to resolve. You will use the Problem Isolation Flowchart in Appendix B to isolate client connectivity issues. In each scenario, you will execute a batch file that will introduce an issue into the system. You will then work through a series of steps to isolate and fix the issue.

Scenario 1: Resolving a "Request Timed Out" Connectivity Issue

A customer has logged a help desk request stating that he cannot access any network resources. He is receiving a "Request timed out" error. You are working at the user's computer to isolate the connectivity issue and either resolve it yourself or pass it on to a systems engineer.

Tasks	Specific instructions
1. Introduce the problem.	a. If necessary, log on as **Paul**, with a password of **Pa$$w0rd**. b. Run **D:\2276\Labs\Mod05\s1.bat**.
2. Isolate the issue.	a. Use the Ping utility to send an Echo Request to localhost. b. Ping DEN-DC1. c. Verify your own IP configuration.

? After you pinged localhost, did the TCP/IP stack function properly?

? After you pinged DEN-DC1, did you receive a successful reply?

? When you verified your own IP configuration, was it correct? If not, what was the issue?

3. Correct the problem.	■	In **Control Panel**, navigate to **Network Connections**, and then click **Local Area Connection** and correct the problem.
4. Reset the computer configuration.	■	Run **D:\2276\Labs\Mod05\r1.bat**.

Scenario 2: User Cannot Access Any Network Resources

A user complains that he cannot access any network resource. He mentioned seeing a dialog box, stating something about a duplicate IP address on the network.

Tasks	Specific instructions
1. Introduce the problem.	▪ Run **D:\2276\Labs\Mod05\s2.bat**.
2. Isolate issues associated with this scenario.	a. Review the IP configuration information by using **ipconfig /all**. b. Determine whether DHCP is enabled. c. Verify that the ARP cache lists a network interface adapter. d. Isolate the issue.
❓ Is the adapter configured for DHCP?	
❓ What is the value of the IP address and the subnet mask?	
❓ When you verify the ARP, what is the response?	
❓ What is the issue?	
3. Correct the problem.	▪ Using **Local Area Connection**, correct the problem.
4. Reset the computer configuration.	▪ Run **D:\2276\Labs\Mod05\r2.bat**.

Scenario 3: Partial Access to Network Resources

A user at a remote office has only partial access to the network. She can access some shared folder files, but the DEN-DC1 computer is inaccessible to her. You are at the user's computer to isolate the connectivity issue and either fix it yourself or pass it on to a systems engineer. For this scenario, you are working to restore connectivity to the DEN-DC1 computer.

Tasks	Specific instructions
1. Introduce the problem.	- Run **D:\2276\Labs\Mod05\s3.bat**.
2. Isolate issues associated with this scenario.	a. Ping localhost. b. Ping DEN-DC1. c. Run Nslookup to query the DEN-DC1 computer.
❓ Can you ping the localhost? Did you receive an answer?	
❓ Can you ping DEN-DC1? What is the response? What is the displayed address for DEN-DC1?	
❓ Was the Nslookup query on the DEN-DC1 computer successful?	
❓ What is the most likely problem?	
3. Correct the problem.	
4. Reset the computer configuration.	- Run **D:\2276\Labs\Mod05\r3.bat**.

Scenario 4: Unable to Access Host by IP Address

A user in the local office is having difficulty accessing the London computer. The user is unable to print to the print device connected to the DEN-DC1 computer and cannot access any of the files located in shared folders on the DEN-DC1 computer. In this scenario, you are working to restore connectivity to the DEN-DC1 computer.

Tasks	Specific instructions
1. Introduce the problem.	▪ Run **D:\2276\Labs\Mod05\s4.bat**.
2. Isolate issues associated with this scenario.	a. Ping localhost. b. Ping DEN-DC1. c. Ping 10.10.0.2.
❓ Can you ping localhost successfully? Is TCP/IP functioning properly?	
❓ Can you ping DEN-DC1 successfully? What does the output of the ping indicate?	
❓ Can you ping 10.10.0.2? What is the reply?	
❓ What is the issue?	
3. Correct the problem.	
4. Reset the computer configuration.	▪ Run **D:\2276\Labs\Mod05\r4.bat**.
5. Complete the lab exercise.	▪ Close all programs and shut down all computers. Do not save changes.

Course Evaluation

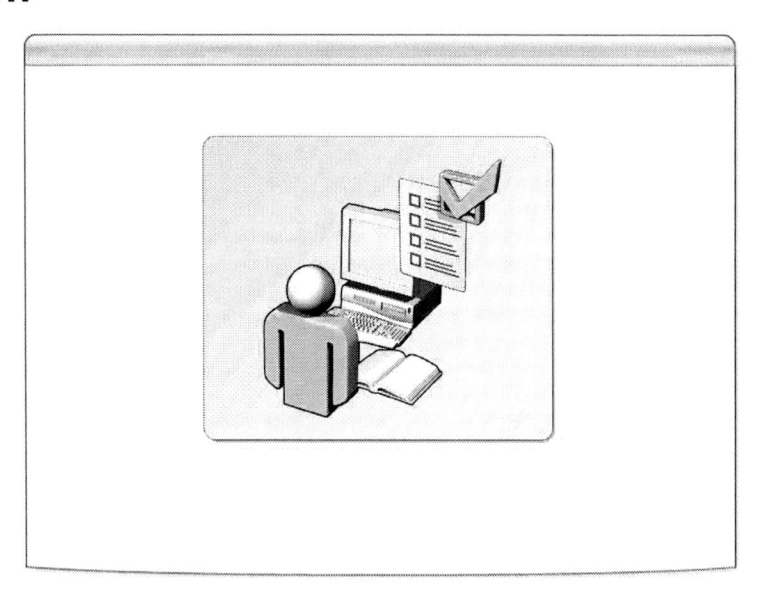

Your evaluation of this course will help Microsoft understand the quality of your learning experience.

To complete a course evaluation, go to the Metrics That Matter page of the Knowledge Advisors Web site at http://www.metricsthatmatter.com/MTMStudent/ClassListPage.aspx?&orig=6&VendorAlias=survey.

Microsoft will keep your evaluation strictly confidential and will use your responses to improve your future learning experience.

Index

Note: Numbers preceding the hyphens indicate the module in which the entry can be found.

A

Active Directory, DNS and, 4-11
address resolution. *See* name resolution
Address Resolution Protocol. *See* ARP (Address Resolution Protocol)
Alternative Configuration feature
   defined, 3-20
   how it works, 3-21
   overview, 3-20 to 3-21
ANDing, 2-19
APIPA. *See* Automatic Private IP Addressing (APIPA)
application layer, OSI model
   defined, 1-3
   role in receiving process, 1-7
   role in sending process, 1-6
application layer, TCP/IP protocol stack. *See also* Internet layer, TCP/IP protocol stack; network interface layer, TCP/IP protocol stack; transport layer, TCP/IP protocol stack
   defined, 1-12
   list of protocols, 1-15
   overview, 1-15
   role in receiving process, 1-19
   role in sending process, 1-18
ARP (Address Resolution Protocol)
   examining packets in Network Monitor, 1-30
   flushing cache by using Network Connections Repair, 5-32
   need for, 1-24
   overview, 1-24 to 1-25
   resolving IP addresses to MAC addresses, 1-26
   role in isolating connectivity issues, 1-25, 5-21 to 5-22
   role of cache, 1-24 to 1-25
   step-by-step process, 1-26
   syntax and parameters, 1-25
   as TCP/IP Internet-layer protocol, 1-16
Automatic Private IP Addressing (APIPA)
   defined, 3-21, 3-22
   disabling, 3-23
   how it works, 3-22
   limitations, 3-22
   testing, 3-24 to 3-25

B

binary numbers
   calculating decimal values, 2-15
   converting to decimal, 2-15
   relating dotted decimal notation to, 2-14 to 2-15
bridges, role in OSI model, 1-8

C

cache, ARP, 1-24 to 1-25
cache, resolver. *See* DNS resolver cache
child domains, defined, 4-10
CIDR (classless interdomain routing)
   need for, 2-40
   notation, 2-42
   overview, 2-40
   role in supernetting, 2-41 to 2-42
Class A, IP address, 2-8, 2-9
Class B, IP address, 2-8, 2-9
Class C, IP address
   overview, 2-8, 2-9
   supernetting, 2-41, 2-46
Class D, IP address, 2-8, 2-9
Class E, IP address, 2-8, 2-9
classes, IP address, 2-8 to 2-9
classless interdomain routing. *See* CIDR (classless interdomain routing)
command-line utilities
   ARP, 1-25, 5-21 to 5-22
   Ipconfig, 3-6 to 3-7, 5-24
   Nbstat, 4-24 to 4-25, 5-22 to 5-23
   Netsh, 5-35 to 5-37
   Netstat, 5-24 to 5-25
   Nslookup, 5-23
   Pathping, 5-31
   Ping, 1-22 to 1-23, 5-26 to 5-29
   Tracert, 5-30
computer names
   choosing type, 4-4
   defined, 4-1
   full, 4-13
   resolving into IP addresses, 4-2

D

data-link layer, OSI model
   bridge operation, 1-8
   defined, 1-4
   role in receiving process, 1-7
   role in sending process, 1-7
   switch operation, 1-9
data-link layer, TCP/IP protocol stack. *See* network interface layer, TCP/IP protocol stack
datagrams, in OSI model context, 1-4
decimal notation, in IP addresses, 2-14 to 2-15
default gateways
   configuring clients for, 2-7
   overview, 2-7
   role in internetworking, 2-7
DHCP (Dynamic Host Configuration Protocol)
   assigning default gateways to clients, 2-7
   benefits of using, 3-11
   creating reservations, 3-17
   creating scopes, 3-16 to 3-17
   defined, 3-10, 3-11
   enabling, 3-12
   how it works, 3-11 to 3-12
   IP address renewal, 3-14 to 3-15
   lease renewal process, 3-15, 5-32
   overview, 3-11 to 3-12
   role of Network Connection Repair in lease renewal, 5-32
   server configuration, 3-16 to 3-17
DNS, as TCP/IP application-layer protocol, 1-15. *See also* Domain Name System (DNS)
DNS resolver cache
   controlling, 4-14
   defined, 4-14
   flushing by using Network Connections Repair, 5-33

DNS suffixes
    connection-specific, 4-13
    multiple, 4-13
    overview, 4-12 to 4-13
    primary, 4-12
Domain Name System (DNS)
    how it works, 4-10 to 4-11
    Ipconfig options, 3-7
    overview, 4-10 to 4-11
    resolver cache, 4-14, 5-33
    resolving host names, 4-7 to 4-17
domains, defined, 4-10
dotted decimal notation, 2-14
dynamic IP addresses, 3-3
dynamic routing, 2-27

F-G

flowcharts. *See* Problem Isolation Flowchart
frames, in OSI model context, 1-4
FTP, as TCP/IP application-layer protocol, 1-15
gateways, role in OSI model, 1-9. *See also* default gateways

H

host names
    defined, 4-5
    maximum length, 4-5
    NetBIOS name resolution process, 4-28 to 4-30
    NetBIOS over TCP/IP and, 4-15
    resolving, 4-7 to 4-17
    ways to use, 4-5
Hostname utility, 5-24
Hosts file
    connectivity problems, 4-9
    overview, 4-8 to 4-9
    sample entries, 4-8
HTTP, as TCP/IP application-layer protocol, 1-15
hubs, role in OSI model, 1-8

I

ICMP (Internet Control Message Protocol)
    examining packets in Network Monitor, 1-30
    as TCP/IP Internet-layer protocol, 1-16
IGMP, as TCP/IP Internet-layer protocol, 1-16
Internet Control Message Protocol. *See* ICMP (Internet Control Message Protocol)
Internet Group Management Protocol (IGMP), as TCP/IP Internet-layer protocol, 1-16
Internet layer, TCP/IP protocol stack. *See also* application layer, TCP/IP protocol stack; network interface layer, TCP/IP protocol stack; transport layer, TCP/IP protocol stack
    defined, 1-12
    list of protocols, 1-16
    overview, 1-16
    role in receiving process, 1-19
    role in sending process, 1-18
Internet Protocol (IP). *See* IP addresses; IP protocol
Internet Protocol (TCP/IP) Properties dialog box, 3-4 to 3-5
internetworks
    defined, 2-7
    role of default gateway, 2-7
    role of routers, 2-26
IP addresses
    assigning in multiple subnet networks, 2-1 to 2-46
    calculating network ID, 2-5
    checking address resolution, 5-21 to 5-23
    Class A, 2-8, 2-9
    Class B, 2-8, 2-9
    Class C, 2-8, 2-9
    Class D, 2-8, 2-9
    Class E, 2-8, 2-9
    classes, 2-8 to 2-9
    communication between networks, 2-11
    communication within single network, 2-10
    configuring clients to obtain automatically, 3-10 to 3-18
    configuring for client computers, 3-1 to 3-25
    configuring for complex networks, 2-13 to 2-24
    configuring for simple networks, 2-2 to 2-12
    dotted decimal notation, 2-14
    local vs. remote, 2-19
    overcoming limitations, 2-35 to 2-46
    private vs. public, 2-37 to 2-38
    renewal, 3-14 to 3-15
    resolving to MAC addresses, 1-26, 5-21 to 5-22
    role of subnet masks, 2-4 to 2-5
    role of VLSM in conserving, 2-39
    static vs. dynamic, 3-3
    and supernetting, 2-41 to 2-42
IP protocol
    routing procedure, 2-28
    as TCP/IP Internet-layer protocol, 1-16
IP routing tables, 2-25 to 2-34
    default, 2-31
    defined, 2-28
    dynamic, 2-27
    modifying, 2-33
    role in forwarding packets, 2-28
    role of routers, 2-30
    static, 2-27
    troubleshooting routing, 2-32
    types of entries, 2-30 to 2-31
    types of routes, 2-31
    viewing, 2-32, 2-33
Ipconfig utility
    displaying client IP configurations, 5-24
    viewing IP addresses, 3-6 to 3-7
IPv6, 2-43 to 2-44

L-M

link layer, TCP/IP protocol stack. *See* network interface layer, TCP/IP protocol stack
Lmhosts
    adding entries to file, 4-29
    editing guidelines, 4-25 to 4-26
    overview, 4-25 to 4-26
    reasons to use, 4-25
logon, analyzing client process, 5-2 to 5-9
MAC addresses
    checking IP address resolution, 5-21 to 5-22
    resolving IP addresses to, 1-26

N

name resolution
    configuring client computers, 4-1 to 4-30
    overview, 4-2 to 4-6
    utilities for troubleshooting, 5-21 to 5-23
namespace, DNS, 4-10 to 4-11
Nbstat utility
    checking NetBIOS name to IP address resolution, 5-22 to 5-23
    how to use, 4-24 to 4-25
    overview, 4-24 to 4-25
    what it does, 4-24
NetBIOS, defined, 4-19

NetBIOS names
    characteristics, 4-5
    defined, 4-5
    flushing cache by using Network Connections Repair, 5-33
    resolution process, 4-28 to 4-30
    suffixes for, 4-6
NetBIOS over TCP/IP. *See* NetBT (NetBIOS over TCP/IP)
NetBT (NetBIOS over TCP/IP)
    how it works, 4-20
    overview, 4-20 to 4-23
    role in DNS name resolution process, 4-15, 4-20 to 4-21
    types of nodes, 4-22 to 4-23
    what it does, 4-20
Netsh utility, 5-35 to 5-37
Netstat utility, 5-24 to 5-25
Network Connections Repair
    accessing, 5-32
    defined, 5-32
    flushing ARP cache, 5-32
    flushing DNS cache, 5-33
    flushing NetBIOS name cache, 5-33
    registering client names with WINS server, 5-33
    registering DNS names, 5-33
    role in DHCP lease renewal, 5-32
Network Diagnostics, 5-34, 5-37
network IDs
    calculating, 2-5
    combining multiple IP addresses into, 2-41 to 2-42
network interface layer, TCP/IP protocol stack. *See also* application layer, TCP/IP protocol stack; Internet layer, TCP/IP protocol stack; transport layer, TCP/IP protocol stack
    defined, 1-12
    overview, 1-16
    role in receiving process, 1-19
    role in sending process, 1-18
network layer, OSI model
    defined, 1-4
    role in receiving process, 1-7
    role in sending process, 1-6
    router operation, 1-9
network layer, TCP/IP protocol stack. *See* Internet layer, TCP/IP protocol stack
Network Monitor
    Capture Summary window, 1-28 to 1-29
    capturing IP frames, 1-30
    defined, 1-21, 1-27
    examining ARP packets, 1-30
    examining ICMP packets, 1-30
    how it works, 1-27
    installing, 1-30
    viewing captured network traffic, 1-28 to 1-29
    ways to use, 1-27
networks
    analyzing client startup communication process, 5-2 to 5-9
    complex, configuring IP addresses, 2-13 to 2-24
    connectivity issues, 5-1 to 5-38
    devices and OSI model, 1-8 to 1-9
    IP communication between, 2-11
    IP communication within, 2-10
    list of common connectivity issues, 5-11
    local vs. remote, 2-19
    OSI communication example, 1-6 to 1-7
    simple, configuring IP addresses, 2-2 to 2-12
    strategies for solving connectivity problems, 5-10 to 5-19
    supernetting by using CIDR, 2-41 to 2-42
    TCP/IP communication example, 1-18 to 1-19
    utilities and tools for isolating connectivity issues, 5-20 to 5-38

nodes, DNS, defined, 4-11
Nslookup utility, 5-23

O
Open Systems Interconnection (OSI). *See* OSI model
OSI model
    architecture, 1-3 to 1-4
    data receiving process, 1-7
    data sending process, 1-6 to 1-7
    defined, 1-3
    how to use, 1-3
    layers, 1-3 to 1-4
    network communication example, 1-6 to 1-7
    network devices and, 1-8 to 1-9
    vs. TCP/IP protocol suite, 1-15 to 1-16
    what it does, 1-3

P
packets
    defined, 1-4
    in OSI model context, 1-4
parent domains, defined, 4-10
Pathping utility, 5-31
physical layer, OSI model
    defined, 1-4
    hub operation, 1-8
    role in receiving process, 1-7
    role in sending process, 1-7
Ping utility
    error messages, 5-28 to 5-29
    overview, 1-22 to 1-23
    sample output, 1-22
    testing connectivity by using, 5-26 to 5-27
POP3, as TCP/IP application-layer protocol, 1-15
presentation layer, OSI model
    defined, 1-4
    role in receiving process, 1-7
    role in sending process, 1-6
private IP addresses, 2-37, 2-38
Problem Isolation Flowchart, 5-16
public IP addresses, 2-38

R
requests for comment (RFCs)
    document maturity levels, 1-14
    document numbering, 1-14
    document status levels, 1-13
    TCP/IP protocol standards, 1-13 to 1-14
reservations, DHCP, 3-17
RFCs. *See* requests for comment (RFCs)
root domain, defined, 4-10
routers
    how they work, 2-26
    overview, 2-26
    role in OSI model, 1-9
    static vs. dynamic routing, 2-27
routing. *See also* IP routing tables
    defined, 2-25
    troubleshooting, 2-32

S
scopes, DHCP, 3-16 to 3-17
session layer, OSI model
    defined, 1-4
    role in receiving process, 1-7
    role in sending process, 1-6

SMTP, as TCP/IP application-layer protocol, 1-15
SNMP, as TCP/IP application-layer protocol, 1-15
startup, analyzing client process, 5-2 to 5-9
static IP addresses
    configuring client computers to use, 3-2 to 3-9
    defined, 3-3
    managing, 3-3
    preferred DNS server, 3-4
    viewing by using Internet Protocol (TCP/IP) Properties dialog box, 3-4 to 3-5
    viewing by using Ipconfig, 3-6 to 3-7
    when to use, 3-3
static routing, 2-27
subnet masks. *See also* VLSM (variable-length subnet masks)
    choosing, 2-20 to 2-22
    how bits are used, 2-18
    need for, 2-4
    overview, 2-4 to 2-5
    valid vs. invalid, 2-4
subnets
    benefits of using, 2-16
    calculating IDs, 2-21
    creating, 2-17
    determining valid IP addresses, 2-21
    IP addresses for, 2-16
    overview, 2-16 to 2-17
    role of VLSM, 2-39
supernetting
    Class C networks, 2-41, 2-46
    determining number of bits required, 2-45
    role of CIDR, 2-41 to 2-42
switches, role in OSI model, 1-9

T

TCP, as TCP/IP transport-layer protocol, 1-15
TCP/IP protocol suite. *See also* IP addresses
    architecture, 1-12
    benefits, 1-12
    data receiving process, 1-19
    data sending process, 1-18
    network communication example, 1-18 to 1-19
    vs. OSI model, 1-15 to 1-16
    overview, 1-10 to 1-20
    published RFCs, 1-13 to 1-14
    stack layers, 1-12
    utilities for monitoring, 5-21 to 5-31
Traceroute (Tracert) utility, 5-30
transport layer, OSI model
    defined, 1-4
    role in receiving process, 1-7
    role in sending process, 1-6
transport layer, TCP/IP protocol stack. *See also* application layer, TCP/IP protocol stack; Internet layer, TCP/IP protocol stack; network interface layer, TCP/IP protocol stack
    defined, 1-12
    list of protocols, 1-16
    overview, 1-16
    role in receiving process, 1-19
    role in sending process, 1-18
troubleshooting
    IP routing, 2-32
    network connectivity issues, 5-1 to 5-38

U-V

UDP, as TCP/IP transport-layer protocol, 1-16
User-Configured Alternate Configuration, 3-21
user logon, analyzing connection process, 5-2 to 5-9
VLSM (variable-length subnet masks), 2-39

W

Windows Internet Naming Service (WINS)
    benefits of using, 4-27
    client requirements, 4-27
    configuring client to use, 4-29
    defined, 4-27
    NetBIOS name resolution process, 4-28
    overview, 4-27
    registering client names by using Network Connections Repair, 5-33
Windows Server 2003, Alternative Configuration feature, 3-20 to 3-25

Notes

Notes

Notes

Notes

Notes

Notes

Notes

Notes

MSM2276CCPN/C90-04744